FIRESIDE

by Vidal Sassoon
SORRY I KEPT YOU WAITING MADAM

A YEAR OF
BEAUTY AND

BEVERLY AND VIDAL SASSOON

HEALTH

with Camille Duhé

Illustrated by Judy Francis

A Fireside Book
Published by Simon and Schuster

Yoga photographs by Norman Eales
Photograph on page 44 by John Adriaan, London Daily Mirror

Copyright © 1976, 1978 by Vidal Sassoon, Inc, and Beverly Sassoon
All rights reserved
including the right of reproduction
in whole or in part in any form
Published by Simon and Schuster
A Division of Gulf & Western Corporation
Simon & Schuster Building
Rockefeller Center
1230 Avenue of the Americas ·
New York, New York 10020

Manufactured in the United States of America

11 12 13 14 15 16
1 2 3 4 5 6 7 8 9 10 Pbk.

Library of Congress Cataloging in Publication Data

Sassoon, Beverly
  A year of beauty and health.

  Includes index.
  1. Beauty, Personal. 2. Women—Health and
hygiene. I. Sassoon, Vidal, joint author.
II. Duhé, Camille, joint author. III. Title.
RA778.S26   646.7'02'4042   75-23286
ISBN 0-671-22123-X
ISBN 0-671-24379-9 Pbk.

To Catya, Elan, Eden and David . . . and all children . . .
for a healthier and happier life.

ACKNOWLEDGMENTS

We would like to thank our very good friend Laurance Taylor, who achieved the impossible by coordinating so many different people—the two of us, Camille Duhé, photographer Norman Eales, illustrator Judy Francis and the various departments at Simon and Schuster.

CONTENTS

AUTUMN

HAPPY NEW YEAR ANY DAY OF THE YEAR!

And let's begin this new year by reshuffling your attitudes about yourself and the world around you. Only by shaking free of crusty old ideas can you be free to make new decisions for a beautiful new way of life.

One of the first tired notions we want you to drop is the one that a new year always begins on January first. For you, a bright new year of beauty and health begins right this minute. NOW. Whether it is April or October, for you it's the beginning of a whole new year of self-discovery.

Turn straight to the chapter for this month—whatever month it is. You will find a program of day-by-day techniques, tools for your new approach to making the most of the looks you were born with. Beside each thing we suggest, you will find a page number. Turn to that page and get full details on special cleansing for your skin type, the right way for you to shampoo, everything you need to know in order to get your new year off to a flying start, right now. . . .

FIRST THINGS FIRST: SETTING YOUR GOALS

In order to get anywhere, you always need to know where you want to go. To make this year work overtime to bring you all the rewards you deserve, you must give yourself a checkup on your store of wishes.

Have a good, long look at yourself mentally and physically. Give yourself some time and strip for action. Stand in front of a full-length mirror and study yourself. You cannot be too thorough in this self-administered physical examination. Review everything about yourself with as much detachment as possible. How is your hair? Posture? Skin? Do you need to lose weight? Do you need a good body toning? Could you use a good pedicure? What are the disturbing areas that require special exercise? What bothers or bores you most about your life, and do you know why?

Use your bathroom scale, your tape measure and record all the results in your diary. Then, beside the current facts, set down the figures as you want them to be. These future figures are your goals for the year. The three of us, working together, will get there. Now that you know where you're going, getting there will be easier.

A GREAT NEW YEAR

Passport people, gossip columnists, and the old-fashioned type of doctor are always interested in chronological age—with how long you've been around. The new breed of doctor has a better way of looking at things. He cares about your true physical age as shown by the state of your body and mind, not by the date on your birth certificate.

No matter what chronological year this is for you, it will be the one you remember as a delightful mental and physical turning point.

It is going to be a year of discovery and exciting adventure. With the help of this book, you can learn about yourself and how to achieve the right balance between vitality and serenity, between self-fulfillment and realistic self-acceptance.

This is not a beauty manual of unrealistic promises and gimmicks. It is a collaboration. We give you the outline and suggestions that we know have worked for us and for our friends, but you are going to write in the important material: the story of the progress and discoveries you are going to be making throughout this year of beauty and fulfillment.

It's going to be new, it's going to be exciting, a watershed from which you will emerge as the healthy, attractive, dynamic person you truly are—and it's going to be fun.

Let's talk about beauty. Real beauty is that self-awareness that makes you like yourself, that makes you face life with poise, confidence, and warmth, so that everyone you are in contact with comes away feeling that you are a very special and attractive person. It's what makes others like and admire you, enjoy your company, and think of you as an asset in any situation. It's the aura of energy and serenity that will make you stand out in any crowd, no matter where you go or who else is there.

Let's put it this way: *There are no plain people in the world.* No child is born unattractive or ordinary. Each of us is a miracle.

There are some whose features are less than perfect. Few of us come up to the current plastic beauty standards. But each one of us is capable of exuding that radiant glow of the confident and attractive person.

How often have you seen perfect-looking people who are so totally locked into themselves that they are completely eclipsed by others? The trick is to feel good about yourself and then to forget your self-image in order to be a vital, interested, and interesting person. It's not your beautiful face but the beautiful person you are inside that will show and will draw others to you.

Through this year of beauty, our greatest hope is that you will learn who you truly are; how to make the best of what you are; to be able to say "I like you" to yourself and mean it; and how to extend that wonderful happiness, self-confidence, and positive vitality to everyone around you.

Even in the middle of a change-of-seasons slump, you can hit the top again if you resolve that right this minute is the time to dare a few changes in the way you look . . . the way you feel . . . the way you will deal with life in the whole, beautiful year that lies before you.

We don't mean drastic, frightening changes. You probably don't need those. Very few people—maybe one in a hundred—need a makeover; but everyone can benefit from a rethink, and now is the time for it.

Take a few of the small risks that put excitement into your looks and your life. Try a new way of looking at yourself, a new way of thinking about yourself. It is essential for healthy growth and change—it's what we call learning to climb.

Whether they are climbing a tree or playing a game, we always encourage our children to climb higher, to play harder, to explore their strengths, to test and expand their capacities.

Testing, learning, and growing are not limited to childhood. We all retain the capacity for wonder and exhilaration that a child knows high up in blue sky on a tree limb. Too many of us deny the child within and wall off the joy and the wonder. Don't be one of them.

Dare something small, experience the delight, and you are on your way to a more exciting, more attractive life. This thrill, this new kind of beauty will never leave you no matter how long you live—if you continue to climb.

THE OTHER BOOK YOU SHOULD HAVE

As we go through this year (and this book) together, keep your own companion volume to this one.

Get yourself a diary—the "week-at-a-glance" kind, or a ruled spiral-bound notebook—with the cover in a rich shade of your favorite color. Our special color is deep chocolate brown. Yours might be scarlet or purple. Whatever it is, the pleasure of color will cost no more than muddy gray and will make using the book far more appealing.

On the first page, record everything you can about yourself. Put down your current weight, measurements, the state of your skin, your hair, your health, and your state of mind. Be frank with yourself, but not cruel—don't confuse honesty with masochism. But remember your diary is completely private, so write it all down.

And put it down in ink. That way you won't be tempted to erase the evidence about the old you as you become a totally attractive new person.Later, this first page will be your satisfying, secret proof of how much you have accomplished during the year.

Use a pencil to record goals for the month. Set a figure for weight loss you would like to achieve this month, or for inches off the waist. Pencil it in on the page for the last day of the month. Weigh yourself at the same time every morning, and write down the figure. By the end of the month you will have a record of how your weight fluctuates with diet, with exercise, and with body cycles. On the last day of the month you may find that the goal you set today has been reached.

And if you don't? Not to worry. Borrow Scarlett O'Hara's maxim that tomorrow is another day; turn the page, start a new month, continue climbing to your goals.

Using some of the new ways we suggest, you will see immediate changes: your hair will look shinier and healthier as soon as you learn the ABCs of a good shampoo; (page 45) your body will look better as soon as you learn to avoid the Seven Standing Sins (page 30). Changing your clothing size or growing healthy new nails takes more time. Skin, nails, and hair change more slowly than your mind, but they do grow and change for the better. Give them—and yourself—time. Even several months may be needed to correct years of neglect in certain areas, or the wrong kinds of attention in others.

Keep at the good new ways. They will soon become second nature. At first you will need dedication and discipline. Lots of both. But if you check your progress weekly in your diary, you will begin to see that the road leads up all the way.

Before you begin new ways of eating and exercising, see your doctor for a complete physical check. Make sure he is a doctor with an awareness of preventive medicine as well as curative medicine.

We've put in a sort of calendar checklist at the start of each month to help you plan your time and set your goals for the month to come. Use it as a guide, but don't be a slave to it.

Add to the calendar, borrow from the next month, or subtract what isn't right for you. Juggle the calendar to suit your life. Because more than our book, this is *your* book. The subject is you, and the object is a happier, healthier, more beautiful life for you.

LISTS MAKE LIFE MORE BEAUTIFUL

Get into the habit of making lists and you will be way out front in the organization game. Since being beautiful is all about smoothly organized living, start now to keep lists. Jot down the next day's schedule before you go to sleep; make notes of chores to be done, letters to write or books to read, what you will need at the market, all the things you plan to do. As you accomplish each thing, check it off the list. The contented smile that results is very becoming.

How about starting with a list of equipment you will want to have on hand for building the new you? Go through the suggestions, check off what you already have on hand, then go out for a brisk walk to the store to get anything else you will need.

IN THE BATH:

Safety Razor. This, along with a good shaving foam and after-shave moisture cream, is the best way to solve the problem of unwanted body hair. The new razors designed especially for women help you shave more easily than ever. It isn't true (according to the American Medical Association) that shaving causes quicker or thicker regrowth. It is true, though (according to us), that depilatories can irritate your skin.

Pumice Stone. The volcano's gift to the world and one of the most valuable additions to the bathroom since electric light. Elbows, knees, feet are all better for a flick of the pumice—but always temper the buffing with a slather of soap on the stone, and be gentle with yourself. Skinned knees are for kids.

Loofah sponge. This coarse natural sponge will scrub up a glow in even the most rebellious winter-weary skin. Once the loofah sloughs dead cells off the surface, your shoulders gleam like satin.

Pleasant to Have, but Nonessential:
Bath pillow. A plastic, air-filled head rest for the bath probably won't knock a hole in the budget, but you can substitute a folded terry towel for this if you like.

Bath brushes. Two or three for different parts of the body are nice to have. A beautiful older friend of ours uses just one brush—the rough, tough kind you scrub floors with—and she has glowing, baby-pink skin. Our suggestions are: for the *face,* a baby's hairbrush; for the *back,* a natural bristle brush with a long handle; for *nails:* a natural bristle brush, the kind with short bristles on one side for scrubbing under the nails, longer bristles on the other side.

IN THE BEDROOM (or wherever you exercise):

Beach ball. The kind you played with as a child, to use now in exercises that whittle thighs and upper arms.

Tape measure. For documented proof that you are winning with your new shape strategy.

Floor mop. The kind that unscrews so you can use the handle alone as a very effective exercise prop.

Bathroom scale. One you can read without bending, even in an early-morning fog. Best time to weigh is the minute you step out of bed (you weigh less then, and that's always comforting); make it a point to weigh yourself at the same time of day every time you weigh.

Kitchen timer. For timing exercises and sunbaths. These are inexpensive, and one in your favorite color (ours is sand beige, yours might be parrot green or purple) costs no more and is nicer to have around.

Jump rope. It's still fun to skip rope, and, according to Dr. Kaare Rodahl of the Institute of Work Physiology in Norway, "for producing the greatest fitness in the least amount of time, nothing surpasses the simple jump rope." Get a good heavyweight one that is the proper length for your height. The local sporting-goods store is the place for this.

Full-length mirror. To make those crucial critiques of your figure and posture. Get the biggest mirror you can and check for wavy distortions before you buy.

IN THE KITCHEN:

Kitchen scale. Get a small, inexpensive one and use it. Weighing the food you eat may seem like a bother, but it's vital to really intelligent control of eating habits. Soon you will become so eagle-eyed that you can estimate the difference between three ounces and six of smoked salmon or applesauce—but it takes practice with the scales.

Electric blender. This is *Key*—the most important single investment in beauty equipment you can make. A high-quality blender costs less than a set of hot curlers, about the same as a blow dryer. Unlike these, it can be used several times every day to benefit every cell of your body.

The most important blender suggestion we have for improving your life is on page 162—a Vitality Drink that will give you 365 days of greater energy, serenity, and beauty. Aside from this magic potion, we will suggest ways to use your blender to save your skin; help your hair; delight yourself, your family, your guests with delicious and body-improving things to eat and drink; and—very important!—to save precious time.

Give the blender you already own a place of honor in the kitchen so it's ready to use at all times . . . or go out and buy one now . . . or save to get one. But get one.

EQUIPMENT FOR YOUR HAIR

Brush. The best one will glide through your hair like a knife through butter. You should be able to use it (on dry hair) exactly as if you were combing your hair with a wide-toothed comb. The idea that a good brush has tightly packed natural bristles is old-fashioned; a tightly packed brush will, in fact, tug at your hair and damage it. The best brush is a Denman type in which nylon bristles with rounded ends are set into a flexible red rubber pad.

Comb. Ivory or tortoiseshell are beautiful for show; inexpensive hard rubber is just as fine for use. Whatever the material, it should have both wide and narrow teeth. As you use a brush to give direction to dry hair, use a comb to section and guide wet hair.

Hot comb. One of the great innovations for short hair.

Curling iron. Be sure to use only a model with Teflon coating and thermostat. Use it for only a few seconds.

Dryers. The *hand-held dryer* used well can be as important as your toothbrush. (We will show you how on page 50). You certainly don't need a *rigid-hood salon type dryer,* but if you have the space, money, and desire for one, a salon dryer is very nice when you are using a conditioning pack or setting your hair in rollers. *Bonnet dryers* are not recommended. We don't like them since they tend to overdry the hair in one area while it remains damp in others.

Hair clips. Certainly easier to use than pins for doing pin curls, but we don't like them. The tight buckle they make on the hair is a little thing, but it makes a big difference. Your hair won't look first-rate when you take the easy way out.

Hairpins. If you use them, we assume you are using the ones with plastic-coated tips.

Heated curlers. Don't make it a daily habit to use them. They are very handy, but constant use of any heating equipment will lead to dried-out hair. Mist curlers are better used in cold, dry weather than in hot, humid weather when the hair tends to be too moist anyway.

Rollers. They should be the foam-rubber-covered ones for gentlest treatment of your hair. They should never be seen out-of-doors. We can't think of anything more unattractive than a woman walking around with a head full of rollers wrapped under a scarf. That sort of thing gives the supermarket a bad name.

Scalp massager. One of the few electric hair helpers you cannot use too often. Massage with fingers or equipment whenever you like, to keep the scalp loose and the circulation brisk.

A SHOPPING LIST FROM THE HEALTH FOOD STORE . . .

There are lots of things in the health food store that can be used for external beauty aids, as well as for eating and drinking. Investigate . . .

Cold-pressed almond oil. A polyunsaturated oil that's great for salad dressing and cooking, and is a beautiful addition to a bath, or a treatment for dry hair.

Avocado oil. For cooking use, and, because of a high degree of absorbency of ultraviolet radiation, worth thinking about when you sunbathe. It's high in beautifying vitamins and minerals for skin, too.

Wheat germ oil. Rich in skin-nourishing vitamin E, it can be mixed into sun lotions, used as an eye oil, mixed into blender drinks for extra vitamin E, and used in salad dressings or cooking.

Oatmeal. Is high in B vitamins (especially inositol, which may help prevent hair loss); and, if you like porridge, cook it. If you prefer leaving the cereal bowls to Goldilocks, use dry oatmeal to mix with water for skin-clearing face and body packs.

Almond meal. Makes a wonderful base for facial masks and body packs; adds texture, flavor, and protein to casseroles. You can make your own almond meal by pulverizing blanched almonds in the blender.

Brewer's (food) yeast. Powdered form is the most economical and goes into the blender to mix well with almost any liquid. Without a blender, the powder tends to resist mixing and clump up in a very unappealing way. That's when yeast tablets are invaluable. Get a big bottle, because you have to take more tablets than you might think in order to get the same benefits that a tablespoon of powder gives. But the benefits are inestimable (as you will read later) for beautiful skin, hair, disposition, etcetera, etcetera—beautiful everything, in fact.

Desiccated liver tablets. Only dedicated sauteed-liver freaks can get enough of the enormous benefits of liver. As it does so much for all of you, be sure you are getting in on the receiving end with a big bottle of desiccated liver tablets. If you don't like liver, these tablets are priceless because you get all the credit (shining hair, glowing skin, energy to spare) without ever having to taste liver itself. The tablets that are low-heat-dried are best.

Herbal teas. The variety is endless. So are the claims of what each one can do: camomile to calm troubled complexions and nerves, wild strawberry as a laxative, papaya to aid digestion, cowslip to aid sleep. Some are delicious, others you might find a bit blah. I would advise making your own sampler of the smallest amounts you can buy of five or six different teas. Try them one at a time, or make your own blend in the same pot (papaya and mint are especially good together). Do try the rose-hip tea—a beautiful pink color and loaded with natural vitamin C. Fine alone or delicious with a little honey and lemon. Start a tea library with small supplies of several teas such as lemon balm, strawberry, papaya, rose hip, camomile, mint; and try new ones for fun every now and then.

Carob powder. Has a chocolaty flavor, but doesn't have a beauty-wrecking crew of ingredients as chocolate does (chocolate contains theobromine, a stimulant that acts just like caffeine, for one). Carob does have B vitamins. Use carob whenever your sweet tooth demands chocolate.

Raw honey. Uncooked honey retains all the trace minerals, B vitamins, natural fructose and glucose. The body can use honey for its requirement of natural sugars without having to work for them (as it must in order to utilize ordinary refined sugar, whether white or the suntanned kind that is called "raw"). Raw honey is a life food. Sugar is a destructive one.

Wheat germ. The part of the wheat responsible for growth. To a stalk of wheat, it's the spark of life; to you, an incredibly rich source of vitamins, minerals and protein, and very economical. It is a nutritional magic cushion. Use it in place of bread crumbs to add value to other foods; use it with milk as a dynamite cereal. You can buy wheat germ either raw or toasted. The toasted kind is tastier; the raw is slightly higher in vitamin E and lower in cost, and you can toast it yourself by spreading it on a cookie sheet for a few minutes in a warm oven. Do get the kind of wheat germ that is most convenient and appealing to you. No good food does you any good if it's just sitting on the shelf uneaten.

Sea salt (or salt substitute). We use a salt substitute on the advice of our doctor. It's wise for everybody to *limit* salt intake (the average diet supplies at least six times the requirement of sodium) in the interests of keeping down weight and blood pressure. Sea salt supplies iodine and other trace minerals that are good for you. If you use salt, use sea salt—the taste is better than that of ordinary table salt.

RESOLVE TO MAKE THIS YEAR A PLEASURE

Armed with your new beauty tools (which you'll learn about as you go along) and a fresh new year ahead, it's natural to think of making resolutions.

For your new year, make resolutions that are pleasurable and positive, not those self-denying negative ones.

You might resolve, for instance, to read one book a month purely for pleasure—a book you are not required to read for work or school. Very important: Resolve to devote one full evening each week of the year to yourself. No TV or telephone, just puttering around and resting, or getting better acquainted with yourself. You might spend the evening on experimenting with new makeup or on a pampering beauty routine you wouldn't otherwise have time for. You might spend it on getting to bed extra early for a long sleep (one of the great beauty aids).

Not only will these pleasure resolutions enable you to look the new year in the face with enthusiasm, but they will have a beautiful effect on the face and body you present to the world and will contribute enormously to your store of positive vitality.

GETTING UNDER WAY

In passing along some of the good things we've learned about looking and feeling better, it's difficult not to get ahead of ourselves and skip over valuable basics to tell you about our newest enthusiasms. Yoga, for instance, can do an enormous amount of good for your skin, your state of mind, and your body. We will talk about that soon, along with exercise, diet, and a great deal more. But first you should know about the thirty-six-hour revolution you can effect in your system; a night and a day that, if your doctor agrees, can advance the whole cause of a beautiful year.

Because we are all exposed to so many poisons in the air, even in the food and water we consume, the body is hard put to produce results quickly from a program of better care. But if you shed these toxins, improvements can proceed more rapidly. That is the purpose of the two-step regime we have called the English Health Farm program. It involves a short fasting period on water and fruit juices followed by a diet of fresh raw foods and liquids for two days. Since shedding these stored toxins and fat is fatiguing for the body, the liquid fast and the two-day Clearing House Diet should only be attempted during a period of rest, such as a weekend. But we think it is so important that we urge you to read the next chapter and consult your doctor, then schedule time on this weekend or the next for this program. Remember, his OK is imperative for the liquid fast. If he feels it would be too strenuous for you, then spend a weekend following the Clearing House Diet as a first step in your new thinking about food.

WINTER

A new beginning. One of the most beautiful prospects ever, and it's yours this season. To make the most of it, start absolutely fresh in everything. Clear away the encumbrance of things past—old notions, old ways of thinking—because shining new ones are in store. A clean slate, an empty canvas to create on, is the immediate goal.

We will discuss the ways you can remove old obstacles to get a head start on the strong, serene new way of living you will enjoy this year, from this minute on. . . .

Set your personal goals, and let's get cracking!

JANUARY

Much of the world is gearing up for a new year now; there are fresh new calendars and appointment books and a second of hesitation before writing the correct date on a check or a letter. Perhaps this is the first month for your new year of health and beauty; perhaps you have been with us for a few months and the new calendar year is just an artificial division of your personal twelve-month program.

Whether you stand at Go or the midway point, January is a demanding month. The twilight closes in early, so you have to get moving early in the day if you are to make the most of it. Experiment with getting to bed a little earlier for one week this month, setting the alarm so that your day begins a little earlier. You may very well find that those extra quiet minutes in the morning are the ideal time for writing a letter to someone you love, for collecting your thoughts and setting your goals for the day, for doing some early morning warm-up exercises you wouldn't otherwise have time for. Having this little slice of extra time in the quiet morning hours may very well contribute to a day-long feeling of serenity and achievement.

YOUR CHECKLIST AND SCHEDULE FOR JANUARY

First Morning of the Month

> Log your vital statistics into your diary (p. 14) *in ink.* Set your goals for the month as to loss of pounds or inches and gains in other areas, such as proficiency at yoga, say, or using the hand-held dryer. Pencil in your goals on the diary page for the last day of the month, and start the program that will help you achieve your goals.

Every Morning

> Seven-Way Stretch   (p. 91)
> Cup of hot water and lemon juice
> Warm-up exercises   (p. 146)
> Clean face and moisturize   (p. 54)
> Makeup   (p. 61)
> Fix hair
> Vitality Drink and nutritional supplements   (p. 94)

Every Evening

> Warm-up exercises to relax
> Feet-up rest with pillows or on slantboard for 10 minutes
> Clean face and moisturize
> Bath and all-over body lotion   (p. 128)
> Clean teeth before bed   (p. 259)

As Often as You Like: At Least Three Times Each Week

> Exercise session of 30 minutes   (p. 242)
> Yoga session of 30 minutes   (p. 96)
> Shampoo and finishing rinse   (pp. 45–46)

Once Each Week

> An evening (or a day) of rest, a time for yourself
> 10-minute protective protein conditioning pac for hair
> Manicure and pedicure   (p. 201)
> Tweeze stray hairs on eyebrows   (p. 167)
> Shave legs and underarms   (p. 166)
> Facial mask   (p. 162)

Once This Month

> One night and one day of rest for the digestive system on either the detoxifying Liquid Fast or the Clearing House Diet (pp. 36–38)
> Haircut and any other professional hair services such as color

or perm. (Your cutter might advise a cut more often, perhaps every three weeks. Follow his suggestion in making out your individual schedule.)

BEVERLY'S MAKEUP BAG OF TRICKS

I really believe that good things come in little packages when it comes to makeup. I buy makeup in small sizes because I like to swing with the moment, and change my makeup from time to time. Small sizes allow for this without leaving behind half-empty bottles and jars of last season's colors.

Another very good reason for small sizes is that you can simplify your life. A bathroom cluttered with makeup, a desk drawer at the office filled with emergency supplies . . . who needs it? That's a messy way to live. You are always having to worry whether you need more of this or that, and where. You wind up with two of this in the office and none at home.

Use your organizational skills to simplify the whole business. Weed out, pare down, and stick to little sizes; then keep all your makeup in one waterproof plastic zipper bag that fits into your handbag and is with you whenever or wherever you need it.

You will be amazed at how much you can put into it. All this goes into mine:

2 eyecolor shadow pencils
1 cake mascara
1 child's toothbrush (for eyebrows)
1 tweezers
1 lash curler
1 hairpin (bent, for applying false lashes)
1 pair false lashes (plus eyelash glue)
1 vial eyedrops
6 pads of sterile absorbent cotton
1 lipstick brush

2 lipsticks
1 lip gloss
1 liquid foundation
1 blusher
1 skin freshener
1 moisturizer
1 small bottle baby oil
1 emery board
1 cuticle cream
1 perfume spray

THE CRUCIAL KEY TO GOOD LOOKS

Here is the key to glowing skin, clear eyes, healthier hair: Take a good, deep breath and let it out.

That such a simple thing as breathing properly can make such a difference is one of the easily overlooked facts. Healthy, active people tend to breathe properly without thinking about it. But sedentary urban people can get into a very bad habit of shallow breathing that leads to tension, a pinched and drawn look and oxygen-starved skin.

There are many therapeutic breathing exercises in yoga. Here is a simple one to do at any time: Inhale slowly and deeply through the nostrils. Take the air all the way down into the diaphragm and hold it there. Extend your stomach as far as it will go, a great round stomach. Hold in the air for a slow count of five, then slowly constrict the stomach muscles to force the air up into the lungs, and exhale through your mouth. At first you might want to use your fingers to guide the stomach muscles: press in and up on the lower part of the stomach as you exhale.

Breathing in this slow, complete way will relax you almost instantly even in a super-tense situation. Try it when you have trouble sleeping. After a few minutes of this yoga breathing you'll be nearer sleep than you would be with a pill. Deep, rhythmic breathing has other benefits. People will soon notice you have begun speaking with a warmer, sexier voice and you will notice that the muscles of your abdomen will knit together for a flatter front: two bonuses along with the clear eyes and skin that advertise healthy circulation.

GETTING UP TO BASICS . . . THE SEVEN STANDING SINS

Now it's time for a great big, and immediate, change in your looks.

The way you wear your frame is the most important thing

about you, but most people—apart from dancers and athletes—carry their bones like so much excess baggage.

Let's change that now. Go over to your full-length mirror. Stand before it in profile and check for:

1. *Floorward forehead:* This stance is perfect for studying your feet, all wrong for anything else. If your head hangs down, so does everything else. You coax double chins into being, add years to your face, and get a head start on a dowager's hump. Decide that all the action is out in front of you, pull your neck up high, get your chin parallel to the floor, and eyes straight ahead. You've just dropped a few years.

2. *Ski-slope shoulders:* These curve down and out in front. Terrible for your skin! Here's why: Hunched shoulders force your lungs into a semi-collapsed state, so circulation suffers. When circulation is impaired, so is the healthy glow and tingle you want. A

rigid little tin-soldier stance isn't the answer. This is: Pull your shoulders up into the most expressive Latin shrug, roll them up and back, relax. The great thing about your frame is that it knows the way and will fall naturally into a comfortable, correct posture if you give it half a chance. Correcting sin number two will help correct sin number three . . .

3. *Saggy Breasts:* Take a deep breath, lift up but not out. Exhale and look at the beautifully feminine line.

4. *Vanishing waistline:* The thickening result of letting your rib cage slump down into your hips. An ugly line that isn't doing bodily functions any good either. Simple corrective—just stand there and pull UP from the base of the spine. Lift the rib cage and inhale deeply. As you exhale, you will feel how much more efficiently the oxygen is coursing through every inch of you. A mirror check will show how much taller and trimmer you look.

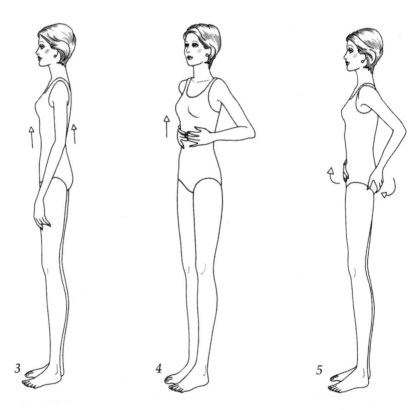

5. *Rear Thrust:* A big fanny is a common figure fault. Diet and exercise are musts to correct it, but you can minimize it by tilting your pelvis forward and up. This tightens both abdomen and buttocks, supports all the lower organs better, and lessens fatigue in the legs and the lower back.

6. *Loose legs:* Even bow legs are correctable with the right stance and a bit of exercise. You have to strengthen the inner muscles of the calves. Do it by standing with ankles together, and pressing the insides of the calves together. Hold while you count to ten, then relax. Do this whenever you think of it, and you will see results in a month or two.

7. *Wayward feet:* Pigeon-toed or duck-footed variety. A long, straight strip of masking tape on the floor in front of your mirror will help. Walk the line with exaggerated heel-and-toe action once or twice a day, and you'll soon be on the right path.

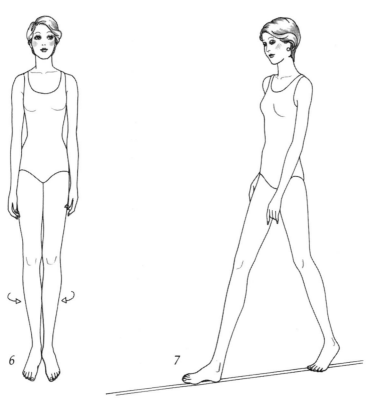

VIDAL ON THE SUPER ENGLISH HEALTH FARM AND THE CLEARING HOUSE DIET

Fasting is something I do automatically for thirty-six hours every month. If you think about it, there can be no harm in missing four of the ninety meals we usually eat in the course of a month.

After one night and one day of taking in no solid food I feel marvelous. It is a great rest for the liver and the digestive system. At the end of a fast, I feel very light, very pure.

Don't undertake a fast when you've a heavy work schedule before you. Fast on a weekend when your time is your own, when you can sleep late and enjoy the great luxury of idleness.

My first fast was about fifteen years ago when I was in a state of nervous exhaustion. A friend, the actor Kenneth Haig, spotted my problem and suggested I pack a sweat suit and a copy of Camus' *L'Etranger* and book myself into Enton Hall, an English health farm, for a week of fasting and much-needed rest.

The English health farms offer a rest for the dynamic as well as a jolt for the sedentary. The body has a chance to rest and renew itself through a fast followed by a detoxifying diet, sleep, massage, high colonic enemas if you choose, long walks in the fresh air and gentle toning exercises. It is an excellent preparation course before embarking on a more strenuous program of exercise.

By cleansing the system, preparing it to be happy with smaller portions of better food, and gradually introducing it to exercise, you insure that the results of a new way of living show up as rapid improvement, not as the sore muscles and hunger pangs that accompany crash courses of strenuous exercise and stringent diet.

There are many English health farms, and I have been to many of them, but I have a special fondness for Grayshott Hall, near London. It was there that, over a cup of yoghurt, I proposed to Beverly.

Even if you don't find the person to share your life with while you follow this program, you will finish it in wonderful shape. You become loose, as a dancer is loose; there is not a trace of nervous tension; the skin is in magnificent shape and without blotches; you are clear-eyed and feel clearheaded.

People say that emotions come from the heart, but the juices surely come from the stomach. During the time you follow the English Health Farm Diet, you are putting your stomach in training—training it to want the right kinds of foods, and in the amounts that the body truly requires. Because you are disciplining your mind and body, you acquire a sense of well-being and even dignity while shedding fat and bad eating habits.

Remember that you are not depriving your body of food; you are rewarding it with rest. When the fast is ended, and you graduate to high-energy foods, concentrate on the good taste, the freshness, the juiciness and flavor, the vitamins and minerals these foods contain—on the good things they are doing for you. If you begin thinking in this way, you will have a hard time ever going back to useless junk food. You will take positive satisfaction in the enjoyment and discipline that healthy eating bestows.

THE FIRST STEP OF THE ENGLISH HEALTH FARM PROGRAM

Before checking in at an English health farm, it is a wise idea to check in with the doctor for a physical checkup. It's also an especially important step before beginning this or any other plan of diet and exercise at home.

There is no reason why anyone in good health could not follow these eating programs, but timing is important.

Begin the thirty-six-hour fasting period at the start of a weekend, or at any time when the demands on your energy and time will be lightest. Then when you are ready to tackle the world again, graduate to two days of the Clearing House Diet plan. Unless your doctor says no, this should be easy to follow. It will do wonderful things for your skin, hair, figure, and energy. If you need to gain weight, or require more calories for a feeling of well-being, increase the portions.

If you are on holiday you might want to prolong the diet to a full week, as you would at Grayshott Hall.

Remember, no feats of endurance for your body during this time. Do the Seven-Way Stretch (p. 91) in the morning, do your warm-up exercises (p. 146), get in some walking or bicycling. If you can get to a swimming pool for a dip every day, or to a masseur, so much the better, because your pleasure in the week will be greater.

Even if not, you will emerge from a few days of this regime feeling—and looking—younger, fresher, and happier than before.

THE THIRTY-SIX-HOUR FASTING PROGRAM

THE NIGHT

Plan an early bedtime. Draw a warm bath and add to the water a cup of apple-cider vinegar. It helps to relax you and draws impurities and dead cells away from the skin. While the water is running, mix a tall fruit-juice drink. This liquid dinner is half spring water and half orange, apple, or grapefruit juice. Sip it slowly while you soak. Rest in the tub for as long as you like. Read or listen to music on your transistor radio. When you feel drowsy, wrap up in a big terry-cloth towel or robe that will blot you dry and crawl straight into bed for a good, long sleep. Don't set the alarm clock.

THE DAY

When you awake, warm up with a long, slow Seven-Way Stretch. Stretch every inch of your body as a cat does. Enjoy the length and suppleness of your body, the luxury of surfacing slowly to the day.

Have a big mug of hot lemonade (unsweetened). Or a tall glass of spring water and orange juice. Or both, if you like.

Do your morning warm-up routine of a shoulder roll and the other de-kinkers, then take a long walk in the fresh air. Or spend the morning at the gentle art of puttering: straighten a closet, write letters, read, or daydream. Listen to music or do nothing. This is your day to give pleasure to yourself, to be free of responsibilities.

As often as you like, every hour or so at least, have a drink of water. Add some fruit juice and a thin slice of lemon to make it seem more festive. A warm cup of herb tea will stave off hunger pangs during this rest for the digestive system. Don't use regular tea, though—you want to cleanse the system, not add caffeine to it.

Later in the day, have a warm shower and wash your hair. Then have a relaxing warm tub. Add cider vinegar or powdered milk to the water. To step up the free flow of perspiration, drink a glass of cool fruit juice and water. When you feel relaxed enough for bed, blot yourself dry, and if you feel a bit restless, have a cup of warm camomile tea to help you to sleep.

ON THE NEXT MORNING, YOU ARE READY TO BEGIN THE TWO-DAY CLEARING HOUSE DIET

Now it is time to reward your body with delicious, easily digested foods that skin, hair, and nails thrive on.

As you begin this second stage of your new thinking about food, the first proof of the good it's doing will be apparent. You should feel a bit lightheaded. Your skin may look clearer already. If not, it certainly will in a day or two.

Food for these two days is mainly liquid, mainly raw, so it contains the full quota of vitamins and enzymes.

Now and always, it's important to take it slowly. Dawdle over your food, stretch the meals out. It takes fully thirty minutes for the blood sugar to rise when you eat, and until the blood sugar rises you continue to feel hungry. So eat slowly, and you will feel full with less food.

As breakfast is the most important meal, start the day with one of the Vitality Drinks on page 94 to kick off your day with lasting energy. Even if you're the sort who cannot face breakfast, you will probably be able to swing it with one of these liquid wonders.

Day One. All the water to drink that you like, plus . . .

Breakfast: Vitality Drink, cup of hot herb tea or decaffeinated coffee (if you wish) and vitamin supplement.

Mid-morning: Cup of hot vegetable bouillon, or hot tomato juice with a teaspoon of brewer's yeast stirred in.

Lunch: Plain yoghurt (stir in some wheat germ or lemon juice if you like), cup of hot herb tea.

Mid-afternoon: Cup of warm skim milk and blackstrap molasses, or lemonade with honey, or hot herb tea.

Dinner: Big bowl of fresh raw vegetables. Toss together grated carrot, chopped celery, chopped cabbage, small edible pea pods, raw spinach, whatever combination appeals to you, and dress with a little yoghurt and lemon juice.

Day Two. All the water you wish, plus . . .

Breakfast: Vitality Drink, plus herb tea or decaffeinated coffee, vitamin supplement.

Mid-morning: Hot vegetable bouillon, or hot tomato juice with brewer's yeast.

Lunch: Big tossed salad of raw vegetables tossed with yoghurt and lemon juice; ripe apple, pear, or other fruit; hot or cold herb tea or decaffeinated coffee.

Mid-afternoon: Fruit juice or hot cup of herb tea or vegetable juice.

Dinner: Fillet of broiled fish with lemon juice; small raw vegetable salad with yoghurt and lemon juice; small bowl of diced fresh fruit drizzled with honey; hot herb tea or decaffeinated coffee.

Bedtime: (If you like) cup of yoghurt or warm skim milk with a little honey or blackstrap molasses.

SPECIALS FOR YOUR FOOD PLANNING

• If you are working off a little poundage you gained during the holidays, have a warm low-calorie drink when hunger strikes. It gives you the comfortable feeling of having eaten something. Cheat the appetite, not the scales, with hot vegetable broth or rose-hip tea. Consult the Sassoon Diet for All Seasons on p. 265 for other delicious low-calorie ideas.

• Every bit of vitamin C helps. It has jobs to do all over the body, forming defenses against colds and viruses, keeping the tissues of your skin healthy. Here is a great blender drink to have hot or cold. As it uses all of the pulp and a little of the peel of fruits, you get a rich supply of the bioflavinoids and other ingredients of the vitamin C complex that are not found in the juice alone.

VITAMIN C POWERHOUSE DRINK

Use 1 lemon, 1 orange, and ½ grapefruit. Peel the fruits, quarter them, and remove the seeds. Liquefy in the blender, a few pieces at a time along with just a bit of the peel. This will be a pale golden purée. Add a little honey if you wish. Mix equal parts of the pureed citrus fruit with hot or cold spring water and drink.

• While you are clearing away and making room in your life for great new things, how about making some room in the kitchen, too? Go through the refrigerator and the shelves and get rid of these:

sugared breakfast cereals	saccharin
white bread	chocolate bars and hard candies

bleached flour	colas and diet colas
refined sugar	sugar-filled jams and jellies
lard, shortening, or other hard fats	commercial peanut butter
potato chips	T.V. dinners

• Anything else that is fake, synthetic, and lifeless goes. For the sake of your vital new life, replace them with liquid golden oils that are polyunsaturated, natural honey, molasses, fresh nut butters, whole-grain breads, and vitamin-rich "nibblers" such as toasted soybean nuts or sunflower seeds, with fresh things to drink such as naturally sweet fruit juices and herbal teas. Consider donating the deep-fryer to the next rummage sale. Frying foods shouldn't be part of your new food style. Foods slivered and quickly sautéed in polyunsaturated oil are easier to fix, more attractive, and much more palatable.

SPECIALS FOR YOUR HAIR

• Keep hair covered in cold weather. In freezing temperatures hair gets brittle and can split. Nourish it over the winter like a hothouse plant with moist warmth (keep a humidifier going indoors) and with protein conditioning pacs.

• It is especially important at this time of the year to avoid too-frequent use of curling irons, electric curlers, and blow dryers. Let your hair dry naturally whenever possible but be sure it is thoroughly dry before you go out-of-doors in cold weather.

• If static electricity devils your hair, moisture is the answer. An oil pack is one way of helping too-dry hair. Don't use olive oil, as old-fashioned recipes usually suggest, but a polyunsaturated oil (cold-pressed almond oil from the health food store or corn oil from the supermarket). Polyunsaturated oils penetrate into the hair shaft better than olive oil. Warm a little oil to body temperature and massage into the hair. Wrap your head in a hot, damp towel and leave the oil pack on for a couple of hours on your weekly night for rest and beauty (you should make sure you have one). Then shampoo (you may need two or even three latherings). Don't forget your finishing rinse or protein conditioner.

• A wide-toothed aluminum comb is helpful in static-electricity problems, too.

• Many factors influence the selection of the perfect cut, but the wearing of glasses never has been, is not now, nor ever will be one of them. The cut must be an esthetic shape that is becoming to you. The glasses you wear should have an esthetic shape that is becoming to you. If the shape and color of the glasses is flattering, then glasses will not compete with, but will complement, any shape and color you choose for your hair. If you suspect that your specs don't do it for you, get new ones. For help in selecting the best haircut, you depend upon the expertise of your cutter. For glasses, listen to the advice of a first-class optometrist. They are very aware of fashion these days.

• If your hair is very fine and you use a setting conditioner, get extra hold by blotting hair damp-dry with a towel first and then applying the lotion.

• Fine hair is happiest if it is cut rather short so the weight of the hair doesn't flatten it at the crown.

• Remember, no haircut will look its very best if you are much heavier than you should be. It is hard for the cutter to suit the cut to bone structure if he can't see the bones.

SPECIALS FOR YOUR BODY

• Your skin is drier now than at any other time of the year. Be very careful of it. Keep baths brief and lukewarm, add milk to the water for soothing. The powdered instant kind is just as good as liquid, and easier on the budget. One pint of milk in the tub will do wonders for skin, soften the water, but won't leave a sticky residue on you. Everybody, male and female, needs skin protection. The same body lotion is great for the whole family. Our favorite is one of the least expensive, and the simplest: combine Johnson's Baby Oil and Nivea Lotion in equal parts.

• Ease into exercise if you've been away from it for awhile. Start with the Seven-Way Stretch and the Warm-ups. But graduate to skipping rope sometime during the first week. Kids love it—remember? It's still fun, and one of the greatest indoor exercises. If it's cold where you are, bundle up, put on plenty of lip gloss and moisturizer, and get out and walk. Really stride along. Even a brisk five-minute walk after dinner is dynamite for circulation.

• Your eyes need moisturizing, too. Use eye drops when you've been out in the cold and the wind.

SPECIALS FOR YOUR MAKEUP AND FRAGRANCE

• When your skin is healthy and very clean, makeup can and should be kept light. Use less all the time for a fresher, younger look. Shed your makeup in slow stages so as not to shock yourself or your audience. Start with your eyes. If you have been wearing a heavy eyeliner, you're aging yourself with yesterday's makeup. Leave off the liner and try drawing the thinnest possible line at the roots of the eyelashes with a fine brush dipped in a soft gray-brown mascara. Or use a gray-brown eye shadow for an even softer effect.

• When it's cold out, be supergenerous with moisturizer. (If you ski, you need moisturizing with a sun-blocking cream. Bouncing off the snow, sun at high altitudes is lethal.)

• Well-dressed ladies used to wear gloves summer and winter. Smart women still do in winter to protect nails and thin-skinned hands from damage, as well as for warmth. And what do they wear under their gloves? Lots of hand and cuticle creams.

• Put on perfume, cologne, scented body oil, or any fragrance while you are still warm and damp from the bath. It seems to "take" better and last longer.

FEBRUARY

Maybe you agree with T. S. Eliot and find April the "cruelest month," but for most people, February has it beat by a mile. Actually, you can hit a little minor snag at almost any time of year—a day when you simply feel a little blue for no good reason. It's perfectly normal—and rather than fretting about why you feel down, why not do something nice that will make you feel up?

Lots of bad jokes used to be made about women buying new hats to cure a bout of depression. The principle, though, is a pretty sound one. Give yourself a treat when you want one. It can be as simple as just dropping the housework to put on a favorite record that makes you feel happier. If you are dieting, you should give yourself lots of nonfood rewards. The money you might have spent on chocolate eclairs could go into a big bunch of tulips to cheer up the living room, or maybe some potted hyacinths to fill it with color and fragrance.

Be prepared in advance for grown-up "rainy days" in the same way that you would keep a bunch of coloring books and special projects in reserve for the kids. For less than ten dollars you can lay in a big supply of paperback books to lose yourself in. A complete set of Jane Austen, maybe, or the collected words of Xaviera Hollander—whatever turns you on. Don't race through them, like eating popcorn, but save them as a first-aid kit for a slump.

If doing something nice for yourself is a help, doing something nice for someone else is surefire. Take time to write a long, chatty letter to a great-aunt or the friends who moved to Portland, and you will feel a nice little glow of pleasure, because you are giving pleasure to someone else. You might double the recipe for the Superloaf in this month's food specials and give a present of fresh, home-baked bread to a neighbor. You might volunteer some time to take an elderly relative on a shopping trip, or do the shopping for them. Have you ever thought of volunteering time to read to the blind? Reading aloud to someone is not only a worthwhile thing to do; it helps you to improve your speaking voice.

If you start thinking about the nice things you could do, you will come up with a long list. The only limit is time. But once you start, you will find it becomes less of a problem. For some strange reason, the more you do, the more you can do. The people who seem to complain most about not having enough time are those who never do much with the time they have.

YOUR CHECKLIST AND SCHEDULE FOR FEBRUARY

First Morning of the Month
> Log your vital statistics into your diary (p. 14) *in ink.* Set your goals for the month as to loss of pounds or inches and gains in other areas, such as proficiency at yoga, say, or using the hand-held dryer. Pencil in your goals on the diary page for the last day of the month, and start the program that will help you achieve your goals.

Every Morning
> Seven-Way Stretch   (p. 91)
> Cup of hot water and lemon juice
> Warm-up exercises   (p. 146)
> Clean face and moisturize   (p. 54)
> Makeup   (p. 61)
> Fix hair
> Vitality Drink and nutritional supplements   (p. 94)

44   *A Year of Beauty and Health*

Every Evening
    Warm-up exercises to relax
    Feet-up rest with pillows or on slantboard for 10 minutes
    Clean face and moisturize
    Bath and all-over body lotion   (p. 128)
    Clean teeth before bed   (p. 259)
As Often as You Like: At Least Three Times Each Week
    Exercise session of 30 minutes   (p. 242)
    Yoga session of 30 minutes   (p. 96)
    Shampoo and finishing rinse   (pp. 45–46)
Once Each Week
    An evening (or a day) of rest, a time for yourself
    10-minute protective protein conditioning pac for hair
    Manicure and pedicure   (p. 201)
    Tweeze stray hairs on eyebrows   (p. 167)
    Shave legs and underarms   (p. 166)
    Facial mask   (p. 162)
Once This Month
    One night and one day of rest for the digestive system on the
        detoxifying Liquid Fast or Clearing House Diet   (pp. 36–38)
    Haircut and any other professional hair services such as color
        or perm. (Your cutter might advise a cut more often, perhaps
        every three weeks. Follow his suggestion in making out your
        individual schedule.)

THE ABC'S OF A GOOD SHAMPOO

It's the only treatment your hair cannot do without. And depending
on how you shampoo, it can be one of the best or worst things you
do for your hair. A good shampoo is tension-relaxing. It can even
be sexy, if your mate and you shampoo together in the shower.
    Here are the ABCs of a good shampoo:

Shampoo in the shower to make plenty of rinsing in lots of
running water easy.

Using lukewarm water, rinse your hair thoroughly to get rid of surface dirt. You'll need less shampoo.

Pour just a little shampoo into the palm of your hand. About a tablespoon or so should do it.

Rub your wet palms together to work up a lather before you apply the shampoo to your hair. You get better coverage this way.

Massage the shampoo into your scalp lightly with fingertips and work out to the ends.

Rinse well. If your hair is very oily, or very dirty, you may want to shampoo again. If you shampoo every day or so, one lathering should do.

Rinse several more times to get all the shampoo out of your hair.

Pour out a finishing rinse, or a quick conditioner, into the palm of your hand, rub palms together and apply it to your hair. Remember, it's hair that needs conditioning, not the scalp. So keep conditioner where it belongs, in the hair. Never skip the finishing rinse or conditioner. This quick treatment helps add protein and shine to the hair and aids removal of the last traces of shampoo.

While the conditioner is working, go about your shower. Then rinse.

Rinse again.

Dry your hair as gently and as slowly as possible. Blot your hair with a terry-cloth towel to soak up excess water. Use a second towel to make a turban around your hair and give it a few minutes to soak up as much moisture as possible.

Unwrap damp hair and untangle it gently with your fingers. Don't pull, just wriggle fingers through it. Comb with a wide-toothed comb, and let hair air-dry or use the drying equipment your style requires.

THOUGHTS, TIPS, AND HOME TRUTHS ABOUT SHAMPOOS

You do *not* need a shampoo with a low pH (highly acid). A highly acid shampoo will give good results at first. Eventually, though, you may find that the hair is duller, actually looks dead. You have overacidified your hair. Very hard water plus an acid shampoo can be a terrible mixture, especially if hair tends to be oily. The very acid shampoo will have a chemical reaction with very hard water that causes the oils and dirt to complex—which means they solidify and do not wash out. A few hours after shampooing, body heat causes these oily solids to melt and your hair looks dirty all over again because it was never really cleaned.

You *do* need a mild shampoo. It should cleanse the hair gently, and leave it in a neutral state on the pH scale of acidity to alkalinity. When every trace of shampoo is rinsed away, then you restore the hair to its normal acidity. This should be done with the use of a finishing rinse or a regular preventive protein pac treatment.

Which shampoo? Ads are wildly misleading. All good shampoos cleanse the hair. I happen to think that our own Vidal Sassoon shampoo is best, but there are many scientifically tested ones—and

they don't have to be expensive—that are excellent. In general, a newer shampoo is a better bet. Many that were introduced ten years ago were formulated for stronger cleansing (in the chemist's term, they are more "active") than newer shampoos.

The reason is simple. Ten years ago, a shampoo was a weekly affair at best for most people, and the shampoo had to work harder. If you shampoo every day or so, your hair doesn't need all that heavy-duty cleansing.

No shampoo is a good one unless you use the smallest amount that will do the job and unless you rinse it out completely. Rinsing it out is as important as putting it on.

A good finishing rinse product is almost as important as the shampoo itself. Every time you comb your hair, you do a little damage through pulling. Comb your hair, of course; but correct damage as a matter of course. Our Vidal Sassoon Finishing Rinse is applied to wet, pre-shampooed hair, then rinsed out in sixty seconds or less. In that brief time, it restores the hair to its natural pH-6 state and adds body, sheen, and control.

Hair will *adsorb* protein in a conditioner, but it will not *absorb* protein. That is, the liquid protein will cling to the hair shaft as a coat of paint clings to a wall. The conditioner will fill in pits along the hair shaft and will coat it with a shiny clear shield to protect it from damage. By using a conditioner you offer your hair the benefit of a buffer against external damages. It will look and behave better with protein conditioning, too. Damaged hair shafts tend to lie tangled together on the head in a lackluster way. Hair gets spring and swing as well as shield and shine from a good conditioner.

Use conditioning products properly. They are made to work quickly, but let them work on your hair—not on your scalp. Pour conditioner into your palms and work it into the hair from ends to roots. Don't just slop it on. Allow it to work for the required number of minutes, then rinse it out.

Shampoo as often as you like. People sometimes shampoo twice daily; I see no harm in it, provided you use a mild shampoo and remember the ABCs on pages 45–46.

Combs, brushes, and anything else you use in your hair (barrettes, clips, or pins) should be cleaned as regularly as your hair. When you shampoo, give your comb and brush a shampoo by soaking them in a basin of warm, soapy water. Add a little ammonia to the water if you like.

Dandruff is a condition characterized by excess scalp cells coming off in flakes, and can have many causes. Any competent hairdresser will send the client to a good dermatologist if he notices any abnormal scalp condition. The dandruff-controlling shampoos are effective in many cases of dandruff. The mild kind containing selenium sulfide is the best for chemically treated hair. Often the amateur will make a mistake in diagnosing a case of dandruff. It might actually be a crusty deposit of shampoo that has been inadequately rinsed away. Subsequent shampooing is not cutting through to clean the scalp. Before you go out to buy a dandruff shampoo, try this: Saturate a pad of sterile absorbent cotton with plain rubbing alcohol. Section the hair and rub the pad all over the scalp. Let it dry on the hair. Brush the hair and then rinse the hair thoroughly and massage the scalp, but do not shampoo.

One application should take care of the flaky condition, but you may repeat it once every two weeks for as long as you like. If your problem is really dandruff, the alcohol rub will not work. Perhaps your professional salon offers FDA-approved dandruff treatments. If not, see a dermatologist or your regular doctor for treatment.

Like everything else in our industry shampoos have changed greatly since I [Vidal] began working in the field at the age of fourteen. I've learned an enormous amount about the nuances of hair-care products over the years. Even so, I got a great education working with Don Sullivan, the brilliant creative chemist who formulated our line of products and many other well-known lines before he joined our organization.

DRYING YOUR HAIR—YOUR LOOK DETERMINES THE METHOD

Many of the new looks don't demand special drying. Air drying or a heat lamp are fine for short, curly hair. For a man or woman with a short, off-the-face style, the hot comb is best. For chunky bobs you can use a hand-held blow dryer.

The hand-held blow dryer, used properly, is a wonderful tool. Unfortunately, most people do not really know how to use it well.

In our salons we give instructions to clients on the best way of using the blow dryer for excellent results.

Here, in words and pictures, is the way.

USE THE HAND-HELD HAIR DRYER LIKE A PRO

Do your hair in two stages. First dry it, then finish off the style. While drying or finishing, keep the dryer in motion. Playing a moving current of air on your hair is fine, but concentrated blasts on a single section of hair will overheat it. Hold the dryer about six inches away from your hair.

Drying:

Section damp hair with a wide-toothed comb into sides, sides back, back, and top front.

Start at one side and work around the head to dry the hair section by section. Dry the front section last.

Starting at the side, brush the hair across the top of the head, keeping the dryer moving. Brushing and drying the hair *against* the natural growth direction keeps the hair from clinging to the head and gives it more volume. Start at the side top and pick up the hair, layer by layer, with the brush.

When the hair is dried, bring it down, layer by layer, with the brush, twirling the hair like spaghetti on the brush. Keep the dryer on the move as you aim it at the hair in the brush.

Now brush this dry section into place and move on to the next.

In brushing the back, start near the top and brush hair upward. (If you can't stretch your arms to bring hair straight up over your head, then brush to the side). Hold the dryer over your head, or to one side, as you brush hair up.

Now bring the hair down, layer by layer, starting at the bottom, with the dryer following the brush. Brush hair smoothly down.

Move on to the next side section. Hold the dryer in your left hand when you dry the left side.

Dry the bangs or top hair last. First brush them back, blowing them dry while brushing. Next, brush them down, following the movement of your brush with the dryer.

Brush hair into place all over. Brushing now means a smoother finished job.

1

2

3

4

5

6

7

Finishing:

To turn ends under, repeat the twirling action with the hair-brush. Start again at the side and work your way around the head, finishing with hair at the front of the face. If your dryer has a nozzle, use it to concentrate the airstream during finishing. Pick up the hair in the brush, twirling it to hold, then draw the brush through the hair, directing air from the dryer to the bottom of the brush. Roll the brush down and under. Go all around the head with the twirling.

To prevent frizziness on the top layer, turn the dryer to the "cool" setting. If your hair tends to frizziness, you may want to repeat the entire finishing stage with the dryer on "cool" this time around.

Brush your hair down again without the dryer, and you are set—the professional way.

THE SKIN GAME . . . KEEPING IT CLEAN

If you ever open a beauty magazine or watch television you can't help having doubts about what you're doing to your face when you wash it. Should you be using a cream or soap and water? If soap, which one?

Before you can decide on the best cleansing program for your skin you must know something about your skin type. Here's a checklist:

Dry skin has very fine pores . . . seldom has a pimple . . . tends to be flaky, sensitive.

Oily skin has visible pores . . . frequently erupts . . . nose and forehead start to shine an hour or so after makeup is applied.

Combination skin has visible pores on the nose, perhaps the chin . . . may break out in blemishes in a monthly cycle, perhaps less often . . . nose and forehead start to shine three or four hours after makeup is applied.

WHAT YOU SHOULD KNOW ABOUT YOUR SKIN TYPE AND CARING FOR IT

Dry skin hits almost everybody after thirty. It is usually dry only on the surface, and proper care can normalize it. Since dry skin tends to be thin skin, delicate care is the order of the day (and night). Oily skin is not exclusively a teen-age problem, but is worst then. Plenty of attention is needed to keep it clean and clear. Combination skin is what "normal" skin is all about. The mask of the face (forehead, nose, and chin) is oily; everything else is dry and delicate. This requires special care to keep all in balance.

HERE'S HOW TO CLEAN YOUR FACE
—IF YOU HAVE DRY SKIN

Morning:

Wash with mild castile soap and warm water. Rinse your face twenty times in warm running water. Apply moisturizer to damp skin, from bosom to hairline. Blot off the excess moisturizer (except around the eyes) with a towel or tissue after ten minutes.

Night:

Use cream or an oil to remove makeup. Then wash and rinse as in the morning. Wet a pad of sterile absorbent cotton with water, then pour a skin freshener onto the wet pad. Rub the pad of diluted freshener all over your face (except around the eyes) to remove any last traces of makeup or soap. Rinse your face in cool water and moisturize.

One night a week:

Once a week at night, wash and rinse as usual, but instead of the diluted skin freshener use an oatmeal or almond-meal cleansing pack. Take a handful of meal and mix it with enough warm water to make a thin paste. Apply this to your wet skin (except around the eyes) then wipe it off very gently with a wet washcloth. The mask will remove all the dry, dead cells that your skin sheds during the week. Rinse with warm running water and moisturize.

HERE'S HOW TO CLEAN YOUR FACE
—IF YOU HAVE OILY SKIN

Morning:

Wash with a mild soap and warm water. Rinse twenty times in warm running water. Wet a ball of sterile absorbent cotton with astringent and rub it all over your face (except around the eyes). Rinse your face again in cool water, and apply a light moisturizer from bosom to hairline. Blot off the excess immediately with a towel or tissue.

Before dinner:

Rinse your face with warm water and use a cotton pad soaked with astringent to remove oil and dirt. Rinse with cool running water, and apply a light moisturizer. Blot it off (except around the eyes).

Night:

Wash with soap and warm water. Rinse twenty times, use astringent on a cotton pad to complete the cleansing, rinse in cool water.

One night a week:

Follow your usual program, but substitute an oatmeal or almond-meal cleansing pack for the astringent. Mix a handful of meal with enough warm water to make a thin paste. Apply it to your wet skin and gently wipe it off with a wet washcloth. Rinse with cool water.

Note: If you have very oily skin, combined with pimples or acne, do *not* use the oatmeal or almond cleansing pack. A medicated skin lotion is a better idea for your skin and will do the same job.

HERE'S HOW TO CLEAN YOUR FACE
—IF YOU HAVE COMBINATION SKIN

Morning:

Wash with a mild castile soap and warm water. Rinse twenty times in warm running water. Dampen a pad of sterile absorbent cotton with water then wet it with skin freshener and rub this around the hairline, across the forehead, and over your nose and chin. Rinse with warm water, and smooth moisturizer over your damp skin from bosom up to hairline. After ten minutes blot off the excess moisturizer with a towel or tissue, but do not remove moisturizer from the delicate skin around the eyes.

Night:

Repeat your morning routine.

One night a week:

Wash and rinse as usual, but do not use the skin freshener. Instead, make an oatmeal or almond meal cleanser to slough off the dry, dead cells the skin throws off during the week. Wet a handful of meal with enough warm water to make a thin paste and apply this to your wet skin. With a wet washcloth, gently wipe off the cleansing paste. Rinse with warm water, and moisturize as usual.

THE OTHER SKIN TYPE, THE SENSITIVE SKIN

It might be an allergic skin, or it might be a sensitive skin. There is a difference, but both types react quickly and unpleasantly to the wrong kind of treatment.

Allergic skin will react to a specific thing—which can be anything from strawberries or roses to formaldehyde—by blotching or swelling or worse.

A sensitive skin is alert to all kinds of mistreatment. It becomes sunburned in nothing flat, wool sweaters chafe it, and the wrong kinds of products make it feel dry and tender.

Sensitive skin and allergic skin are more common problems than the insensitive would think. The boom of companies that produce irritant-free makeup is proof of that.

Here are a few tips on care of sensitive and allergic skin. To discover the specific irritant to allergic skin, you will have to do some work with your doctor or dermatologist. But every delicate skin should know that:

The term "hypo-allergenic" means a product contains fewer irritants, it doesn't mean it is 100 percent irritant free. Hypo-allergenic products are fragrance-free, mild formulations in which every possible care has been taken to minimize the possibility of allergic reaction. That includes production in sterile laboratories as well as leaving out irritating chemicals and perfume oils.

Perfume belongs on the clothing and not the skin of the sensitive ones. Use perfume atomizers and spray colognes.

Protection is paramount. Shun the sun when you can, and wear a good moisturizing sun block. But avoid those sun blocks that contain PABA (para-aminobenzoic acid). These can irritate your skin.

Moisturizer is vital for all skins. Your skin needs it even more.

Take care when choosing and using skin fresheners and astringents. Diluting them is a good plan. Add a few drops of astringent to a sterile cotton pad after you have soaked the pad in water.

Buy your hypo-allergenic cosmetics and skin care products in small sizes, and get fresh ones frequently. Since they do not contain the chemical preservatives that give long shelf life to regular products, they may not last as long. Preservatives will make the other products look better longer, but since they won't make *you* look better, forget them. It's a fresh face you want, so use fresh makeup.

MOISTURIZE AS IF YOUR SKIN DEPENDED ON IT—IT DOES

Remember "What one book would you take to a desert island"? If you play the game with beauty products and your answer is "moisturizer"—you win.

The most important thing you do for your skin—and the quickest—is moisturizing. It should take you just fifteen seconds flat to protect your skin from bosom to hairline, including your ears. And include hands, too. But nothing else you do for your skin will count for much if you omit that quarter minute. A good makeup needs moisture down below for full bloom.

Make it second nature. Moisturizer is your second skin—and your first skin depends on it.

How Much Moisturizer?

The tiniest blob—just enough to cover the tip of the index finger should do it. So many women use moisturizer like cake icing. It's not only a waste, it looks awful.

Use a pea-sized drop of moisturizing cream and spread it all over on damp skin, working up from the bosom. That is enough also to moisturize the ears (skin is both exposed and thin there) and hands (they really need moisturizing because the skin is thin, and gets very dry). Then blot off any excess with a tissue after ten minutes, and apply foundation.

WHEN?

Because the idea is to trap moisture inside, next to your skin, *always* apply moisturizer on clean damp skin, right after washing your face. Moisturizer spreads more smoothly, too, on damp skin, so there is less drag on the delicate skin tissue.

WHAT IS THE MOST PENETRATING MOISTURIZER?

No moisturizer really penetrates the skin, and you wouldn't want it if it did. A moisturizer should act exactly like Saran Wrap—to provide a film over the surface of your skin to prevent moisture from seeping out from inside, and to protect the skin against anything that might seep in from outside: that includes makeup and all the dirt and fumes in the air around us.

WHAT IS THE DIFFERENCE BETWEEN A MOISTURIZER AND AN EMOLLIENT CREAM?

None. "Emollient" means softening, and that's what a moisturizer's mission is—to soften the skin by keeping moisture present in the top layer of the skin, where the air can dry out and roughen dead cells.

AND HUMECTANTS?

Are bad news. A humectant is a substance like glycerine—smooth and slippery. Glycerine can make your skin *feel* softer, but it acts like a sponge: it loves moisture, and draws all it can from the air. But if the air is dry, glycerine will draw its moisture quota right out of your skin. Small amounts of humectants in a cream are O.K. But avoid anything that is "rich in humectants"—your skin will be poorer for it. Old-fashioned glycerine-and-rosewater hand cream is one of grandmother's pure, natural products you are better off without; the same goes for glycerine soaps.

How About Hormone Creams?

Steer clear. Pre-menopause, your body produces the hormomes it needs; post-menopause, you run the risk of inducing a skin cancer. It's a very slight risk, but why chance any risk? Hormone creams can plump up the skin and make it look younger, but only for sixty days. Then the metabolism of your skin has been changed, and no further improvement is seen. But since you've upset the metabolism of the skin, you have to go on feeding it the hormones it didn't want but now demands. Once you've hooked the skin on hormones, you have to go on supporting its expensive habit. Do you need that?

Can You Skip Moisturizer in the Summer Since Oil Glands Work More Freely?

Moisturizer is indispensable clothing for your skin—in January you are happier in warm woolens; in July, in thin cottons. You might be happier with a light oil in summer, and a heavier cream in the winter. You might like to use the same cream moisturizer all year round, but to use it a little more lavishly in the winter. Never plaster it on, but do blot off a little more in the summer.

You need *more* moisturizer in the summer if you go off on vacation by plane. Pressurized cabin air is dry as a bone.

Use less moisturizer in summer, but moisturize more often. You'll be splashing more cool water on your face, bathing more frequently, and perspiring more. All these wash away that invisible shield—so reapply.

Does an Oily Skin Really Need a Moisturizer?

It might sound like coals to Newcastle, but even an oily skin needs help in the quick-dry areas around the eyes, the mouth, on the throat and the hands. But easy does it. Be miserly with moisturizer, and after ten minutes blot well—especially on the forehead.

Shouldn't an Older Skin Have a Heavier Moisturizer?

As you get older you need more B vitamins, more ego-boosting, more money, and more moisturizing—but it doesn't have to be heavier moisturizer. Just go lightly when you blot off the excess. In fact, you might not want to blot at all. That moist look isn't called the bloom of youth for nothing, and a moisturizer can help create it while the sweat and sebaceous glands are slowing down.

How Much Should You Spend on Moisturizer?

Whatever you want. A superexpensive moisturizer probably has ingredients that you don't really need, but if you like the smell, or the texture, the color, or the idea of moisturizing with strawberry cream—why not? Even the most expensive moisturizer is usually not a big expenditure because you use so little. There are many good ones at reasonable prices. And if you really want to economize, or if you should run out of your moisturizer—head for the kitchen. Cold-pressed soy oil or almond oil will work as a moisturizer. They won't smell or feel the same as your moisturizing cream, but they're better than a naked skin.

And don't forget to moisturize your throat! Your bosom! Your ears! Your hands! Your feet!!!

VIDAL ON: WHY I CAN'T HATE HAIR SPRAY AS MUCH AS I WOULD LIKE TO

Without it, some heads of fine hair are going to just fly away between the salon and home, so hair spray becomes an evil necessity. Especially in the rotten weather that is a late-winter specialty.

If you remember that spray is to protect your hair from the elements and *only* for that, you should be fine.

Once you are indoors, brush the spray out of your hair. No gales are sweeping through your living room, so why wear a hard, unsexy helmet?

Get the lightest, gentlest spray you can and use it with diligence. Hold the can at least eight inches away from your head. Shield your face. Keep the spray can moving—no concentrated blasts.

Please brush it out as soon as you can. Hair spray and candlelight are a lethal combination. The only thing that's worse is lacquered hair in bed. Enough of that kind of "plastic woman" behavior and there would be zero population growth in no time at all.

BEVERLY ON: MAKEUP—THE OLDEST, MOST PERSONAL ART

It may not be one of the major arts, but it is one of the oldest and the most personal. The nice thing is that you don't hang your finest creation in a gallery but wear it for the world to enjoy.

Every artist learns to paint by painting. The more you paint, the better you paint.

That means more often. Not more paint.

This is one art where less definitely is more. The skill and the artistry comes in knowing how and where to place a little makeup for a lot of effect. You can spend eighty dollars on makeup, but unless you hold back in applying it, you'll look awful.

Even in little bottles, makeup seems expensive. But it lasts for a very long time, if you use it properly. Always buy the best you can, in small sizes. Tell yourself that this bare minimum has to go a long way and last a long time. You will find yourself hoarding it, using much less than you think you need. And that should be just the right amount. If the result is *too* washed-out, you can add more color. But remember, it's easier to put on than to take off and heavy makeup is always aging.

Another good reason for a very few things in very small sizes is that—like your mind, the seasons, and everything else—makeup is always changing.

Only a few years ago, eyes were the whole story. They were rimmed with heavy black goop and the rest of the face was a zero. Remember? It was always a bore to apply, not very becoming, and now it's as dead as the Twist—deader, because the Twist is still a great waist exercise in private even if it's passé on the dance floor. Raccoon eyes are bad news everywhere now. Yet you still see women wearing them and aging themselves in the process.

Check what's new in makeup by going through the editorial beauty pages in the magazines. You can see what the makeup geniuses like Way Bandy or Pablo Manzoni are up to, what they forecast. Then swing with the moment.

Don't simply fall in line with fads. But try the new. Adapt it, and tone it into your forecast for yourself. Adjust it to suit your critics. My critics are the kids. When my daughter asks "What's that stuff on your eyes?" I know it's time to issue a revised forecast.

Even when they seem far out, the magazines are safer guides than the old-line department-store makeup saleslady. There is a whole new attitude going on there, too, but there are an awful lot of salesladies who feel they have to be all done up in Daisy Duck false eyelashes with green and purple and orange plastered on their faces. When one of *those* women says to me, "Well, dear, I'm wearing . . ." I rebel and don't even want to think about wearing makeup.

To be fair, they probably do a great job technically, and their job is to get all the makeup out there and sell it. The makeup men in the movie studios used to specialize in heaviness and technical perfection, too, when I first started as an actress. But some of the perfect on-camera effects looked pretty weird off camera.

There have been a lot of changes behind the camera and behind the makeup counters in the past few years, but you are still your own best makeup artist. If you practice.

Practice makes for speed, too,

Because of yoga classes that have improved my complexion enormously, and the lighter trend in everything, I usually spend only about five minutes a day on my makeup. In winter, or when skin isn't up to par, I need foundation, and that adds to the minutes. Still, I can make it in less than fifteen minutes at most. That really isn't so much time to spend on making yourself look as attractive as you can.

Once makeup is done, then I forget about it. But it's like your diet. It has to be a consistent part of your life. Neglect is bound to catch up with you, and you find that instead of saving time, you lose it by trying to get back in practice.

Barring a weather catastrophe, my makeup gets only a one-minute touchup to dramatize it a little if we are going out in the evening.

This is my plan of action:

1. You must have a clean canvas before you paint. We've already covered the all-important washing and moisturizing step;

never start to make up without that. I usually skip from moisturizing to step #4 on days when I do yoga, or in summer. Otherwise, the next thing is . . .

2. Foundation. The color depends on your skin tone. Mine is very pink, almost ruddy, so I use an ivory foundation. No matter what your skin tone, don't apply foundation until you check it with what you'll be wearing. Get that out of the closet and make sure that it won't be wrong with your foundation tone. If it will, switch to another foundation before you start. I like liquid foundation best for two reasons. The finish has a natural, youthful sheen. Cake or pressed-powder foundations tend to build up in any little lines or crevices so that even when you keep a straight face you have little smile creases. Foundation under the eyes, and the application of it, should be several times lighter than a butterfly's wing. In addition to being very delicate and easily harmed by heavy fingers, the skin under the eyes is a network of tiny, tiny wrinkles even on a sixteen-year-old. Foundation will pinpoint them. Flutter on the least foundation possible with the little finger.

If last night was a late one, you may want to use a cover stick on dark circles. However, I really don't recommend it.

I find cover stick is always noticeable, and so I don't like to use it. Better to use your regular foundation. Or you could try this trick: Use the cover-up just *under* the dark circles rather than *over* them. When foundation is applied over the cover-up, the eye will somehow be distracted away from the circles and to the lighter area at the top of your cheekbone.

With the tip of the little finger, I tap on three dots of my foundation on the right side of the forehead, and very gently blend it up into the hairline. Next, the same thing on the left side, and continue blending to even out both sides.

The reason for doing first one side, then the other, is so blending can be done while foundation is at its wettest. Next, two little dots on the top of each cheekbone just below the eye socket. Blend across and up into the temple, then in, down, and under across the cheeks. One side at a time for the best blending. Again, go easy with foundation under the eyes. It creates a buildup in tiny lines there. Go easy with the blending, too. *Never* rub under your eyes—just the most delicate fluttering with the fingertips. One or two tiny dots in the hollow of the cheek. Blend. Four dots along the jawbone, blended down the jawbone and upward on the throat from

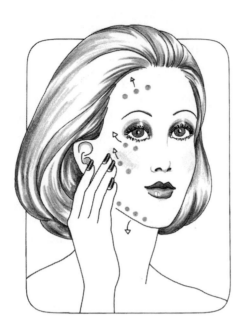

the neckline of your clothes. Never forget to carry the color down onto the throat and neck. If makeup stops at the chin it looks like head and body don't belong to the same person.

3. Shading. A blusher stick in pinky-beige is the tool for me. The effects can be fantastic. Most of these effects, however, are better left to models, who really sculpt their faces for the camera with shading. A professional makeup artist like Way Bandy can use shading to make the most lopsided face look symmetrical. Noses can get straightened, jawlines narrowed. But daylight isn't kind to makeup magic, as most of us practice it, so save the tricks for evening or for when you are having your picture taken, play them down, and when you shade, *blend!* Here is the one bit of shading, however, that I think works for day, for most women: use a light flick of the blusher just under the chin and blend up to the bone and across toward the edges of the jaw (it helps correct a tendency to multiple chins, but neck exercise is a better bet). You can also drop your lower jaw, suck in your cheeks, and put a light twist of blusher in the hollows. Blend well.

Now I do my eyes.

4. Curl the upper lashes with a eyelash curler and brush the eyebrows up with a child's toothbrush.

5. Lowlights and highlights with shadow. Lowlights are the true shadows, tones that recede, and cast an area into shade as if your thick, thick lashes were doing it. All the browns and grays, the smoky neutralized blues, greens, and mauves are lowlights. Highlights are the pretty pale ones you use to point up the eyelids, the eyebone, to pull some light and sparkle in around your eyes. Primrose yellow, shell pink, pale lavender, silvery blue, true silver and real gold are highlights. Texture plays a part in all this, too. Beige can be a highlight if it's gleaming and frosted, lowlight if it's powdery and matte.

When you want prominent eyes to recede, you shadow them with smoky, soft, matte shadows. You pull them out of hiding with shiny highlights on the lids, pale shimmer on the eyebone.

I usually stick to gray, gray-brown, or gray-blue shadow and pinkish highlights on occasion. They all look more natural to me than emerald eyelids—at least as natural as rings of shadow over the eyes is ever going to look. If you do like positive color, try mixing several different pastels together. It's softer, more becoming than any one color alone and makes you feel like more of an artist. In summer, I sometimes blend pale pink, pale yellow, and a little silver frosting. It's a pretty, pale-peachy effect that looks cool and festive. Try mauve and light gray-beige with pale blue.

Matching shadow color to eye color is not the most effective way to "bring out" your eyes. The two blues, or browns, or whatever, almost never really match. I find that a sort of golden brown can make blue eyes look bluer and truer than ever. It's the opposite of blue on the color wheel, and the contrast is fantastic. Russet brown to winey tones can do the same for green eyes.

Cake eye shadow or very soft eye color pencils are the easiest to blend with the least pressure on delicate skin around the eyes. Use a very soft brush. Make shadow even lighter, easier to blend by holding the brush vertically and poking up and down in the shadow. You'll pick up all the shadow you need on the tip of the brush.

I draw a little sidewise V in the corner of the eye. Smudge and blend up into the crease of the lid, and inward to the center of the lid. I never take shadow closer toward the nose, or all the way over the eyelid. It's too heavy and makes eyes look close-set. As with foundation, I do one side at a time, blend, then do the other side to

check balance and be sure that both sides match. I brush very lightly at the line of the lower lashes to the middle of the lower lid. This is very, very light with most of the shading over the eyes.

6. Now come false eyelashes (on occasion—otherwise, I skip to the next step). I prefer the term Estée Lauder uses for these, "supplementary lashes," because the point is just that: to supplement your own lashes and make them look thicker—not to get a stuck-on look. Individual lashes look more natural than any others. They glue on here and there between the real lashes and last for a week or so. I don't have the time or patience for them, and I have a thing about washing my face (tricky with lashes on) and about sleep. How can you sleep naturally if you're worried about bending your lashes?

I'll stick to lashes in strips. They can be as bristly as you like or as delicate. They come nicely feathered, or you can trim to taste by using a single-edge razor blade in a rocking motion. You can also cut up the strip so you supplement only at the outer corner, or almost to the inner corner. I say almost because lashes look very unnatural if they go beyond the outer two-thirds of the eye. Using them on the lower lid will only close up your eyes. Mascara is the only supplement for lower lashes.

Putting on lashes takes a little practice, but not much. A wooden toothpick is the best tool. Dip the tip in surgical glue. Get the smallest amount and spread with the toothpick along the lash strip. Pick up the lash and hold as close as possible to the lash line. With the toothpick in the other hand, I use it to press false lashes downward with little vertical strokes so both lash lines meet. So there is no joint visible, I wet an eyeliner brush and dip it in my eyeshadow. Then I draw a thin line at the lashes. A little mascara (dark or medium brown, dark gray, *never* black—too harsh!) over real and false lashes makes them look uniform.

7. Lips come last, but they have got to be there. In fact, you could skip, as I often do, from moisturizing straight to mascara, but you must never omit the fifth and final step.

Whenever you look at someone, you make contact with either lips or eyes. A pale, thin mouth puts me off. I like the look of very moist, sensuous lips. They need not be vivid crimson. In fact, unless your teeth are up to a TV commercial for toothpaste, you will do them and yourself a favor by wearing not bright, but soft, rose, peach, or apricot lip color. But to have a beautiful mouth you have to wear something. It needn't be color. Clear lip gloss, cocoa butter, anti-chap stick, anything. But something. Twenty-four hours every day. But since color is such as easy way to make yourself more beautiful, why not use it?

Lips should be soft, but the outline shouldn't. Get the clearest shape with a lipstick brush. Here's how: balance the elbow of your drawing hand on a table. Rest your chin in the three fingers and heel of the palm of that hand. Use the thumb and index finger to hold the brush. Go from corner to center of the mouth.

Outline first in a color one shade darker than your lipstick and feather the color down into the lips. Fill in the outline in the lighter shade. Clear lip gloss goes over this to protect the color and put a shine to it. You can use lip gloss under color, too. Outline, then use lip gloss, and fill in over it. If lipstick darkens or gets the blues later, use more lip gloss.

Blotting went out with the Edsel.

Following the natural outline of lips looks better to me. It might pass at a distance if you paint way over or way inside your lips, but up close it just calls attention to the natural shape you are trying to camouflage. If you feel your lips really need this kind of over- or underplaying, spend your evening this week practicing with the lip brush to see just how close to the natural line you can go without losing the effect you're after.

SPECIALS FOR YOUR FOOD PLANNING

• Bake some bread. It might sound demented, when you're trying to watch your weight, to suggest eating bread, let alone baking it. Believe me, this bread is something else. First, it is packed with protein from whole grains and nuts. So it helps your body, all of it from hair to nails. The body also demands carbohydrates for storage of proteins. Your brain thrives on the energy from properly utilized carbohydrates. No matter what your eating plan, one or two slices of whole-grain bread each day is a wise idea. The U.S. Olympics teams eat two-day-old bread, by the way. It's easier to digest, according to Hermann G. Rusch, food supervisor for the U.S. teams. If you can stand to wait, you can keep the following easy-to-make bread for two days before using it, but it won't be easy. The smell of it as it bakes is so good that it might even go into the list of fragrance suggestions for the season.

SUPERLOAF

2½ cups whole wheat flour
1 teaspoon baking soda
1 teaspoon sea salt or salt substitute
1 teaspoon baking powder
pinch of cinnamon
    Sift together into a bowl. Add:
½ cup molasses or raw honey
¼ cup polyunsaturated oil
1½ cups buttermilk
½ cup chopped walnuts or cashews
1 tablespoon grated orange rind

    Stir everything together. Pour into a loaf pan and let stand for 20 minutes. Bake at 375° for 45 minutes to an hour.

• How do you take your coffee? Seldom, I hope, because it can bedevil your system. A patient at Walter Reed Medical Center was sent to their psychiatric clinic because of his apprehension, dizziness, and trembling. Treatment gave no relief until it was discovered that he drank fourteen cups of coffee and a few colas each day. Cutting down on caffeine cleared up the symptoms within a month. A bit of protein such as cheese and crackers along with coffee might help prevent caffeine nerves. If you do drink coffee and drink it sweetened, try honey instead of sugar. We find it has a much smoother taste as well as being better for you

• C.S. stands for clear soups and for carrot sticks. Both are great low-calorie foods for the menu this month.

• If it's ever inexpensive, beef is lowest in price from winter to spring. Budget cuts are lower in fat, too, and make good soups. Make a soup the day before you plan to serve it. Refrigerate. Before serving, remove the congealed fat and reheat to get protein value without saturated fat. Lamb is a good buy through late spring, and an even better protein buy than beef on a ratio of protein to calories. (Refer to the chart on page 120.)

SPECIALS FOR YOUR MAKEUP AND FRAGRANCE

• Which comes first, clothes or makeup? Clothes do. Always. But especially if you are wearing a difficult color or are trying to match the beigy foundation you usually wear to a new beigy dress. In these cases it's wisest to have the outfit in front of you for checking before you fit yourself out in makeup.

• If you try to match lip color to nail color, you are dating yourself and boring your audience. Do your hands a flattering favor and put a pale color on nails. Use a richer one in the same family on lips. The lighter color on nails makes your hands look longer and more graceful. Try it. I don't know the reason myself, but it works.

• About your nails. Always have a pen or pencil with you. Not for doodling on nails, but saving them. Use the pencil to rummage through your handbag; use the eraser end for telephone dialing and button pressing. Use the business end of the pencil to make a note in your diary to lay in a good supply of cuticle cream. You need little dabs all the time, especially at this time of the year.

• A pencil-poke through your bag should unearth a spray cologne or spray perfume. Women who complain that perfume doesn't last on them are usually asking for too much lasting power. Four hours is a long run. Give yourself and your scent a lift with a quick refresher after four hours.

SPECIALS FOR YOUR SKIN AND BODY

• Get hold of a slantboard, or rig one up for yourself: Prop a narrow padded board (an ironing board is perfect) up securely on a fifteen-inch slant. The support might be a wooden box or a chair. The chair should have its back to the wall so it can't slide. If you use a wooden box, tack nonskid rubber to the bottom, or nail box and board together for security's sake. The idea is to lie on the slantboard with feet elevated and spine straight for fifteen minutes at a clip—longer if you have time. This position speeds the blood back up to your head and heart, away from the legs. So you take potentially dangerous pressure off the legs (varicose veins) and wake up the complexion.

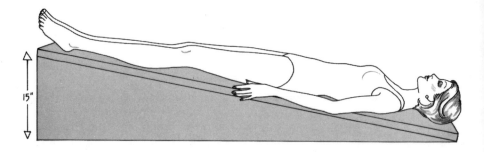

• Never draw a bath without adding a few drops of oil to the water—at least until the warm weather. For now, quick baths with bath oil added are your best bet. If you bathe right before bedtime (or earlier if you are staying in) you'll give your skin a long, soothing opportunity to replace natural oils before you meet the elements again.

• Don't forget elbows in the moisturizing scheme. Quickest way to treat them: whenever you cream your hands, cup a palm to your elbow. Rub. What would be excess cream on your palms will get put to good use.

SPECIALS FOR YOUR HAIR

• If you use heated rollers to curl your hair, wait until hair is dry. It is elastic while wet, and will shrink tighter and tighter around the curler as it dries and you will have ugly tight curls.

• Massage your scalp often. Use the balls of your fingers and really rub to keep scalp loose and the blood circulating. An electric scalp massager is one of the few hair helps you can't use too often. If there is someone around to give you a scalp massage, so much the sexier.

• Scalp massage brings up the subject of traction alopecia. That's the technical term for hair loss that occurs when the hair is pulled too tight for too long. It's particularly threatening to children. I saw a child in New York who showed early signs of it. Because she wanted her beautiful long hair out of her way, it was tied back in a ponytail, but she would keep tightening it through the day. A real hair loss showed about the hairline in time. When her hair was cut short, the hair loss stopped and everyone was happy. I strongly recommend short hair for a child. A girl will have lots of time to wear long hair later—but not if she loses it at seven. If you wear your hair in a ponytail or chignon, make it a loose one. Use a fabric-covered elastic to hold hair, never a twisted rubber band. Cornrow hair styles for black women can be artistic triumphs, as Cicely Tyson has proved. But they take hours to do, and I can well understand the reluctance to undo all that work, even though the hair is pulled dangerously tight. But unless you undo it, it will be the undoing of your hair. Save such hairstyles for special occasions, and keep hair clean and free the rest of the time. Or set aside the extra time for daily redoing. Any time spent on heightening your morale and pride in yourself is time well spent.

MARCH

At the end of this month, winter goes out and spring comes in. The tag end of the winter season can seem like the longest part of the year, so make the month one that is filled with new adventures that enliven the next four weeks.

It may be too cold where you are for outdoor exercise. How about giving a twist to indoor exercise by doing something that's really fun. How about learning to belly dance? Seriously. It really is exercise even though it seems like a lark. Or how about fencing? Or tap dancing. Tap dancing is having a big revival, not because it happens to be a terrific workout, but because it's so much fun.

If your idea of fun is on the quieter side, how about planning a series of little dinners this month? Just four of you to try out the recipes you've collected but never used for Chinese dishes or for paella. Or how about a film festival at home? Not movies of your last vacation, but maybe a different Hitchcock classic every week. Hundreds of great films (and the projector to show them) can be rented for nontheatrical showing at home. Costs of this could be defrayed by making it a group project with friends and the theater could be a different living room each week.

Color, in big doses, is more welcome now than ever. Do you have a long drab hallway or a basement that could stand a jolt of cosmetic color? Since a hallway isn't a place to linger, it can be decorated in an uninhibited way. You might like a really eye-opening color on the walls and ceiling, or to repeat the brightest accent color in your scheme in shiny enamel on the doors and woodwork, or a different color on every door. Get out the rollers and do it.

Or you could paint a mural. Painting on a grand scale, across an entire wall, has freed the hidden artist in many people who "could never draw a straight line" on a little scale. Drawing a straight line isn't the point, anyway. A file of big, naïve sunflowers marching down the walls of a hallway can be very crudely drawn, with crooked stems, and be just that much more effective for their unpolished air. Think of the charm of a child's painting. Some of that charm lies in a free, open response to the beauty of the world and the simple joy of playing with paints.

Open yourself to that kind of unselfconscious action and there need never be any dreariness to late winter (or any other season) that you cannot overcome.

YOUR CHECKLIST AND SCHEDULE FOR MARCH

First Morning of the Month
> Log your vital statistics into your diary (p. 14) *in ink.* Set your goals for the month as to loss of pounds or inches and gains in other areas, such as proficiency at yoga, say, or using the hand-held dryer. Pencil in your goals on the diary page for the last day of the month, and start the program that will help you achieve your goals.

Every Morning
> Seven-Way Stretch   (p. 91)
> Cup of hot water and lemon juice
> Warm-up exercises   (p. 146)
> Clean face and moisturize   (p. 54)
> Makeup   (p. 61)
> Fix hair
> Vitality Drink and nutritional supplements   (p. 94)

Every Evening
> Warm-up exercises to relax

Feet-up rest with pillows or on slantboard for 10 minutes
Clean face and moisturize
Bath and all-over body lotion   (p. 128)
Clean teeth before bed   (p. 259)
As Often as You Like: At Least Three Times Each Week
Exercise session of 30 minutes   (p. 242)
Yoga session of 30 minutes   (p. 96)
Shampoo and finishing rinse   (pp. 45–46)
Once Each Week
An evening (or a day) of rest, a time for yourself
10-minute protective protein conditioning pac for hair
Manicure and pedicure   (p. 201)
Tweeze stray hairs on eyebrows   (p. 167)
Shave legs and underarms   (p. 166)
Facial mask   (p. 162)
Once This Month
One night and one day of rest for the digestive system on the detoxifying Liquid Fast or the Clearing House Diet   (pp. 36–38)
Haircut and any other professional hair services such as color or perm. (Your cutter might advise a cut more often, perhaps every three weeks. Follow his suggestion in making out your individual schedule.)

HAIR COLORING

Color has become one of the most exciting aspects of our profession for a very good reason—after the supercut, color is the most becoming change you can effect in hair.

Even beyond the colorist's ability to flatter eye and skin tone with new highlights and shadings, color can help the structure of your hair. It can give extra body to fine hair, as if an extra layer had been added.

To enjoy the benefits of color, you needn't change your natural shade. A color conditioner that matches your own hair color exactly will give your hair incredible sheen, new lights, and new body.

Almost every woman can benefit from the advances in products and techniques available to the colorist today. But I cannot urge you too strongly to have your hair colored by a professional who has studied for years to perfect skills and sensitivity to colorings and shadings.

Granted, there are products that the amateur can use at home, and these are carefully formulated not to harm the hair if you use them with the same care that went into making them. Do not attempt or expect, however, to make extreme color changes at home. (You should not expect to be able to do the same job as your dentist when it's a question of filling cavities, although you can brush your teeth and care for them on your own.) I think home coloring should be limited to temporary rinses.

Before we go further into the subject of color, let's discuss coloring agents.

There are three kinds of coloring.

Temporary: These are rinses. They coat the hair shaft with clear color to darken or highlight. On light to medium hair, a rinse can add burnished gold or copper highlights, it can fire up the red in the hair or tone it down, it can add dramatic deep lights and brighten with shine. Rinses are good as toners on already colored hair that has oxidized to brassy, greenish, or too red a color. Rinses can add some color to help tone in gray hair, but they will not cover it. A rinse will not lighten your hair, because it contains no bleach.

With your next shampoo, the rinse washes away completely. Should you choose not to use it on your hair again, not to worry. A rinse does not penetrate the hair shaft or change its structure, so you have no problems of porosity or other damage to cope with. You should not use a rinse before having a permanent. Coloring and permanent should be spaced two weeks apart. That goes for any coloring, not just rinses.

If you follow our advice, a rinse is the *only* coloring agent you will ever use at home. Get one that has built-in conditioners, and be very careful with it.

Semipermanent: That means approximately one month. Semipermanent colorings are similar to temporary rinses, but they do change the structure of the hair to a certain degree. They coat and slightly penetrate the hair shaft. Each time you shampoo, a bit of the color is washed away until it goes completely with enough shampooing. If you don't like a semipermanent color, you can speed it on its way by shampooing often. If your hair has been previously tinted and is, therefore, more porous, a semipermanent color can become permanent as it penetrates deeper into the hair shaft. Semipermanent coloring does more of what a temporary rinse does—it can darken more dramatically, add brighter color. But you cannot lighten your hair with a semipermanent color. Like a rinse, it has no bleach.

To our ears, semipermanent sounds serious. There are semipermanent colorings available to the home doer, but for anything that will change your looks for a whole month, we think you should go to a professional. You are getting better-looking all the time; why set yourself back by an easily avoidable mistake?

Permanent: This group is just that. Using bleach, tint, or dye means altering the structure of your hair. For good. Or for ill, if anything less than an expert job is done. It should only be done by a professional colorist. So rather than tell you about the kits and products that are on sale in the drugstores to help you harm your hair, we would prefer to speak of the absolutely marvelous and beautiful ways that a professional can color your hair to make it more flattering to your individual beauty than ever.

You can give your hair a cool shade to tone out reds and bright yellow, or you can add brightness with a warm shade.

Fair hair can be switched to a striking dark color that will make the fragile coloring of your skin more dramatic by contrast. Dark hair can be subtly lightened around the face to soften the features.

These are simply generalizations, and we could go on listing the possibilities for pages, and still not cover them. As you are a unique person, the perfect color treatment for you will be absolutely unique.

Before you do anything about color, do keep in mind these basic guidelines:

Color should be scheduled not sooner than two weeks after hair is permed.

Extra conditioning treatments—a month of them—are a good idea for your hair before you color to get best results.

Be honest with the colorist about your time, money, and life. If you want a radical change of color, you must be prepared to come back frequently for touch-ups and treatment. But you can help yourself to color magic even if you can only afford the time and money for two visits a year to the colorist. Henna treatments and highlighting techniques will need attention only every few months. Between the two of you, a great color plan can be worked out that is perfect for you and your life.

Give color a chance. The true effect of color depends on the natural oils of your hair, and the new color will really sing only two days after treatment.

There are a million beautiful possibilities, and only one rule: *Color must suit the eyes and the skin tone.*

This basic rule will always be true—but the days of flat, all-one-color hair are over. The colorist now mixes up to a dozen separate tints to use on a single head of hair so that enough, just enough, of the natural shading remains to flatter the complexion; but the over-all effect is of dramatic new color that enhances your life in a way that was impossible before.

If you are a brunette, you can become a blonde. Not a hard platinum woman, but an alluring and feminine creature with soft and sexy blond hair that has warm rose and honey lights in it, or tawny and smoky depths to it.

If your hair is gray, you can change it completely, make it any color you like, or turn it into a tremendously elegant silver frame for soft, youthful color in your skin and eyes so they flash with color as they never did at twenty.

In the salons, we have been using color for an asymmetrical effect that is smashing. Not streaking, but perhaps doing one side of the head in a marvelous Titian red that sweeps around and blends almost imperceptibly into warm brown on the other side.

Henna, one of the oldest colorings, is popular again, and can give some remarkably beautiful lights to even black hair. Black henna used on almost-black hair can give it deep lights like a ripe black plum; or henna can put a sort of fire-down-below gleam like polished rosewood into drab brown hair. Use natural henna for body.

I said before that hair color must be uniquely yours, and I meant it. There are a few general rules of thumb for specific situations that should be borne in mind:

If your hair is gray, or graying, you should not do the unimaginative thing and just "go blond." With the lighter skin tone that often accompanies gray hair, blond can simply tire the face. In coloring we prefer to work some of the gray in along with both warm and cool highlights in blond to brown tones. It gives a better, and younger, glow for the skin and a more natural look.

Black women can enjoy the drama of the jet-black hair that is harsh and witchy with paler skin tones. I have seen some beautiful color jobs with reds for black women. Provided, of course, that it suits her skin tone, a black woman with deep auburn hair can be a knock-out. Since most black women have very porous hair, it's important to be very careful with color. A dramatic change—to strawberry blond or pale coppery red, for example—should be done with a wig rather than by overtreating the hair.

If you are Oriental, we beg you to keep your hair blue-black and shining. Oriental hair is the strongest of hair, if well cared for, but I don't think it should be dyed. We have seen every variation of blond, brown, and red hair worn by Oriental women and it just doesn't work, as far as we are concerned, with the delicate tints of your skin. Give your hair a smashingly beautiful cut and keep all the color and shine naturally intact.

COLOR IS DIFFERENT FROM SEASON TO SEASON

Not that phony malarkey that you read in magazines that this is the season to be a redhead, or the year of the blonde. But your hair and your color thinking vary with the seasons.

Because of more sun, everyone's hair looks lighter in late spring and summer. You may want to accentuate the effect with highlighting, or lightening the hairs that frame the face. Individual hairs can be lightened to make a kind of airy, golden lacework around your face even if you don't touch the rest of your head.

Richer color seems to suit fall and the richer colors worn then. Fall is a good time for temporary rinses that will put a deep glow into your natural color and will mask any oxidation that has changed tinted hair over the summer.

Winter is peak season for flagging spirits, and hair color may want help. You can brighten or lighten your hair, or you can deepen the color, but darkening is trickier in winter since the contrast with winter-pale skin can be a little severe.

Ever and always, however, hair color must suit the skin tone and the eye color—and a professional colorist is the best judge!

VITAMINS—YOU NEEDN'T BE A CRANK

We agree on vitamins—up to a point. The point is that everybody needs them. Vidal takes so many vitamin pills that if you shook him he would rattle. But everything was prescribed for him. I take one multi-vitamin capsule with breakfast, extra vitamin C in the morning and the evening. We both are happy with our very different vitamin programs.

You and your doctor must be the ones to decide on what is just right for you.

You should know the guidelines and the suggestions before you go out to shop for vitamins. And there is new information all the time. The first vitamin, vitamin A, wasn't isolated and named until the eve of World War I. New discoveries are still going on.

The United States Food and Drug Administration has revised its thinking on vitamins. The old minimum daily requirement (MDR) has been changed to a higher recommended daily allowance (RDA). You'll find the list on pages 83–84.

Lots of vitamins is the usual prescription these days to look beautiful, stay youthful, feel great. Without the right supply and the right amount of vitamins you won't be any of those things. But you should know what you're going.

You won't overdose on vitamins (with a few important exceptions such as vitamin A) because most are water-soluble and the body throws off what it doesn't need or want. You need minerals to work with vitamins, and we know less about them than we do about vitamins. Studies are going on now, in fact, to determine whether an overload of minerals might actually speed up aging!

You needn't be a crank to wonder what you need and don't need.

We've put together charts with everything we could find out to help.

Before getting into the individual vitamins, let's clear up a few general points.

GET AN O.K. FROM THE DOCTOR?

A balanced supplement is a good idea for everybody. If you have hypoglycemia or diabetes or high blood pressure or have had rheumatic fever, then your case is special and your doctor will probably want you to have more of some vitamins, perhaps less of others.

IS A SUPPLEMENT NECESSARY?
CAN'T YOU GET EVERYTHING IN FOOD?

All the vitamins and the minerals that the government recommends, in the amounts you need (and sometimes exceeding them) are available in food. Of course, you might have to eat an awful lot of food. It takes a whole 1,095 calorie loaf of whole wheat bread to supply the day's needs of vitamin B_1. We did a research project to find out the minimum amount of food that would supply you with all the vitamins and minerals you need for the day. You get the quota and then some if you eat everything on this list every day:

4 glasses tomato juice	1 cup raw wheat germ
1 cup fresh grapefruit juice	3 cups skim milk
10 tablespoons brewer's yeast	8 ounces beef liver
1 grated carrot	2 shrimps
1 cup canned tuna	5 whole dried apricots

If you ate all of these every day you would be full of vitamins and minerals, but bored to death, and the lack of balance wouldn't make for very beautiful skin, hair, or health. Why not put as many of these foods, really wonder foods, into a richly varied diet to boost your vitamin intake (and your looks) and add a vitamin supplement for extra insurance.

NATURAL OR SYNTHETIC—DOES IT MATTER?

Beauty and nutrition experts Linda Clark and Adelle Davis have written that natural vitamins are superior. Erwin DiCyan, Ph.D., says in his book *Vitamins in Your Life* that synthetic vitamins are the equal of natural ones. You must be the judge. We feel that in a world where food shortages and famine are a horrible fact of life, it is irresponsible to process foods into vitamin tablets when a synthetic alternative exists. Apart from ethical considerations, natural vitamins are more expensive. If your finances won't allow for them, then there is no question.

WHAT ABOUT MEGAVITAMINS?

This term means, simply, massive doses of vitamins. Taking vitamin C in the large doses recommended by Dr. Linus Pauling for colds is an example. Any time you take vitamins in amounts that are higher than the U.S. RDA, you are taking megavitamins. If you think you are in need of massive doses of any vitamin for therapeutic results, check it out with one of the new breed of doctors who specialize in preventive medicine. We cannot repeat too often that you need a balanced supply of the full alphabet of vitamins. Make up some lopsided program for yourself (lots of this, a bit of that) and you open a Pandora's box. A chilling example of where it can lead is the case of the canary-colored corpse. A forty-eight-year-old Londoner devised for himself a vitamin A cure: a gallon of carrot juice and 1,000,000 IU (international units) of vitamin A each day. In ten days he had turned bright yellow, and was dead of cirrhosis.

WHICH IS THE BEST TIME TO TAKE VITAMINS —MORNING OR NIGHT?

Breakfast is the ideal time. Swallow your tablets or pills along with the morning Vitality Drink. Since blood sugar is at low ebb in the late afternoon, you might want another vitamin pick-me-up around three or four o'clock. Have a glass of skim milk or tomato juice with a little brewer's or food yeast stirred in, along with your vitamin pill, and you get an energy boost of B vitamins. Since vitamin C is so easily destroyed, yet so important, have a vitamin C tablet before bed. If you smoke, you should probably take vitamin C even more often—each cigarette destroys 25 milligrams of vitamin C!

WHAT ABOUT B$_{12}$ FOR ENERGY?

If you get B$_{12}$ all by itself you are wasting money and not achieving anything worthwhile. The B vitamins—all of them together and in the proper balance—are essential for becoming the beautiful person you can be. Here is the proportion you want:

B$_1$, B$_2$, B$_6$, folacin . . . . .approx. 2 milligrams of each
niacin, pantothenic acid . . . . .approx. 20 milligrams of each
PABA (para-aminobenzoic acid) . .approx. 40 milligrams
choline, inositol . . . . .approx. 1,000 milligrams of each
B$_{12}$ . . . . .approximately 1 to 3 micrograms

A microgram is just one 1,000th of a milligram, so you can see how little the requirement of vitamin B$_{12}$ really is. So don't waste your money on separate B$_{12}$ pills; get those that supply you with all of the B complex.

THREE THINGS YOU SHOULD NEVER DO

Never take vitamins on an empty stomach. Vitamins must combine with the proteins, minerals, and enzymes in food to work. You will also wind up with a strong, unpleasant aftertaste, and possibly an upset stomach.

Never diagnose vitamin-deficiency symptoms on your own. Cramps may be a sign of deficiency of B$_1$, or they may be tied in with menstruation. Dry, itchy skin can stem from a need for vitamin A, or for a milder soap.

Never take supplementary vitamin E and iron together. Most iron salts destroy the E. Have E with breakfast, iron after dinner. Female hormones also destroy vitamin E. If you take hormones, space them as you would iron.

VITAMIN CONTRADICTIONS

One excellent reason for getting good professional advice on vitamin supplements is that there are so many "experts" with such conflicting "expert opinions." The only one to listen to is the one who really knows about your individual needs. Each of us is unique in so many ways; doesn't it stand to reason that we should be unique in our vitamin and mineral requirements? And that these requirements should vary as our daily life varies?

Dr. Linus Pauling says that the daily requirement for vitamin C varies from 250 milligrams daily to 10 grams daily. His estimate of the minimum requirement is more than four times that of the Food and Drug Administration and allows for a vast difference in individual needs predicated on many factors.

In undergoing a complete series of physical examinations at the famous Leahy Clinic in Boston, I was told by the doctors there that supplementary folic acid or supplementary vitamin B_{12} would upset my body's particular balance of the B vitamin complex. But while I need not and should not supplement with these vitamins, they may be exactly what you require.

The only way to know is to consult a doctor who knows this field. He cannot really judge your nutritional needs just by looking at you, but he can give you a blood test and urinalysis, then, based on your dietary pattern, he can prescribe the vitamins you need—and tell you what you don't need, too!

It may sound expensive, but it's far cheaper and healthier than spending money and time on taking the wrong vitamin supplements.

VITAMINS AND MINERALS—Which Ones You Need, How Much, and One Food That Meets the Total Daily Quota

VITAMIN	U.S. RDA		SOURCE
A	5,000 IU		1 grated carrot
B_1	1.5 mg.		1 T. brewer's yeast
B_2	1.7 mg.		2 T. brewer's yeast
B_3	20 mg.		6 T. brewer's yeast
B_6	2 mg.		4 glasses tomato juice
Folacin	.4 mg.		4 T. brewer's yeast
PABA		(40 mg.)	10 T. brewer's yeast
Pantothenic acid	10 mg.		10 T. brewer's yeast
Biotin	.3 mg.		10 T. brewer's yeast
B_{12}	6 mcg.		1 slice beef liver (8 oz.)

Cholin	(1,000 mg.)	1 cup raw wheat germ
Inositol	(1,000 mg.)	
C	60 mg.	1 cup fresh grapefruit juice
D	400 IU	1 cup canned tuna
E	30 IU	1 cup raw wheat germ
Calcium	1 g.	3 cups skim milk
Phosphorus	1 g.	
Iodine	150 mcg.	2 shrimp
Iron	18 mg.	1 slice beef liver (8 oz.)
Magnesium	400 mg.	1 cup raw wheat germ
Zinc	15 mg.	1 cup raw wheat germ
Potassium	(5,000 mg. per T. of salt in the diet)	5 whole dried apricots
Copper	2 mg.	8 oz. beef liver

Figures in parentheses are suggested requirements by Adelle Davis in *Let's Eat Right To Keep Fit* and are used as indications of possible need for those vitamins and minerals for which no U.S. RDA has been determined.)

VITAMINS: WHAT THEY DO FOR YOU AND WHERE TO FIND THEM

Vitamin A is for skin and hair and nails and teeth and eyes and . . . The possibility of a deficiency is very remote, so don't diagnose one for yourself. Vitamin A is one of the few that the body stores, so you *can* overdose with it. If you eliminate fats from your diet, you're asking for trouble with vitamin A. It needs fats to be used by the body. You can get all the A you need from food: 1 grated carrot meets the daily requirement, one ounce of beef liver triples it.

Vitamin B₁ (Thiamin) is vital for vitality, for muscle tone, for skin and hair. Too many carbohydrates, too much liquor, tension, very cold weather, or very hot weather increase your need for it. Brewer's yeast, wheat germ, and sunflower seeds are the richest sources. Almonds, cashews, and pecans have it, too.

Vitamin B₂ (riboflavin) is for good vision and firm tissue; it also protects you from infection and breaks down fatty acids. Without it, you'll be anemic. But get it with the other B vitamins. You need all of them working together for you. Here we go again—liver, brewer's yeast are the richest sources.

Vitamin B₃ (niacin) is for whipping up the circulation, reducing cholesterol, and turning carbohydrates into food for the brain. Without enough, you will be moody and depressed. Liver, tuna, chicken, brown rice, halibut are rich in niacin.

Vitamin B₆ (pyridoxine) is for the brain, too. It also helps the body deal with fats, proteins, and amino acids. If you take The Pill or tranquilizers, or are on a very high protein diet, you need more pyridoxine. Without enough, you retain water and get migraines. Wheat germ to the rescue.

Vitamin C is a complex, too. It is made up of ascorbic acid, rutin, bioflavonoids, citrinoids, chalcone, and quercitin. All elements of the complex are found in the pulp of citrus fruits, but not everything is together in synthetic vitamin C tablets. So take your supplements, but don't skip natural sources of C. Eat oranges, tangerines, lemons, limes, papayas, broccoli, sweet green peppers, strawberries, grapefruit, to give C a chance, yourself a treat.

Vitamin D is the one that helps calcium and phosphorus build bones, teeth, and tissue. You need fat to use it, as with vitamin A, and like A, it is stored in the body. To work, it needs to be in partnership with vitamins A, K, and E, as well as with good polyunsaturated fats. Dr. Alexander Schmidt, Director of the U.S. FDA, says that the RDA of 400 IU of vitamin D is "rational, reasonable, and rather puny." Adelle Davis's recommendation was for 5,000 IU daily. One cup of canned salmon will put you somewhere in between. Milk is usually fortified with D.

Vitamin E is for protecting every cell in your body against aging by oxidation. It protects your lungs against pollution and prevents the liver spots and varicose veins that are outwardly aging, since it aids the circulation and keeps red blood cells from being destroyed. Whether it increases your sexual performance is up to you. Although polyunsaturated fats are the best kind to keep your cholesterol level down, they do use up vitamin E to keep from turning into saturated fats. So step up vitamin E in your diet by 100 IU for each tablespoon of fat. Add E gradually, no more than 100 IU a day. Liver and wheat germ are rich in it.

Folacin is for building red blood cells and metabolizing proteins. A deficiency might occur if you take The Pill, *but* any supplementation must be on doctor's orders. It can be very dangerous if you get folacin and B₁₂ in the wrong balance. Orange juice has folacin along with the big three—wheat germ, brewer's yeast, liver.

Pantothenic acid is for the adrenal glands, along with all the things that B_6 helps. Alcoholics are the only ones likely to be deficient in it, and they are deficient in all the B vitamins. Avocados, eggs, and brewer's yeast will give it to you.

Biotin is for your hair and skin. Another liver and yeast specialty.

Vitamin B_{12} is the one that keeps your digestion peppy, your energy high. Deficiency is common among vegetarians and alcoholics. The need is small in most of us (higher if you take The Pill) and is supplied in liver, brewer's yeast, eggs, meat, and oysters.

Vitamin C is the miracle worker when it comes to destroying poisons, bacteria, virus infections, while it heals wounds, prevents fatigue, (maybe) lowers cholesterol, prevents allergies, and goes on to build healthy blood vessels, teeth, tissue, and bones. You can't have enough of vitamin C's kind of help. The only possible shadow on megadoses of C is that some researchers suspect it may act against the dissolving of crystals of uric acid, so kidney stones may form in time. If you save the megadoses for times when you need them, and get a healthy supply the rest of the year, not to worry. When you need a megadose is at the onset of a cold. Then you should have up to 1,000 milligrams per hour, every hour. Dr. Alan H. Nittler, in his book *A New Breed of Doctor*, suggests that you take 1 kelp capsule, 1,000 milligrams of vitamin A, and 41 milligrams of calcium lactate along with the vitamin C. He also recommends 2,000 milligrams of vitamin C hourly for poison ivy; massive doses of vitamin C along with vitamin E for burns. Lots of vitamin C is a good idea if you smoke. Twenty-five milligrams per cigarette are destroyed. The daily requirement is 60 milligrams.

This is a vitamin, but not a necessary nutrient: *Vitamin K* is for guarding the body against hemorrhage and is manufactured by your body with no outside help. It's also found in many foods, especially leafy green vegetables.

This next one is not, strictly speaking, a vitamin, although research is going on now to isolate a new vitamin that is found in it. We are talking about *lecithin*. Lecithin is a group of substances; your liver manufactures a certain amount of lecithin, so it is not absolutely necessary to supplement this nutrient. It is a miracle worker, though. It keeps fats moving through the bloodstream. It has been shown to reduce the cholesterol level substantially for many, many people—in some cases by almost half, even on a high-cholesterol diet. It may have a role in protecting the lungs and in preventing blood clots. We are being overcautious in all of this, because real proof is impossible to find until all the evidence is in. We are as tired as you are of wildly exaggerated claims for this or that one vitamin (or one face cream or anything else) that will do everything for whatever complaint you have. We do know that lecithin is found in seeds, and few of us eat many seeds. It's found, for instance, in soybeans. Cigarette smoke destroys it in the lungs. The liver manufactures some, but not enough for most people. We ourselves take two tablespoons of powdered lecithin in our break-fast Vitality Drink every morning. If you are concerned about your cholesterol level, or the fat in and on your body, you might want to add lecithin to your program of supplements. If you do, get more calcium. Lecithin is very high in phosphorus, (which must be balanced with calcium).

MINERALS

You know that your body needs them along with the vitamins; but minerals are a less well-charted territory.

There are some you must have, and in precise amounts. Others are adequately supplied by a good balanced diet and should be supplemented only if your doctor prescribes this. There are some other minerals that can be death-dealing.

Do not supplement your diet with:

Cadmium

Nickel

Selenium

Fluorine (it's no problem in water or toothpaste, though)

Tin

Vanadium

Sodium (you need *only* up to 1 g. daily. Even salt-free diets usually contain up to 6 times that. Sodium is in almost everything)

Do not supplement (except under prescription and supervision) with:

Chromium   Manganese   Potassium

Cobalt   Molybdenum

That leaves us with seven minerals that you may have to add if your diet doesn't supply the amounts of each you need daily. These are:

Calcium (1g.)   Iron (18 mg.)

Phosphorus (1 g.)   Magnesium (400 mg.)

Iodine (150 mcg.)   Zinc (15 mg.)

THE MAJOR MINERALS: WHAT THEY DO FOR YOU, AND WHERE TO GET THEM

Calcium, along with Vitamin C, forms collagen to keep skin firm and prevent stretch marks. Calcium works with phosphorus to form bones and teeth. Calcium is also the natural tranquilizer that can calm nerves, help you to sleep. Although calcium and phosphorus requirements are equal, you may have to take additional calcium because it is not so prevalent in the usual diet. Most of us get far more phosphorus than calcium (meat, for instance, is high in phosphorus, but not in calcium). Any excess phosphorus will combine with the calcium supply and leave the body as waste material. If a calcium imbalance is created, the body will take calcium from the bones to meet its needs. Cigarette smoking causes a further loss of calcium. Oranges, natural cheeses, green leafy vegetables, pineapple, yoghurt, and milk are all high in calcium and low in phosphorus. When combined with wheat germ, milk is an even better source of calcium. Adding vitamin D to milk improves the body's absorption of calcium.

Phosphorus works along with calcium to the same ends. It also helps turn B vitamins into energy and helps you use carbohydrates. Beef, beans, and Brazil nuts are high in phosphorus, not so high in calcium. Tuna is high in phosphorus, and grapefruit is balanced 50-50.

Iodine is needed throughout your life, but more than ever during adolescence and pregnancy. Iodized or sea salt, seafood, spinach are all rich sources of iodine, the real mission of which is to keep the thyroid gland functioning properly.

Magnesium is necessary for the brain to function well. It joins with phosphorus and enzymes to help the muscles and the nerves. Wheat germ has all you need.

Zinc works in producing collagen tissue to keep skin firm and elastic. Zinc is also important for sexual development. It helps in keeping circulation brisk, healing wounds, and preventing high blood pressure. Oysters, liver, and wheat germ are loaded with it.

Copper has a little mystery to it. No one is sure, but it probably works with zinc to reduce cholesterol. Beef liver has it, so do oysters.

Iron is vital for your blood and for your liver. You need lots of iron while you are growing, lots during menstruation, lots after menopause. You have an ironclad lifelong need for iron. All you want is to be found in liver, eggs, dried apricots, blackstrap molasses, and meats.

BEVERLY AND VIDAL ON: SLEEP— THE NO-COST BODY INSURANCE

VIDAL: Some medical researchers say that the human body requires very little sleep; other studies seem to indicate that we really do need the standard eight hours or more. I believe you have to know your own needs, know your limits, and get the amount of sleep that's right for you. If necessary, I can get by with only six hours of sleep per night for a week at a stretch, but then I will need ten hours a night for two nights in a row. It may be true that sleep before midnight is more valuable for the body, but the night that goes on until three or four in the morning has always been very rare for me. I leave the party by midnight whenever I have a morning show or meeting. It is unfair to oneself and to others to show up at less than peak form because of fatigue; unforgivable, if you are tired because of a night out on the town.

BEVERLY: I have to have eight or ten hours; if I have less, my skin shows it. It's dry and lifeless, it just doesn't fit. One of the great luxuries is to get some of your sleep in an afternoon nap, an hour's nap if you can make it—but even fifteen minutes lying with your feet propped up on pillows in a dark room is wonderfully restful. Of course, if you sleep too long, you'll want to stay up all night, and then you blow it. If you have trouble getting to sleep, try this to eliminate the urge to take a sleeping pill (they really are terrible for your looks, and they don't induce the kind of sleep you should have): Soak for ten or fifteen minutes in a warm bath. No vigorous scrubbing, just a warm relaxer. For super-luxury, bathe by candlelight, with very soft music playing on a transistor radio. Then blot yourself barely dry and crawl into bed. Drink a glass of warm milk (a little sherry or malted milk powder makes it even more soothing) and swallow three or four calcium lactate tablets with the milk. Calcium is a natural tranquilizer that works—I mean really works! You'll be out almost before you turn off the light.

VIDAL: When I have no desire to sleep, I feel it is because the body doesn't require sleep at that moment. When everyone else in the family is asleep and I'm fully awake, that's my time for meditation, or for putting on my earphones and listening to Sibelius' *Second Symphony*, Mahler's *Eighth,* or an Ellington *Nocturne,* or for reading a not-too-taxing book. Gradually I relax and at last I feel sleepy. Often, if I have been kept awake by a problem, I can relax into sleep in this way, and, although I haven't been concentrating on it, I often find that the problem has been solved at some point during a refreshing sleep.

One very important point about a refreshing sleep is this: *a hard mattress is essential.* Sleep gives the bones, the muscles, and the mind a chance to recover. If you sleep in a slumped, uncomfortable position, sunk into a hollow mattress, you will wake up aching. Because of my business I travel a great deal and very often the first thing I must order in a hotel is a bedboard. How hotels can continue to have those soft mattresses is beyond me. I guess nobody complains—except Bev and me.

If your mattress at home is soft and lumpy, get rid of it. If you can't afford to replace it now, put a bedboard under it and start saving for a new mattress.

Another way to improve your bed is to raise the lower part of the mattress. I think everybody should sleep with the feet elevated. It's the ideal position because the blood flows back up toward the heart and away from the feet. You can help prevent varicose veins and other circulatory problems by sleeping with the feet elevated. It's healthy even if you sleep on your stomach. With the feet up, you will then be in the position of a good swimmer, really. And that's fine for the back.

To raise the mattress, you can tuck a small suitcase with hard sides between the mattress and the springs. More esthetically, you can insert a wedge-shaped bolster of foam rubber. This can be bought in a department store, and mail-order houses offer them as well.

THE SEVEN-WAY STRETCH

Now that you've had a refreshing sleep, don't throw your body into shock by jolting out of bed. Coax your body into peak performance with an easy warm-up of muscle and frame, heart and lungs.

Before you arise, lie flat on your back for a five-minute session of slow, lazy stretching. Imitate the relaxed luxury of a sleek cat. If you make this an every-morning ritual, you will find that you move with the panther's grace that is everyone's ideal.

If your schedule is super-tight, we promise that the Seven-Way Stretch pays far higher dividends than five minutes of extra sleep.

THE SEVEN-DAY-A-WEEK SEVEN-WAY STRETCH
TO START THE DAY

1. Stretch both arms straight up toward the ceiling. Stretch hands open, fingers wide apart like an opening fan. Slowly lower arms to your sides. Slide them in a sweeping outward movement and backward over your head, as a child does to make "angel's wings" in the snow, and back down. Rest.

2. Arms at your sides, raise right leg to point to the ceiling. Stretch your foot from the ankle and point your toes. Rotating your foot from the ankle, draw circles in the air with your toes—seven circles; then slowly lower right leg to the bed. Repeat with the left leg. Rest.

3. Lying flat on your back with arms close to your sides, raise pelvis as high off the mattress as you can and slide your hands under the buttocks for support. Feet flat on the bed, slowly walk feet backward to raise the buttocks as high as possible. Hold for a count of seven, and slowly walk back down to the original position. Rest.

4. Lying flat on your back, raise right knee to the chest. Clasp the knee with both hands. Pull knee as close to the chin as possible.

Lower the right leg slowly, lowering against the pressure of your clasped hands. Now repeat with the left leg. Rest. (You have just done your first yoga pose.)

5. Lie flat with arms stretched out at your sides. Raise your arms and clasp hands above you. Keeping left arm straight, bend right elbow and bring it down to the bed, stretching your left arm. Hold for a count of seven. Reverse. Repeat. Rest.

6. Lying on your right side, roll your left knee up to your chin. Clasp it with your hands, hold for a count of seven. Lower and swing the left leg down and out behind you. Reverse. Rest.

7. Lie flat on your back and raise your head. With lips closed, lower your chin as far as you can to your chest. Hold for a count of seven and return your head to the bed. Stretch your neck slowly to touch right ear to right shoulder, now slowly to the other side. Relax.

Now, up and at it.

BEVERLY ON: VITALITY DRINKS FOR BREAKFAST . . . TO MAKE IN MINUTES FOR ALL-DAY ENERGY

Like everyone else who never cared much for breakfast and was watching the scales besides, I have gone through long periods of having a cup of tea and maybe half a grapefruit for breakfast. But busy days lately have changed that. I have finally come to realize something Vidal has known for years: a good, high-protein breakfast gives you long-lasting energy for hours.

We have a cup of hot water and lemon juice first; then I mix our favorite energizer in the blender.

PROTEIN DRINK FOR TWO (Vitality Drink)

2 tablespoons powdered protein (from a health food store or pharmacy)
1 tablespoon granular lecithin (from a health food store or pharmacy)
1 large banana
1 raw egg
2 cups low-fat or skim milk

Toss everything into the blender and let it whip up for 30 seconds.

Drink this slowly while you get ready for the day. It tastes delicious, and while you sip you might think about the benefits of the drink. The egg is high in complete protein. Protein from the protein powder, egg, and the milk builds every cell of the body, carries life, and guarantees reproduction. The digestive juices break protein down into essential amino acids. Some of these make up red blood cells, some are rushed to the constantly growing fingernails and hair, some are sent to the brain to rebuild cells. Lecithin is capable of breaking down fat into tiny particles which can pass through the tissues, and it breaks down fat that would otherwise tend to form clogging deposits on the walls of the arteries. The banana is an easily digested fruit that contributes valuable vitamins, natural fruit sugars and minerals (especially potassium). The milk in the drink supplies calcium and B vitamins as well as proteins.

There is nothing ironclad about the Vitality Drink except for the guarantee that it will fill you with energy. Make your own variations on it, though. If you do not tolerate milk (many adults lack an enzyme that allows the system to assimilate milk) use yoghurt instead. Add honey, wheat germ, and/or brewer's yeast to the drink. You may want to add a little more protein powder and leave out the raw egg. Try using 1 cup of yoghurt and 1 cup of fresh orange juice. In place of the banana, throw in a beautiful ripe peach one morning, or a handful of juicy strawberries.

You can make more than 365 variations on the Vitality Drink, but do have a Vitality Drink for breakfast 365 days a year. Have your vitamin and mineral supplement with it, have a slice of whole-wheat toast with it if you like, but be sure to have this miracle mix every morning and then go on to sail through the day.

BEVERLY ON: THROWING SOME LIGHT ON YOUR CLOTHES AND MAKEUP

Why not get a warm little glow going for yourself? Even if the sun in your area is pale as lemonade (or invisible) at this time of year, it's a good time for treating your complexion to the clean flattery of soft or bright color.

An ivory crepe-de-chine scarf at your throat will give a clean, pretty line on dark winter clothes and reflect a flattering light on your skin. It's a little early in most parts of the country for pale-colored clothing that flatters the skin and hair, but you can always play scarf tricks with soft peach, buttery yellow, and robin's-egg blue. Or you can go deep: marshy green is a wonderful, clarifying color for some pale complexions; rich Chinese lacquer red is marvelous for almost everybody.

Oddly enough, makeup in the softest, most muted colorings is your best bet under colorless skies, and it's more flattering to winter-weary skin than jewel-bright color. As a matter of fact, I would avoid going too bright with makeup at any time of the year. Go lighter and pinker in the summer, richer and warmer in the winter; note too that grayed blues and browns, russet pinks and warm beiges make your eyes and teeth look whiter and brighter, make you look younger, healthier, and more feminine.

BEVERLY ON: YOGA, THE EASY-DOES-IT EXERCISE
(and a Fourteen-Pose Program to Reap Yoga Benefits This Month)

It was Nancy Dinsmore, the West Coast editor of *Harper's Bazaar*, who sparked my interest in yoga.

I ran into Nancy at the health food store and saw that she had never looked better. There was a big change, but I couldn't decide what she had done. Next time I saw her I decided to ask.

The better-than-ever Nancy was due to yoga classes with Yogi Bikram Choudouri in Beverly Hills. I went in right away for a beginner's class.

I found myself doing the type of exercise I like best—slow, controlled, graceful, but giving the heart and the muscles enough of a workout so that the perspiration flows and the oxygen is really coursing throughout the body.

You go into a pose slowly and hold it for ten or twenty seconds. During that time you concentrate on what the body is doing (and the first time you touch your toes to your forehead, it's so incredible that you couldn't think about anything else if you wanted to!) and you try to sense the good that the pose is doing for you. One of the great goods that yoga does is strengthening the spine—and a strong spine equals a healthy body for life.

Between each pose you rest for ten seconds to regenerate the body. The regeneration part is not just hype. After a class I find myself feeling very light, very airy, almost high.

The yoga serenity lasts for hours afterward and you are less easily frazzled for the day. Of course, if I go home and the kids are squabbling, that blows it sooner. Still, I go into my peacemaking role more peacefully since I started yoga.

It was early in October that I started classes with Bikram, and I could see big results before Thanksgiving.

One great result of spending time in yoga classes is that I spend less time in making up. When I do yoga I don't need foundation to correct my skin tone, even in winter. My circulation, thus my complexion, is so much better that I only use moisturizer, lipstick, and eye makeup. That improved circulation is keeping wrinkles at bay, too.

Much more important, yoga is a builder of strength, flexibility, and balance as well as of self-control, patience, and concentration. How's that for a winning ticket?

With yoga you do not see the almost immediate improvement in muscle tone that calisthenics can give. On the other hand, you never feel sore after a yoga class, and you can continue yoga well into old age to retain the kind of supple, graceful body people think of as youthful.

The muscle tone comes, but in time. Yoga is not at all a hurry-up thing; it is the antithesis of rushing. You relax into an *asana,* or pose, slowly and relax slowly out of it. You do only a few *asanas* at first, then as your spine strengthens and your balance and suppleness develop, you move on to more complicated poses. As you practice, you visualize yourself in the perfect achievement of the pose. When you see perfection with the eye of your mind, you will eventually see it in your mirror.

Perfection takes time and practice. Ideally, Bikram says, you should undertake yoga with a one-hour course every day for a month. O.K., that's ideal. Reality?

For Shirley MacLaine, Alexis Smith, Marge Champion, and many of Bikram's other students, a daily yoga class is reality. It's a justifiable professional investment of time and money.

I go to classes as often as I can, but with my family and my work, I just can't afford to go every day. So I do yoga at home for thirty minutes on the days I don't go to class.

Anybody can, once they have the basics. Fortunately, almost every YWCA in the country offers yoga classes at very low cost. Enroll in one and go as often as you can this month. By next month you will be able to continue at home on your own. If you can't get to a class, get hold of one of the illustrated books on yoga and work with a friend. Friend holds the book, you do the pose, and friend tells you how close you are to doing it the way the picture shows.

Whether you are able to get to a class in yoga or decide to hold classes on your own, take it slow; don't let your mind race ahead of your body's capacity.

Take yoga easy, and yoga can help make everthing else easy for you.

Much more than a system of exercise, yoga is, in Bikram's phrase, "the union of objects in the universe." It is a way of life designed to bring every aspect of living into a harmonious union. It involves a balance of the mental, spiritual, and physical.

The physical side of yoga, known as hatha-yoga, is the first to be studied. This is because proper mental and spiritual balance depend on the well-being of the body.

Hatha-yoga has been developed over the centuries into some eighty-four basic yoga poses that concern parts of the body.

On the next few pages you will find fourteen of these poses that are good as an introduction to yoga and that you will continue to do even when you become very advanced.

To repeat myself, on purpose: *Go slow.* Add only one pose a week, if you like; it takes time to get it right. And getting it right is one of the great satisfactions of yoga.

Important: Yoga can be performed on various surfaces, but beds and bare floors are not among them. A bed has too much give, and you can strain your back; a bare floor is just too hard and cold. An exercise mat is ideal, of course, but a large blanket or two beach towels folded on a carpeted floor will do just fine.

Very important: Yoga is a gentle, beneficial form of exercise, but before you begin your yoga practice, call your doctor and tell him what you plan. Yoga poses strengthen and stretch every single part of the body. There may be parts of your body that *shouldn't* be stretched. Some yoga poses are definitely not recommended for those who suffer with, say, stomach ulcers, while other poses are especially beneficial for these people. Your doctor can advise the areas of caution, your yogi can advise the best *asanas* for your individual yoga practice. As in everything else, your yoga regime is uniquely your own.

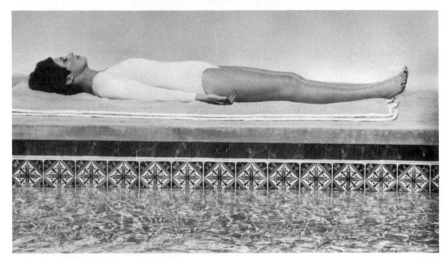

1. *Savasana (Dead Man Pose)*

   Lie flat on your back with the legs stretched out loosely, arms out at your sides, with the palms facing up. Inhale and relax. Rest in this position and think of new energy that has filled your whole body as you rise slowly.

2. *Pavanamuktasana (Gas-Relieving Pose)*

   Lie on your back and inhale deeply as you raise the right leg. Bend the knee and pull it in close to the chest, using both hands. Lower the right leg very slowly and exhale. Repeat with the left leg. Rest; then repeat the pose with both legs simultaneously. Relax feet.

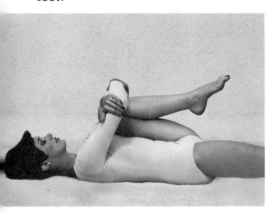 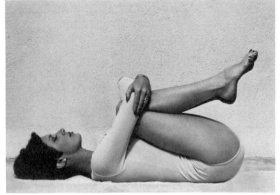

3. Bhujangasana (Cobra Pose)

Lie on your stomach, palms flat on the mat at shoulder level and elbows close to your sides. Slowly raise your body from the hips, arching your back and tensing the muscles of the buttocks. (Try to use muscles of the small of the back to strengthen these muscles.) Use your palms for support. Raise your head as high and

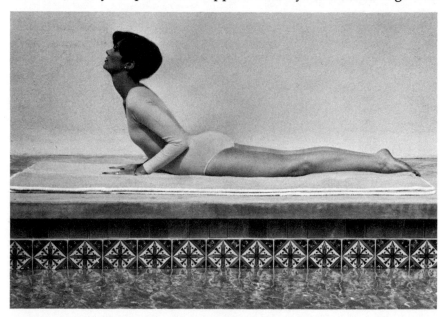

as far back as possible. Hold the pose for twenty seconds, breathing normally, then relax for ten seconds lying on the mat with your arms stretched loosely at your sides. Repeat. Your legs should be stretched straight, with toes pointed.

4. Salabhasana (Locust Pose)

Lie with your chin on the mat, legs straight and toes pointed. Place the arms under your body, your hands, palms down, under your thighs. Breathe normally and tense the body. Raise one leg with knee straight. Stretch it up and out as far as possible. Hold the leg up and out, then exhale as you lower it. Repeat with the other leg. When you become adept at this, which is the Half-Locust, go on to the *Poorna-Salabhasana* or Full Locust: raise both legs at once, using muscles of small of back. Great for the back.

4. *Salabhasana (Locust Pose)*

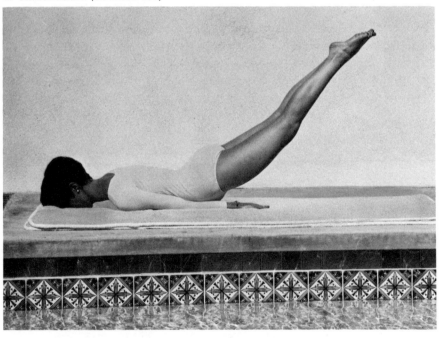

5. *Ardha-Chandrasana*
(Half-Moon Pose)

5. *Ardha-Chandrasana*
(Half-Moon Pose)

5. *Ardha-Chandrasana (Half-Moon Pose)*

Stand with feet together. Raise arms straight up and close to your head. Clasp hands together above your head. Bend to right side, pushing hips to left. Keep arms straight and elbows close to ears. Reverse for left side.

Arms over head with elbows straight and close to head, drop head completely back. Lower arms and arch back as far as possible. Breathe normally and hold each pose for ten seconds. Repeat. Great for the back.

6. *Pada-Hastasana (Hands-to-Feet Pose)*

Stand with the feet together and raise arms over your head. Exhale slowly as you bend forward grasping heels, fixing forearms

to calves. Bend the knees slightly and bring the face as close to the knees as you can. Straighten knees. Breathe normally and hold the pose for ten seconds. Inhale as you return to the starting position. Rest ten seconds and repeat the pose.

7. *Trikanasana (Triangle Pose)*

7. *Trikanasana (Triangle Pose)*

7. *Trikanasana (Triangle Pose)*

7. Trikanasana (Triangle Pose)

Stand with your feet spread wide apart. Raise arms until they are straight out at shoulder level with palms turned down. Look at the right palm as you bend slowly to the right. Bend knee until thigh is parallel to floor. Arms outstretched. Slowly lower right hand to right foot. Keep your eyes on the left palm as you bring the left arm in close to the left ear and perpendicular to the floor. Hold for ten seconds, return to the starting position, and reverse. Rest in a standing position for ten seconds and repeat the Triangle pose.

8. Dhanurasana (Bow Pose)

Lie flat on your stomach. Bend legs at knees and reach back to grasp the ankles with the hands, keep the arms straight, like a stretched bowstring, as you raise your head, chest, thighs. Arch your back, lifting feet straight up and letting all your weight rest on the lower abdomen. Inhale on rising, breathe normally while holding the pose for twenty seconds, exhale as you return to starting position. Rest, then repeat the Bow pose. Great for strengthening lower back. Contracts all vertebrae.

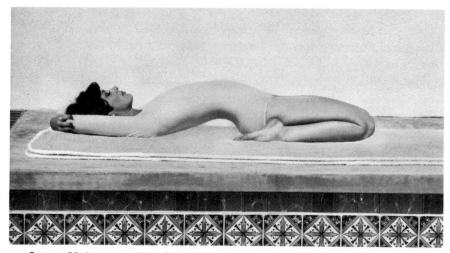

9. *Supta-Vajrasana (Fixed Firm Pose)*

Kneel on the mat, heels next to hips, buttocks on floor. Stretch backward slowly, thrusting the pelvis out and bending backward as far as possible. Hold onto the ankles for support, bend your elbows and rest on them as you let your head touch the mat. When you are all the way down, fold your arms behind your head and hold the pose for ten seconds. Return slowly to the original position and rest for ten seconds. Help yourself up with your hands.

10. *Ardha-Kurmasana (Half-Tortoise Pose)*

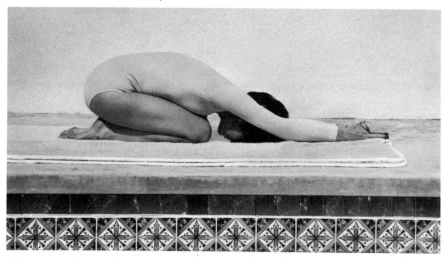

10. *Ardha-Kurmasana (Half-Tortoise Pose)*

Kneel on mat and then sit with feet tucked under you, spine upright and palms resting on the knees. Raise your arms up, keeping them close in to the head. Bend forward to touch the mat with forehead and fingers. Breathe normally as you hold the pose for twenty seconds. Return to the starting position, rest for ten seconds, and repeat the Half-Tortoise pose.

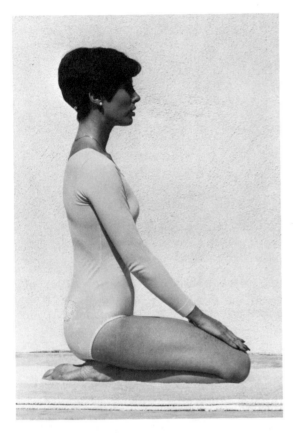

11. *Kapalbhati-in-Vajrasana (Blowing-in–Firm Pose)*

Kneel on mat with knees together. Lower buttocks to rest on heels. Rest hands, palms down, on knees. Blow out your breath forcefully while forcing the abdominal muscles in and up. Relax and inhale normally, but exhale with force, pressing in and up with the abdominal muscles. Repeat sixty times.

12. *Ustrasana (Camel Pose)*

Kneel with knees and feet six inches apart with the spine upright and the toes pressing against the mat. Slowly lower the head and arch back as if to look behind you, while contracting the spine.

As you bend backward, place palms of hands on soles of feet. Breathe normally and hold the pose for twenty seconds. Return to the starting position and rest for one minute. Repeat the Camel pose.

13. *Sasangasana (Rabbit Pose)*

Begin as for the Camel pose, but bend in the opposite direction to touch forehead to the knees and the crown of the head to the mat. Hold onto your ankles with both hands and roll forward slowly to stretch the spine. Hold the pose, breathing normally, for twenty seconds, then relax into the Savasana pose, lying flat on the mat for one minute. Repeat the Rabbit pose.

13. Sasangasana (Rabbit Pose)

14. *Janushirasana (Head-to-Knee Pose)*
Lie on your back on the mat and stretch both arms out over your head. Hook thumbs together and exhale. Inhale and hold your breath as you raise yourself to a sitting position with arms over your head. Exhale as you bend forward slowly to clasp the toes with thumbs and index fingers. Breathe normally and hold the pose for twenty seconds. Return slowly to the original position. Rest for one minute and repeat the Head-to-Knee pose.

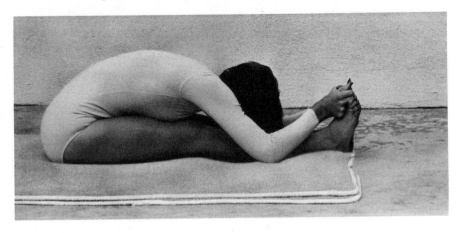

SPECIALS FOR YOUR HAIR

• Time to uncover your hair and give it some freedom in the bright, clear light of spring. If the color isn't all you would wish, this is a good month to do something about it. Make your color decision now and spend the time until your appointment with the colorist in all-out conditioning. Even the healthiest hair takes color better after an extra measure of conditioning treatment.

• If a permanent is part of your hair program, slate it for two weeks *before* your coloring appointment for best results.

• Much of the external damage done to hair can be prevented internally. Tension, poor diet, and poor circulation are major culprits in the alarming incidence of heavy hair loss. Up to 100 hairs per day is normal loss, but many men and women lose more hair than this each day. Much male pattern baldness is genetic in origin, but not all. Tension stimulates the oil glands, but because the scalp is unhealthy due to poor circulation, the excess oil remains just under the skin, while the hair is thin and dry. In this condition it is weak and very susceptible to external damage. Cigarettes and alcohol, along with lack of exercise, impair the circulation. Help your hair and scalp with proper diet, exercise, and scalp massage. See a hairologist or dermatologist for diagnosis and treatment of any unusual scalp condition.

SPECIALS FOR YOUR SHAPE

• Lingering twilights are a specialty of the season. Use the longer days and milder weather to get some outdoor exercise before dinner (you will feel wonderful, look fresher, and eat less). Walk briskly for five minutes, then jog for five minutes, and decelerate on the walk back home.

• Where climate permits, start polishing your tennis serve and your golf stroke, to put yourself ahead for the games of summer. If it's cold out, take horseback-riding lessons. In some areas it's warm enough for sailing; in others, cold enough so that you still can ski. Make the most of what your community has to offer.

• Beat spring fever indoors with skipping rope, breathing and stretching exercises. Here's one you can do to limber the spine without getting out of your chair: Put your hands on your knees. Slowly stretch your neck and your back up and back so that the back is arched and the head tilts back. Let your head fall all the way back. Now let your head fall forward, bend your elbows and let your torso curl forward to follow your head down toward your lap. Return to an upright position slowly, with stomach muscles tight and shoulders loose.

• Yawn deeply and often (when no one is looking) to relax muscles in the face, and in the throat for a pleasanter voice (when someone is listening).

SPECIALS FOR YOUR MAKEUP AND FRAGRANCE

• Skin can look a little sallow or pale for many of us this month. If yours is a little too yellow to suit you, true, clear pinks will neutralize the yellow. Avoid golden melony tints and spicy brownish corals. Go for American beauty reds down to pale, true carnation pinks. Pink is nice to highlight your eyes. It shows you know spring is on the way, but shadow with cool grays and browns without a trace of yellow.

• Do you curl your eyelashes? Start doing it now if you don't. It has a great eye-opening effect. And it takes only a second.

• You're working toward lighter, thinner makeup, right? Here's a trick I learned from the great makeup professional Way Bandy when he did my makeup for a TV commercial: In your palm, blend tiny drops of foundation color with a few drops of your skin freshener. You get better coverage with less makeup.

SPECIALS FOR YOUR FOOD PLANNING

• Delicious as your Vitality Drink for breakfast is, you might be in the mood for a little variety. Here's a super go-getter to try. It makes enough for a family of four.

VIM AND VIGOR BREAKFAST

1 cup sprouts (alfalfa or mung bean or winter wheat)
1 cup sunflower seeds
6 apples with skins, seeded, cored, quartered
3 tablespoons brewer's yeast
3 tablespoons raw honey
½ cup powdered nonfat milk
½ cup wheat germ
juice of 3 lemons
    Liquefy everything in the blender. It's sweet and nutty.

"Raw sugar" isn't raw. In case you are still using sugar, but have switched from white to raw or turbinado sugar hoping that it would be better for you, here's the straight dope: Turbinado is Spanish for "spun." It is the product of a spinning process that separates molasses from sugar crystals in refining. White sugar with all the vitamins and minerals removed by refining is 99.9 percent sucrose. Turbinado, or raw sugar, is usually 97 percent or 98 percent sucrose, tinted with vitamin-and-mineral-rich molasses to make up the other 2 or 3 percent. That minute amount isn't going to help you at all. Satisfy your craving for sweets with raw honey. It doesn't use up B vitamins, and it gives you minerals and vitamins.

• When you eliminate sugar from your life, get rid of chocolate too, and get delicious, chocolaty flavor from carob powder. Here's what chocolate has that carob doesn't: theobromine. This is a stimulant that works just like caffeine to jangle your nerves and upset your stomach, along with interfering with your body's absorbing the calcium it needs for healthy tissue, bones, and nerves. Carob doesn't have theobromine, but it does have B vitamins. Like honey, it is utilized by the body without robbing it of vitamins or minerals. Carob is also called St. John's bread, and if not exactly a staff of life, it can make the sweet life far less dangerous.

SPRING

There is a beautiful rush of stirring and growth in the world around you. The quiet season of late winter gives way to bright-colored activity, a fiesta of change. Beautiful and remarkable changes have been going on for you, too.

You move and carry yourself in a beautiful new way. The Seven Standing Sins have been so long corrected as to be almost forgotten. You breathe in the beautiful, deep, natural way without thinking. That simple change has brought immense changes in every atom of the new you. A morning Vitality Drink, a Seven-Way Stretch, and your new habits of organization have given you stores of effortless grace for even the most hectic days. The new care and cleansing regimes for your hair and skin, plus the good food, the treasury of vitamins and minerals, are paying off in a dazzling change. The good work you have done for yourself has altered the way you look for the better, and forever.

There are many more changes in store, but at the threshold of a new season, concentrate on ways to put your newfound energy and beauty to work for the good of the world around you. Giving pleasure to those you love will increase your own pleasure in the new projects you undertake.

APRIL

With the arrival of April comes the first blossoming of the fruit trees and magnolias and the misty green of new leaves. It's an exciting time of year because everything seems bright and new. And this month can be a time of growth and exciting change for you as well as for nature.

However, sometimes when we begin to make changes a slight uneasiness comes over us and we stop and reflect on what our goals really are. It's very human to question a program that says you should make every effort to look and feel your very best. A lifetime of warnings about the sin of vanity cannot be forgotten overnight. There may be a dark, nagging doubt that all this *is* vanity and you're becoming narcissistic.

It just isn't so.

The most important mission you have is to contribute your mind, your energy, your talents, and your love to improving whatever situations you have control over. If you can pass along to others some of your talent, if you can make the people around you feel better, make life in your home, your neighborhood, your community, richer, then you are a powerful force.

This force, this power, is blocked or destroyed if you neglect the marvelous machine that is your body. Unless you are in peak physical condition, your morale will be low. Your store of energy, of positive vitality, will be wasted. You cannot contribute to the world if your mind is occupied by fretting over how terrible you feel and look.

Doing the most for the world means doing the most for yourself so that you are always ready to face pleasure or crisis with the stamina and the real beauty that affect the world for the better.

To contribute to the world, you must be involved in the world and aware of its beauty and mystery. As the year moves toward the high tide of spring, plan to get out more and enjoy the awakening beauty of the world about you. The new season is a wonderful time to put more delight into your life through new enthusiasms, new projects.

Have you ever thought of taking a nature walk, guidebook in hand, to see the birds, the wildflowers, and the trees that are to be found in your part of the country? It is a real treat and teaches you to see the world through new eyes. A walking tour of historical buildings in your city some bright spring day will give you a fascinating new understanding of the place you live in. Going to a local botanical garden or arboretum will inspire you to new feats with plants at home. Perhaps you have the space for a windowsill herb garden or even for a small vegetable garden? Working a garden is one of the most rewarding ways of using time. Even a tiny one can provide a summer full of tempting fresh food for you and your family.

YOUR CHECKLIST AND SCHEDULE FOR APRIL

First Morning of the Month

Log your vital statistics into your diary (p. 14) *in ink.* Set your goals for the month as to loss of pounds or inches and gains in other areas, such as proficiency at yoga, say, or using the hand-held dryer. Pencil in your goals on the diary page for the last day of the month, and start the program that will help you achieve your goals.

Every Morning

Seven-Way Stretch   (p. 91)

Cup of hot water and lemon juice
Warm-up exercises   (p. 146)
Clean face and moisturize   (p. 54)
Makeup   (p. 61)
Fix hair
Vitality Drink and nutritional supplements   (p. 94)
Every Evening
Warm-up exercises to relax
Feet-up rest with pillows or on slantboard for 10 minutes
Clean face and moisturize
Bath and all-over body lotion   (p. 128)
Clean teeth before bed   (p. 259)
As Often as You Like: At Least Three Times Each Week
Exercise session of 30 minutes   (p. 242)
Yoga session of 30 minutes   (p. 96)
Shampoo and finishing rinse   (pp. 45–46)
Once Each Week
An evening (or a day) of rest, a time for yourself
10-minute protective protein conditioning pac for hair
Manicure and pedicure   (p. 201)
Tweeze stray hairs on eyebrows   (p. 167)
Shave legs and underarms   (p. 166)
Facial mask   (p. 162)
Once This Month
One night and one day of rest for the digestive system on the
  detoxifying Liquid Fast or Clearing House Diet   (pp. 36–38)
Haircut and any other professional hair services such as color
  or perm. (Your cutter might advise a cut more often, perhaps
  every three weeks. Follow his suggestion in making out your
  individual schedule.)

SOME THOUGHTS ABOUT DIET

Whether your plan is to lose, gain, or maintain, there can be no
beautifying and lasting effects from a quickie program that you
drop in three weeks. Begin a new and lifetime pattern. No rigid
plans that will bore and eventually defeat you. Just make a positive

resolution to eat the positive, healthy foods that will make your body and your life more beautiful. To start you off on a great new way of eating, see The Sassoon Diet for All Seasons on p. 265.

It's a big help to keep a record in your diary of everything you eat for one week. Start now. Remember to list the size of the portions you eat. Go back over the list at the end of the week. Make a rough estimate of the calories—or a precise count if you are good at math and calorie tables. Next, take a bright-colored pen and put a check mark next to any food you think is bad for you. Obviously bad are such negative foods as potato chips, soft drinks, candy bars, and white bread. Check anything that is filled with calories and empty of nutrition. Look at the marked items, and you will probably be shocked to see how much nonfood you have eaten. If this were subtracted from the week's intake, would you really have a weight problem?

Prevention is the best cure for overweight, as for so much else. Five pounds is easily dropped, but if you have to lose quite a bit of weight, the Weight Watchers program is great. It is adapted from a plan by the late Dr. Norman Jolliffe, a major figure in dietary research who was head of the New York Public Health Department. Weight Watchers was endorsed by the late nutrition writer Adelle Davis. It has worked for millions and is easy and satisfying to follow.

As you weigh yourself, so should you weigh the food you eat, both on the scales and in your mind. Get a kitchen scale—not to weigh every pea, but to know what four ounces of chicken or cauliflower looks like. It will help you in estimating serving sizes when you eat out. Need we say that food gets weighed before cooking? Use your mental scales, based on the facts you now have about vitamins and food, to judge relative weights of calories to beauty value. One ounce of lima beans has more calories than one ounce of cottage cheese, and it's lower in protein. The cottage cheese is the lightweight choice you should make if you want to be lightweight too.

Get active. When you go on a diet, that's the time to go in every department. An active life leaves less time for sitting around thinking about food. If you do your moving on foot, you will be saving gas and spending calories—visit the local museums, get out and *do* something you will enjoy.

HOW MUCH FOOD DO YOU REALLY NEED?

Calories are sneaky things. You can't see them or feel them. Then one day you both see and feel them, and it means you've had too many. Another treacherous little habit they have is piling up as the years do. If you and 1700 calories a day were the best of friends at twenty, they will turn on you viciously and start putting pounds around your middle when you're forty-five. The rule is very simple: more years, fewer calories. The chart below, from the Food and Nutrition Board of the National Research Council, will give you the idea. It tells how many calories you need to *maintain* your weight.

DESIRABLE CALORIC INTAKE

(At mean environmental temperature of 20¼° C. (68.45°F.), and assuming average physical activity)

DESIRABLE WEIGHT	CALORIE ALLOWANCE		
Pounds	25 years	45 years	65 years
99	1700	1550	1300
110	1800	1650	1500
121	1950	1800	1650
128	2000	1850	1700
132	2050	1900	1700
143	2200	2000	1850
154	2300	2100	1950

You know better than we do how much you should weigh, how much you want to weigh so that you feel really well—not to be a frantic diet fanatic who looks haggard from chasing an unhealthy skinny ideal that won't work with her bones, nor a sluggish, always tired fat lady. We do know that if the calorie allowance for your weight and age is 1650, and you cut down to 1,200 calories a day you will lose a safe 1.3 pounds per week at least. If you exercise and if you switch from foods high in saturated fats, the weight loss will show up quickly in lost inches, and will be accelerated.

SMART PROTEIN SHOPPING STARTS WITH FISH—
Because It's Low in Calories, High in Vitamins

FISH	CALO-RIES	PRO-TEIN	CAL-CIUM	B_1	B_2	NIACIN
Lobster (3 oz.)	78	15.6 g.	55 mg.	.03 mg.	.06 mg.	1.9 mg.
Crab (3 oz.)	89	14.4 g.	38 mg.	.04 mg.	.05 mg.	2.1 mg.
Shrimp (3 oz.)	110	23.5 g.	98 mg.	.01 mg.	.03 mg.	2.8 mg.
Salmon (3 oz., canned)	122	17.4 g.	159 mg.	.03 mg.	.16 mg.	6.8 mg.

I'm for anything that gives you all that protein, B vitamins, calcium, minerals, and polyunsaturated fat. The fact that Vidal is mad about fish helps, too. He calls bouillabaisse, the Mediterranean fish stew, "one of the great food tastes of all time." I think he would probably fly all the way to the south of France for a great bouillabaisse. I invented Bouillabaisse Salad to keep him at home.

BOUILLABAISSE SALAD

1 cup canned crabmeat
1 lobster tail, cooked and sliced
1 pound boiled Shrimp
2 heads Boston lettuce
1 bunch watercress
1 tablespoon chopped chives

1 small onion, thinly sliced (optional)
2 tomatoes, peeled and quartered
1 cup chopped celery

Arrange the seafood in a pretty way on top of the greens. Put celery into a medium-sized bowl and pour boiling water over it. Drain celery and add to the salad. Place tomato quarters around the edge. Pile onions on top (if you like them), if you are feeling extravagant, sprinkle with lumpfish caviar and chopped egg yolk.

Prepare this dressing in the blender or a shaker jar:

BOUILLABAISSE SALAD DRESSING

½ cup wine vinegar
2 tablespoons dry vermouth
1 teaspoon salt substitute

½ teaspoon paprika
½ teaspoon dry mustard

CHOLESTEROL AND SHELLFISH

Ten years ago shellfish fell into very low esteem when they were listed as high-cholesterol foods and were forbidden on low-fat diets.

Well, as you saw in the section on vitamins, research never stops. New discoveries are made, and official attitudes are sometimes reversed.

The National Heart and Lung Institute has issued a new edition of its diet manual for the control of cholesterol levels. To quote from *The New York Times*, "A health official said that a dieter was probably better off eating clams or other shellfish than a steak. Shellfish was added to the revised diets after the Department of Agriculture developed better data in cholesterol levels, based on new measuring techniques."

BEVERLY ON: SOME OF THE MEALS OUR FAMILY ENJOYS

What follows is a variety of dishes that we like and enjoy often throughout the year. You won't find any rules here: Tuesday eat this, Wednesday eat that. You know your own tastes, and your family's, so you can take from this menu and that, put it together in the way that will satisfy your needs. You are not only unique, but also intelligent—you now have the information and have done the thinking that will enable you to tailor an eating plan as individual as your hair, your eye makeup, your outlook on life.

We can all use a few new ideas, though—especially new ideas on what to have for dinner. We hope you can find a few here.

You will not find dishes that are complicated or time-consuming to prepare. Every woman is busy today with her career or her family, or both. Time spent with the people you love is time well spent. Time spent stirring a rich sauce isn't. The heavy sauce just masks the fresh flavor of food, and makes you heavy, too.

So, these are tasty, simple, body-improving . . .

SMOOTH AND CRUNCHY QUICK LUNCH

I don't like going out to lunch in restaurants. If I'm alone at home, I stop for a quick lunch break. And if I have time, I would much rather see my friends for lunch at home. Either way, this open-face sandwich is quick to prepare, filling, and attractive enough for guests. It's also high in B vitamins, A, C, D, and E, calcium, lecithin, and iron, and has an interesting variety of textures and tastes.

Spread a slice of whole wheat bread thinly with mayonnaise. Cover with a layer of sliced avocado, then sliced tomato; top with a slice of mild, hard cheese made from raw milk. Put it into the oven until cheese melts (1 minute, 15 seconds in a microwave oven; 3 to 5 minutes in a regular oven). Sprinkle with alfalfa sprouts, sesame seeds, and Bac • O bits (they taste like bacon, but are made from soybeans).

A Dinner Menu That My Family Likes; Festive Enough for Guests:
    Cold Consommé on the Rocks
    Lemon-Roasted Cornish Game Hen
    Steamed Fresh Green Beans
    Mixed Salad
    Cinnamon Grapefruit

Consommé is served in a small wineglass, with a thin slice of lemon. Madrilène cold, but not jellied, looks especially pretty—it's ruby red.

ROASTED GAME HEN

These are small, so one per person isn't too much. Rub the bird well with lemon juice. Cut some very thin slices of lemon and lay them on the breast. Baste with dabs of margarine and put into a 350° oven to roast for 45 minutes. Run the hens under the broiler during the last 10 minutes to get brown and crisp.

GREEN BEANS

Just wash and snap as usual. Put them into a vegetable steamer if you have one (these perforated metal collapsible baskets hold the vegetables above the water in the pan and allow the steam to cook them preserving all the vitamins and minerals. An ordinary metal colander will work, too.) Put beans in steamer; spread them as thinly as possible. Put some water into a large pot with a lid, and when it boils, lower the steamer into the pot. Don't let the beans touch the water! Cover the pot and let it steam for 10 minutes at most. For an extra taste treat, toss 1 tablespoon dried dill weed into the water so the beans will herb-steam. The taste addition is subtle, but good.

MIXED SALAD

Anything or everything you like. Do try some of the other green, leafy things in addition to lettuce. Spinach, chicory, and escarole have lots of vitamin A, shredded cabbage is high in C and calcium, as well as A.

CINNAMON GRAPEFRUIT

Section grapefruit halves, sprinkle with powdered cinnamon (drizzle on a very little honey, if you like) and put them into the 350° oven while the hens are browning for the last 10 minutes. Take grapefruit out along with the hens. It will stay warm in the kitchen until you are ready for it. Or turn off the oven, leave the door ajar, and grapefruit inside until serving time.

Vary the menu by Substituting:

ORANGE BAKED CHICKEN

It's similar to Rock Cornish game hens, but easier on the budget. One chicken will serve 2 to 4 people, depending on appetite and your shape planning.

Dry chicken with paper towels, rub all over with salt substitute and a spoonful of thyme, sage, and savory mixed together. Put into 300° oven and let bake until brown. Baste every 10 minutes or so with orange juice (fresh or reconstituted frozen).

Terrific soups are great psychological warmers, and good for you if they aren't rich in fat, but are rich in vitamins. This one is:

VEGETABLE BROTH

Make enough for an army, or for one. Use the quantity you like of these:

carrots (washed but not peeled—you retain the vitamins that way. Slice them)
green beans or pea pods
mushroom stems
celery (slice it or chop roughly and use the leaves too)
yellow unpeeled squash or zucchini (washed and sliced)
onion (peeled and roughly chopped)
spinach, watercress, or parsley (wash and tear—don't chop—into small pieces)
water (use about 2 cups of spring water for liquid. Soup should be thick, and vegetables will surrender lots of moisture. Add 1 bay leaf to season)
   Put everything in a big covered pot over a very low flame. Let it barely simmer for several hours while you go about something else that's interesting. Stir occasionally if desired, but this soup can take care of itself. Season lightly with sea salt and freshly ground pepper before serving. With crusty bread, perhaps a raw mushroom and bean sprout salad, it makes a great one-dish meal.

Fish for Dinner
   Grilled Sole, Bluefish, or other fish
   Sliced Cucumbers
   Mushroom, Egg, and Spinach Salad Bowl
   Lemon Freeze

GRILLED FISH

For 4 people, get 1 fish that weighs about 3½ pounds, or 2 smaller ones. Sea bass, striped bass, red snapper, whitefish, and bluefish are all good to grill. Have it split and cleaned. Put a film of margarine on a foil-lined pan. Lay the fish on it, skin side down. Scatter a little dried tarragon, salt substitute, and lemon juice over it. Dot sparingly with margarine, if desired. Broil for not more than 7 minutes, very close to the broiler flame (about 3 inches is the maximum distance. Fish "weeps" if it's far from the fire). Baste it with the pan juices and give it another 5 minutes. Baste it again and test it with a fork. It may want another minute to broil, but get it out the second it's ready. Dry fish is unappealing.

SLICED CUCUMBERS

Great as they both are separately, fish and most cooked vegetables don't seem to take kindly to being served together. Use icy sliced cucumbers to make the fish plate look prettier, less barren. Do them this way:

Pare thinly and slice thinly 2 small cucumbers. Sprinkle them with the juice of 1 lemon, add ½ cup tarragon vinegar, 1 cup cold water. Let them rest in the refrigerator for about an hour before dinner.

MUSHROOM, EGG, AND SPINACH SALAD BOWL

A separate vegetable course is the best way to serve vegetables along with fish. Asparagus, which is presented as a separate course in France, is one great idea for spring. Artichokes as a first course is another. This is one I like: Make a big green salad of well-washed raw spinach. Tear off the tough stalks, and save them to go into a vegetable-broth stock or vegetable puree. Tear the leaves into manageable pieces. Slice 1 or 2 hard-cooked eggs, add them to the bowl along with Bac • O bits (optional) and sliced raw mushrooms (use the whole mushroom or save the stems for vegetable broth).

Dress with vinaigrette: 3 tablespoons wine vinegar, 6 tablespoons olive, almond or other polyunsaturated oil, ½ teaspoon each of dry mustard, paprika, salt substitute. Put in a shaker jar and exercise your wrist and arm muscles for a couple of seconds to mix.

LEMON FREEZE

¾ cup fresh lemon juice
grated lemon rind
4 cups water
2 teaspoons artificial sweetener

Mix everything together and put in freezing tray. Freeze until it begins to solidify. Stir to break up frozen portions. Repeat process several times. Then heap into pretty small bowls or cups. Orange or limes make nice variations on it. Frozen raspberries pureed in the blender will make a beautiful low-calorie sauce to dress it up. Spoon just a dribble of raspberry puree over each portion.

FATS—THE GOOD GUYS AND THE BAD

Fat is not a pretty word, and it's what nobody wants to be. But never make the mistake of cutting all fats out of your diet in order to be slim and beautiful. It won't work. Mr. and Mrs. Jack Spratt probably both looked like hell. Your skin and hair will reflect it in a lackluster look if you attempt a fat-free diet. You need fats in order to make use of vitamins A and E, to handle cholesterol, to burn foods for energy, and to nourish the skin. Learn to separate the bad fats from the good, and cut out the former.

BAD GUYS

Coconut oil	Hydrogenated fats (read the labels on margarines and other products to find out whether
Cream	
Lard	they contain hydrogenated fats and oils;
Butter	many do)
Processed cheese	Animal fats (cut away all the fat you can see in meats and poultry; skim fat from soups before serving. Longer cooking renders out more fat from meat but does not lower the protein content)

GOOD GUYS

Avocado oil   Sunflower oil
Corn oil   Soy oil
Peanut oil   Wheat germ oil
Safflower oil

All these "good-guy" oils are polyunsaturated. Technically, that means rich in unsaturated chemical bonds. Practically, it means that these oils do not combine in the blood stream to form fatty deposits on the walls of the arteries. Any oil you use for cooking should be a polyunsaturated one.

Also use:

Natural cheese

Margarine (if not made with hydrogenated fats or oils)

Peanut butter (*if* you get natural peanut butter from the health food store or if you make your own in the blender from fresh, whole peanuts. Commercial peanut butters are full of hydrogenated oils in order to look appealing on the grocer's shelf for months. That long-shelf-life product has no place in your life)

BEVERLY ON: BATHS WITH EXTRA BENEFITS

Everybody in the family thinks I'm loony when they see me headed for the bathroom with a quart of milk. But if milk baths were so good for Cleopatra . . .

Try one tonight. Pour about a pint of fresh whole milk (or one cup of instant powdered milk crystals) into a tub of warm water and swirl it around with your hand. You will feel the difference immediately. Bathing in it is like swimming in a soft, warm, white cloud. The bath doesn't smell funny, or leave you feeling sticky as you might think it would. You will be amazed at how it softens and gentles the water, and how satiny smooth your skin is after this protein treatment.

I'm also partial to almond oil in the bath, especially when I have to cope with hard water. Milk and almonds together make a delicious combination for special pampering of skin and soul.

Actually, your bath can do a great deal for your mood. Here are a few bath plans to suit special states of mind.

WHEN THE WHOLE WORLD HAS BEEN GUNNING FOR YOU SINCE DAWN . . .

To a very warm tub, add about half a teaspoon of oil of almonds. Make a little cheesecloth bag filled with herbs (dried rosemary, mint, or lavender, perhaps) to hang from the tap. Water running through the bag will turn this into a fragrant herbal bath. While the water is running, set out loofah, pumice stone, orange stick, and a fascinating book within reach of the tub. Soak for a few minutes, read awhile, then with pumice in hand you can lightly buff away any toughened skin on your heels, knees, or elbows. Use the loofah (a vegetable sponge) to remove dead skin cells that are covering up silky shoulders. Splash yourself with a warm rinse. Pat yourself dry, then moisturize all over with body lotion. Put extra cream on your feet, hands, knees, and elbows. Push cuticles back gently with orange stick. Top it off with a quick spray of cologne.

WHEN YOU'RE TIRED, BUT THE SHOW MUST GO ON . . .

The same reviving effect on you that aspirin has on roses comes of using lots of Epsom salts in the bath water.

WHEN YOU WANT HELP IN FALLING ASLEEP . . .

Draw a bath that's just a touch hotter than usual. Have a cup of yoghurt before the bath, and take a cup of herb tea to sip in the bath. Food tends to draw the blood away from your head so you will relax more easily. Douse the electric lights and bathe by candlelight. A scented candle (in a safe place, of course) would be lovely and so would some very soft music on your transistor (never fool with electrical equipment in the bath). Soak cotton pads with eye lotion or cool water. Just lie there like a princess for a while. Lather slowly and gently. Use a big, soft sea sponge to wash with. Rinse with warm water. Blot yourself dry with a big terry towel or robe. Slather on body lotion. Blow out the candles and sneak straight into bed.

WHEN YOU PLAN UNDERWATER EXERCISE IN THE BATH . . .

Sea salt, half a pound of it, tossed into the water will make it buoyant, and it's super for cleansing the pores. This is a trick of Carol Channing's.

WHEN YOU ARE WOUND TIGHTER THAN A WATCH SPRING . . .

The bath had better bubble, look good, and smell good. Pitch a little too much of everything into it: a spoonful of almond oil and a quart of milk to gentle the skin you would like to jump out of. Add some Technicolor with a bubble bath so the water looks like an Esther Williams production number. Have a glass of wine and an absorbing, trashy novel at hand. No scrubbing. Just lie there reading and soaking for as long as you please. If you have a big terry bath sheet, wrap up in it when you step out of the tub. Let it do the drying—you've had enough work for one day. Massaging lots of body lotion into your damp skin isn't work. It's a relaxing self-indulgence. Do it. You deserve it, tonight especially.

WHEN YOUR SKIN FEELS FLAKY, AND SO DO YOU . . .

Add a cup of natural cider vinegar to the bath. Great for dry, flaky skin, it also has the effect of a pick-up and a relaxer in one. Slough away the dead skin cells with bath brush or loofah. Rinse off with lots of fresh warm water. (Without the scrubbing, this is a great bath idea if you have a sunburn.)

WHENEVER YOU HAVE A BATH . . .

Always have a warm bath or a tepid bath or a very warm bath. Never have a hot bath (hard on skin and heart, and it dilates tiny capillaries that can burst into angry little red marks on the skin); and never have a cold bath (constricts the blood vessels). Body temperature, or a little warmer, is best. Always bathe in the evening, if you can, rather than the morning, to give skin eight hours to replace natural oils before you go out-of-doors.

BEVERLY ON: WATER, THE WONDER DRINK

Water is the only thing that will plump up and soften your skin. Really. A sliver of dried, calloused skin soaked in oil will stay dried and calloused and hard. Soaked in water, it softens.

A moisturizer will keep the water where it belongs—next to your skin—but first you've got to get the water there to begin with.

You do that by drinking it. To supply your body with all the water it needs for all vital functions requires about five pints a day.

Don't worry about water retention. Now that your diet is high in protein your body will utilize the water properly. Among the other healthy jobs water does is to sweep away wastes, to keep your skin clear, in perfect shape. If you are troubled with abnormal water retention the problem might be (as it is in so many other disfunctions) The Pill. Check with your doctor on that; but don't give up water and don't under any circumstances take diuretic pills without a doctor's advice. They wreck your system and your looks.

Don't count the liquids you drink as water—coffee, tea, or milk don't make it for this purpose. Sure, they contain lots of water, but there is a build-up of side orders like caffeine, tannic acid, and fat. What you want is pure water.

I'm a great water drinker, and I get up in the middle of the night to drink water. If you look at water more like W. C. Fields did, maybe it's because of the kind of water you have been drinking. Or rather, not drinking.

In some cities, what comes from the tap is unpolluted, to be sure, but it's unpalatable, too. Try putting a big kettle of the local product on to boil. Let it come to a rolling boil. Boil for five or ten minutes. Then let it cool down, pour it into screw-cap jars and let it spend the night in the refrigerator.

I promise you that after you've driven off the chlorine and other foreign substances in this way, water will taste better than ever.

For even better taste, at a price, buy bottled waters. These come in a world of labels, prices, and tastes (see p. 255). You can go from pure, almost tasteless waters to those such as Vichy, which have a very definite flavor of their own.

If you're doing the thirty-six-hour English Health Farm Liquid Fast, you'll almost certainly want to lay in a few small bottles of various mineral waters to sample. It's a good way to discover which ones you like, and the difference in tastes gives a little interest to the idea of drinking water all day.

VIDAL ON: THERAPEUTIC TOUCHING

If the words "massage" and "parlor" go together in your mind to form a dirty picture, you have the wrong idea about one of the most beneficial forms of therapy that exist.

True massage is a form of exercise that involves the manipulation and relaxation of the muscles, pressure, and stroking that rest the body after periods of physical exertion or mental stress.

Even if you haven't had a workout in the gym, your body can be calling out for a massage after a day of sitting still, particularly if tension has caused you to hold your body rigid, if you slouch in a chair or hunch over a typewriter.

If you have access to a massage at your health club, by all means take advantage of the opportunity to further the good you are already doing for your body by having a massage when you can. Even a massage once a month is a treat for the mind and the body.

The basic form of massage that you will encounter is the European massage. It's called Swedish massage usually, sometimes French massage or German massage, and it involves a set number of hand manipulations: *Tapotement,* a firm tapping with the sides of the hands or with cupped palms, which melts away tension, *Effleurage,* a flat-hand stroking in long, upward movements along the body to help circulation; *Petrissage,* a kneading of the muscles to de-kink them; *Friction,* a rubbing with the fingers to move the joints and relax them; *Vibration,* a delicate tapping and circling movement with the fingertips to stimulate circulation without exerting pressure. All these movements are used in the course of the massage, according to the body's need.

There are other more complicated and more ambitious forms of massage.

Allen Cruse, the masseur at my health club in Los Angeles, uses a massage system based on the theories of Dr. Wilhelm Reich. This revolutionary psychoanalyst believed that "chronic muscular hypertension represents an inhibition" and that this unhealthy protective armor could be broken down through psychotherapy that included physical pressing and squeezing that would clear the body and the mind. *Rolfing* is another form of massage aimed at mental and physical balance. Ida Rolf, a biochemist, developed a program of structural integration including a deep-compression massage that hurts as the body is literally forced out of long-held incorrect alignments. As proper bodily alignment is achieved, the equilibrium of body fluids and processes (including the mental process) is felt to be balanced for a new self-confidence and new awareness. *Esalen* massage involves relaxing the muscles as well as increasing sensory awareness through touch and nonverbal communications. It comes from the Esalen Institute in California.

Massage is only one tool in developing your positive vitality but it is an important one.

Smart Protein Shopping: Your Twenty Best Buys for the Most Protein at the Lowest Calorie Cost

Ideally, you should have one gram of protein every day for every two pounds you weigh. If you weigh one hundred twenty pounds, try for sixty grams of protein every day. Even more is even better. The protein you eat is real beauty food for your whole body.

All too many people equate protein with steak and therefore conclude that protein food is expensive. Anyone with a calorie-counting chart knows that steak is expensive in terms of calories, too. A little more research would show that steak is really quite a bad protein buy. A three-ounce portion of sirloin steak supplies twenty grams of protein, and has three hundred and thirty calories. So the ratio of protein to calories is only one gram of protein to sixteen calories. But three ounces of inexpensive canned sardines will supply the same amount of protein at exactly *one half* the cost in calories (not to mention the saving in money).

To show you how to get the most protein in the fewest calories, we have put together a chart of your twenty best protein buys. Any one of them, or any combination, will give you sixty grams of protein in fewer than five hundred calories a day.

Although the cost in money wasn't the object, you will be surprised at the number of inexpensive foods that make the Top Twenty.

SPECIALS FOR YOUR FOOD PLANNING

• Vegetarianism? We don't believe in it, although we have many friends who do. We see animal proteins as quick boosters to prevent anemia, as fast energy sources, and as necessary for the simplest insurance that you are getting the vitamin B_{12} and the amino acids you need.

The vegetarian way of life requires more study and knowledge of nutrition than most of us are willing to devote time to acquiring. Methionine and lysine are two essential amino acids. Both are present in vegetable sources, but not often together. Rice has lots of methionine, but it is low in lysine. Beans are just the opposite. If you eat rice with soybeans, red kidney beans, or even with soy sauce added, you get complete protein. Rice and beans together are inexpensive and delicious. If you are interested in working at a vegetarian diet, you will probably derive great physical and mental satisfaction, as many of our friends have. Do make sure that you are getting the fats and carbohydrates you need. Also make sure of your supply of vitamin B_{12} (not present in vegetable sources) by eating cheese, eggs, yoghurt. But we think you'll be happier if you simply reduce your meat eating, as we do, and avoid fanatic extremes of anything.

Having said that, let us give you a breakfast recipe that would fit perfectly into a vegetarian diet. It's a delicious lunch special, too.

BREAKFAST SALAD (for 4)

Mix together:
2½ cups wheat sprouts
1 cup sunflower seeds
3 apples with peel, grated
3 bananas, sliced
½ cup raisins
½ cup plain yoghurt

THE 20 FOODS WITH THE HIGHEST PROTEIN IN THE LOWEST NUMBER OF CALORIES

AMOUNT	FOOD	CALORIES	PROTEIN (IN GRAMS)	(CALORIES TO PROTEIN)
3 oz.	shrimp (canned)	100	21	(or 1 gram protein in 4.10 cals.)
4 oz.	cottage cheese (uncreamed)	85	17	(or 1 gram protein in 5 cals.)
3 oz.	crabmeat (canned)	85	15	(or 1 gram protein in 5.10 cals.)
3 oz.	clams (raw, meat only)	65	11	(or 1 gram protein in 5.10 cals.)
3 oz.	chicken (broiled)	115	20	(or 1 gram protein in 5.15 cals.)
2 oz.	dried chipped beef (uncooked)	115	19	(or 1 gram protein in 6.02 cals.)
3 oz.	fish (non-oily types, baked)	135	22	(or 1 gram protein in 6.03 cals.)
2.4 oz.	round steak (lean only, broiled)	130	21	(or 1 gram protein in 6.04 cals.)
2.6 oz.	lamb (lean only, chop, broiled)	140	21	(or 1 gram protein in 6.14 cals.)
3 oz.	turkey (roasted)	93.6	13.4	(or 1 gram protein in 7 cals.)
3 oz.	salmon (canned, meat only)	120	17	(or 1 gram protein in 7.01 cals.)
4 oz.	bean sprouts (from soybeans, raw)	23	3	(or 1 gram protein in 7.02 cals.)
3 oz.	tuna (canned, meat only)	170	24	(or 1 gram protein in 7.16 cals.)
3 oz.	hamburger (lean only, broiled)	185	23	(or 1 gram protein in 7.24 cals.)
4 oz.	oysters (raw, meat only)	80	10	(or 1 gram protein in 8 cals.)
1 T.	brewer's food yeast	25	3	(or 1 gram protein in 8.01 cals.)
1 oz.	swiss cheese (natural)	105	8	(or 1 gram protein in 8 cals.)
3 oz.	corned beef (canned)	185	22	(or 1 gram protein in 8.09 cals.)
2 oz.	liver (beef, fried)	130	15	(or 1 gram protein in 8.10 cals.)
3 oz.	sardines (canned, meat only)	175	20	(or 1 gram protein in 8.15 cals.)

• This is good time for fresh salmon. It is the basis for a beautiful spring dinner.

    Clear Vegetable Bouillon
    Oven-Baked Fresh Salmon
    Fresh Asparagus Vinaigrette
    Tomato and Romaine salad
    Golden Fruit Sherbet Cups

OVEN-BAKED SALMON

A 3-pound salmon steak will serve 6. Rub with ¼ cup lemon juice, paprika, and grated lemon peel. Put in broiling pan and bake at 350° for 20 minutes. Run under the broiler to brown.

GOLDEN FRUIT SHERBET CUPS

Combine in the blender:
1½ cups fresh orange juice
¾ cup fresh lemon juice
3 bananas
3 cups cold water
2 cups skim milk
artificial sweetener, if necessary
    Pour into a mold or hollowed-out orange halves and freeze.

SPECIALS FOR YOUR MAKEUP AND FRAGRANCE

• Shop for the brighter, clearer color you will want for spring and early summer makeup. You can start wearing zippier colors from this minute on.

• Test some fresh, light fragrances while you're shopping. You will want a change of pace in your fragrance wardrobe, too. Only three scents to a session of testing when you shop. More than three at a clip will tire and confuse your sense of smell. Since there is no real rush, why not try just two, one on each wrist this go-round. Pick your favorite of those, then try two more on a later visit, then pick the one of four that is ideal for you. Shop alone for scent, by the way. What is wonderful on a friend will sway your judgment, and what you choose may not suit your body's unique chemistry. Remember, too, that time of the day and time of the month alters the chemistry of your body, and the perfume that goes on it.

• Most eyeshadow plans are to make eyes look wide-set. But if your eyes are too far apart, here's what to do—shadow in the inner corner only, and blend out to the center of the eye.

• Eyebrows are important. Always cream them when you are cleansing your face. Skin there will get flaky if it's ignored.

SPECIALS FOR YOUR SKIN

• Warmer weather means more active oil glands. You may want to rinse your face more frequently with cool water. Do not use soap more often, though, than twice a day. Washing more than that strips away the natural acid and oils skin needs for good looks and good health.

• The "acid mantle" beauty editors and dermatologists talk about refers to the normal healthy state of acidity that exists on your skin. The acidity is measured on the pH scale, which runs from 0 to 14. On this scale, 7 represents neutrality. Number from 7 to 0 represent increasing acidity, with 0 a totally acid state. Numbers above 7 represent increasing alkalinity. Healthy skin ranges on the pH scale from a pH of 3.0 to a pH of 5.5, and this slight acidity enables the skin to resist bacteria and fungi. Whether you use an acid or alkaline soap is not so important as that you rinse off every trace of soap. No matter what you are told, you will not have to splash something acidic on clean skin to "bring it back" to a healthy pH. One more marvelous thing about skin is that it returns, all by itself, to its normal pH. High acidity can cause itching skin just as high free alkali can. The skin that is slow to return to its normal acid state from an alkaline state will be just as slow to return to that state from one that is highly acid. Rather than giving your face an acid rinse it might not want, or be able to handle, just give it a good clear water rinse and give your skin a chance. A moisturizer in the 3.0 to 5.5 pH range is ideal.

• Stretch marks don't come only from pregnancies, but I learned something about them the last time I was pregnant. These breaks in collagen fiber beneath the skin's surface are caused by rapid changes in weight. Pre-Natol, an all-over body lotion recommended for pregnant women, can be a real boon to every woman who is concerned about stretch marks. This cream, which has a nonsticky texture and a pleasant fragrance, helps restore elasticity to the skin and prevent collagen breakdown.

SPECIALS FOR YOUR SHAPE

• What about "cellulite"? You surely have heard about what is called "the fat you just can't seem to lose." In theory, cellulite is patches of fatty tissue that hold fat, water, and wastes in clumps on the upper arms, the thighs, and other parts of the body. "It's for the birds," according to Deborah Szekely Mazzanti, who owns one of the best and most famous luxury health spas in the world, The Golden Door. "The test for cellulite is supposed to be that you squeeze your cellulite-filled arm or thigh and see an 'orange peel' effect that indicates cellulite is present. Hair follicles in the skin are responsible for the effect—not cellulite. A woman can squeeze her face (and it can be very fat) but she won't see the orange peel effect because she doesn't have the hair follicles there." Mrs. Mazzanti, along with other experts on nutrition and weight control, does agree that the cellulite diet and exercise suggestions are perfectly reasonable. Raw fruits and vegetables are recommended, high-calorie foods and sugar are not; lots of water is advised and lots of exercise. All these are perfectly sensible for anyone who wants to prevent or take off the bulges of overweight. Massage of "cellulite" flab or any other flab will not reduce it, though. Only proper calorie intake and energy output will do that.

• Start a program of active exercise to add to your Seven-Way Stretch, warm-up and toning, and yoga exercises. Whatever you choose should be fun—jazz dancing, fencing lessons, tennis lessons, or indoor swimming.

• To aid in sticking to your exercise and eating program when you are losing weight, put a coin in a piggy bank for every day you don't eat like a pig. The money is for a bikini in the smaller size you will be by beach weather.

SPECIALS FOR YOUR HAIR

• The perfect cut that is a breeze to care for is now part of your way of life, we hope. I feel we must say a word or two about setting lotions—not the lightweight setting conditioners that are very helpful and good for holding a shape in fine hair, but the heavy goo many people feel is a requirement. When hair needs a heavy gel to hold a shape, that means the cut, the style, and the shape are wrong for your hair. When you attempt to force hair into an unnatural position it will rebel, like anything that is healthy and living. You give beauty to your hair only by encouraging it to follow its own growth pattern in the most becoming way. When your hair is well nourished and well cared for, it is like a body in peak condition. The body is strong and limber, but you cannot force the bones to bend backward—not without breaking them and injuring the body, at any rate. If your hair has shine, if it is as thick at the ends as at the roots, you have the perfect head of hair. And it is beautiful, whether straight as a board or curly as a corkscrew. Encourage the natural pattern into the most becoming form. Don't torture it with setting gels or anything else into unsuitable shapes. You will only make your hair less beautiful.

MAY

This is the time of year when the whole world seems soft and full of promise. If you are just beginning your year of beauty and health, you have picked a splendid time for it. As the world around you develops with a new beauty that is at first fragile and hesitant, then fully developed and vivid, so too you will see great changes both physical and mental in yourself, and they will reflect and keep pace with the changes in the world you live in. Long walks and pleasurable outdoor exercise are inviting prospects now, so you can get your new year off to a flying start and begin to fulfill your own promise.

If you began this year in the cold, short days of the fall or the winter, all the diligence you have put in so far is paying off now. You will have already seen and felt the wonderful changes in yourself before you see the stirrings of new growth in nature. You have begun to focus and direct your own shining quality.

Spring fever can deflect the beam from anybody's light, however; and confusion and stress occur in all seasons. This is no time to relax the discipline that alone will bring you the maximum rewards on the investment you are making—time spent on realizing your fullest potential. When spring lassitude strikes, double up on the stretching and breathing exercises—they are great invigorators. Planning your diet so that the bulk of the calorie intake comes earlier in the day, with a hearty breakfast, fairly substantial lunch, then a light, refreshing evening meal, is one very effective way of keeping energy levels high on warmer days.

For both energy and serenity you might want to sample two of the systems that we find to be of great value: hatha yoga and transcendental meditation. The section on yoga is on page 96, and the one on meditation, page 156. Look into them and then you be the judge. If one of these works for you, then add it to your schedule and work with it. This is the month, and the year, when you are free to explore anything and everything that helps you realize your own potential.

YOUR CHECKLIST AND SCHEDULE FOR MAY

First Morning of the Month
>Log your vital statistics into your diary (p. 14) *in ink.* Set your goals for the month as to loss of pounds or inches and gains in other areas, such as proficiency at yoga, say, or using the hand-held dryer. Pencil in your goals on the diary page for the last day of the month, and start the program that will help you achieve your goals.

Every Morning
>Seven-Way Stretch   (p. 91)
>Cup of hot water and lemon juice
>Warm-up exercises   (p. 146)
>Clean face and moisturize   (p. 54)
>Makeup   (p. 61)
>Fix hair
>Vitality Drink and nutritional supplements   (p. 94)

Every Evening
>Warm-up exercises to relax
>Feet-up rest with pillows or on slantboard for 10 minutes
>Clean face and moisturize
>Bath and all-over body lotion   (p. 128)
>Clean teeth before bed   (p. 259)

As Often as You Like: At Least Three Times Each Week
  Exercise session of 30 minutes   (p. 242)
  Yoga session of 30 minutes   (p. 96)
  Shampoo and finishing rinse   (pp. 45–46)
Once Each Week
  An evening (or a day) of rest, a time for yourself
  10-minute protective protein conditioning pac for hair
  Manicure and pedicure   (p. 201)
  Tweeze stray hairs on eyebrows   (p. 167)
  Shave legs and underarms   (p. 166)
  Facial mask   (p. 162)
Once This Month

One night and one day of rest for the digestive system on either the detoxifying Liquid Fast or the Clearing House Diet. (pp. 36–38)

Haircut and any other professional hair services such as color or perm (your cutter might advise a cut more often, perhaps every 3 weeks. Follow his suggestion in making out your individual schedule).

VIDAL ON: WHAT THE GYM TEACHER TAUGHT ME

His name is Terry Robinson, and in the 1940s and 50s he ran the gymnasium at M-G-M, keeping stars like Clark Gable in great shape. Now he's involved with the Century Health Club in Century City on the site of the old Twentieth Century-Fox movie studios, and he is still keeping many of the new stars in shape.

Even more impressive than his work with adults, though, is his teaching of gymnastics to children who are victims of cerebral palsy. He gets no money for this, and no money could be enough. It's true love.

He has helped me get over an atrophied muscle in my leg. I go in for an hour and a half three times a week, and some of Terry's comments during our sessions together are so true and interesting that I'd like to repeat them:

—"Exercising can't guarantee that you live longer, but it will guarantee that you live better. You will stave off old age and you will really live each day."

—"Bad posture is the most common crime against the body. A child should be trained in correct posture from the first second it can stand alone. Women often have worse posture than men because they become shy when their breasts develop. They start caving in their chests and slumping; high heels throw the body further out of alignment and they develop sway backs."

—"Number one requisite for a beautiful life is a strong lower back, and exercise should be aimed at that. Always stand tall, sit tall, and walk tall to strengthen the back."

—"Plato said, 'Give me the children at the age of six. They will learn gymnastics for the balance of the body; they will learn the arts for the balance of the mind.' "

—"The body is a bilateral machine, and the best exercise for it is swimming because it is a rhythmic, bilateral exercise. Hiking and jogging are next in importance. If you add weight lifting to develop the body, you can't go wrong. But lifting weights must be done under supervision."

—"If you want long muscles like a swimmer's, then you lift a ten-pound weight fifteen times. If you want big muscles and brute strength, you lift a fifty-pound weight five times."

—"My idea of correct eating is more vegetables and fish than meat, and lots of water—except at mealtimes. Meals should be eaten dry. If you chew properly, salivary glands will supply all the moisture you need. Drinking liquids while you eat will interfere with digestion."

—"To stay in shape, don't be a weekend athlete. Work all the time at building strength and endurance; continually exercise the heart muscle. Inactivity breeds inactivity, and the body goes to pot. Even while watching TV, you can constrict the muscle of the diaphragm, then relax it, constrict it, relax it, and you will help keep your abdomen in shape. If you do regular exercise for a year or two, then stop, you are looking for trouble. Your muscles can atrophy as easily as if you had never exercised at all."

—"Proper breathing is essential. Take deep breaths from the diaphragm. Throat breathing is emergency breathing only used to tide you over after a spurt of activity until you can regain control of the abdominal muscles."

—"Gable was a big believer in the medicine ball, and so am I. He used to get round about his middle between pictures. Before he would start work, he would come in and say 'Let's throw the ball, Terry,' and we would put in some long sessions. Hippocrates, the father of medicine, invented the practice of throwing a big leather ball to work up a sweat to lower fever. It's still a great treatment for an out-of-shape body."

—"The gym can save a marriage. Many guys come in here like tigers, straight from the office and all keyed up. They go in and tear hell out of the punching bag, shower, have a hot whirlpool bath, and relax. If they had gone straight home, they would have been tearing into their wives and kids. . . . Many surgeons come in to exercise before performing a grueling surgery and then come back afterward. It relaxes and awakens them so they are mentally and physically alert."

—"The most valuable physical study you could undertake is gymnastics. In it, you learn to walk beautifully, to take care of your body, and to carry it like the beautiful work of art that it is."

TEN THINGS TO KNOW BEFORE YOU GO INTO YOUR ACT

1. Timing is important. Never rush an exercise. Slowly and gracefully is best.

2. Exercise to music when you can. Rhythmic movement is developed that way, and pleasure is increased.

3. Get your mate or your children to exercise along with you. It's more fun that way, and good for them, too.

4. Breathing is crucial to proper exercising. Always inhale with the movement, and exhale on the return—lungs work when the body does and relax as the muscles do.

5. Dinner time and exercise time should be separate. A few minutes of exercise before a meal is fine (may cut your appetite, and will probably relax you so digestion is improved); but allow a couple of hours to elapse before you exercise after a meal.

6. Never collapse in the middle of an exercise. If you start to

feel the pull in a strenuous exercise, relax the position slowly rather than simply falling in a heap.

7. Except for the Seven-Way Stretch in the moring, the bed is not the best place for exercise. Regular exercise demands more support for the back than a mattress will provide. A thin exercise mat is great, but a carpeted floor or a folded blanket on the floor work very well to cushion exercise routines.

8. Clothing counts. A leotard lets you see how your body is working. A sweat suit keeps you cozy. Wear whichever you prefer. The idea is not so much modesty as protecting your warmed-up body from possible drafts and chill. If you want to combine exercise with nude sunbathing in a very private place on a very warm day, that's fine. But do have a big terry robe to wrap up in immediately after your workout.

9. Use the time you spend at housework or at your desk to do some unobtrusive figure improvers. Tightening and relaxing the muscles of the abdomen or the buttocks will go unnoticed but will help your muscle tone. Stretching relieves tension and helps keep you in shape. (Specifics on these quick figure improvers are on page 243.)

10. Don't overdo it. Many people get so intense about exercising that they turn the whole thing into an ordeal. Yes, you need exercise—but don't feel you absolutely need a daily workout. Three sessions of thirty minutes each is almost ideal for the week. But don't neglect a stretch and warm-up each morning if you want to feel your best.

BEVERLY ON: EXERCISE FOR WOMEN

A woman has to be careful to keep from developing muscle. You want firmness, tone, suppleness, grace, a lean line—but not muscle. So there are some exercises I won't do, and won't suggest to you. I will do anything that helps prevent flabby inner thighs, but I skip the ones that build muscle from hip to knee on the outer thigh. My exercises concentrate on the areas where most women have problems—fanny, inner thighs, stomach, upper arms—and on general limberness.

It works. I promise that once you have tried any or all of these when you are really tired, you won't be tired a few minutes later. Instead you will be taking deeper breaths, feeling the oxygen pump through for brighter eyes and skin. And you will feel tension and fatigue sliding away. None of these is a real sweater. They are to be done slowly and gracefully, but they get the job done.

For a real workout I like to go to a yoga class or to a gym—not for a more strenuous program, but for the uninterrupted routine, which helps me stick to what I'm doing. I don't stop for the day because the phone rings.

WARMING UP

Automobiles shouldn't go from "off" to "top speed" right away. Neither should your body. Always begin your exercises with a short warm-up. Even if you haven't time for a real exercise session, a warm-up is a good idea before you start sprinting through the day's chores.

Do the Seven-Way Stretch in bed (if you didn't do it when you got up).

De-kink with a shoulder roll: shrug your shoulders way up to your ears. Hunch them way forward and down, then over, way back and down. Now reverse the roll. Relax.

Hold your arms straight out at your sides. Let the wrists hang limp, and flap your hands up and down briskly for a count of ten. Relax and drop your arms to your sides.

Pull your chin as far down as you can on your chest. Then, with your eyes following the motion, roll your chin over to your left shoulder, then all the way back and over to the right shoulder and down to starting position again. Relax. (This is great to do at any time to relieve tension in the neck.)

BEVERLY ON: A FEW EXERCISES FOR PROBLEM PLACES

Hips, fanny, inner thighs:
Kneel on the floor, tuck your pelvis forward, and support your-

self by holding on to a chair or table. Raise right leg up and swing it out behind you in a back kick. Bring it back and repeat with the left leg. Repeat as many times as you like.

Double chin:

Stick out your chin and pull lower teeth up over the upper ones. Nod your head Yes, up and down as you turn from far right to far left. It looks silly, but it's good. Do this in the morning while waiting for the water to boil, while brushing your teeth, whenever you think of it—and are alone.

Legs:

Knees flexed, pelvis forward, feet comfortably apart, hold onto a chair with one hand. Rise on your toes, then bend down to the floor, holding your body straight and staying on tiptoe. Return to standing position and repeat at least ten times.

Inner thighs: (two to do at the kitchen sink)

1. Lift left foot, point the toe, and swing foot out as high as you can go to the left side. Let the leg swing back. Do for as long as you like, first one foot then the other, while busy at something else.

2. Plant feet flat on the floor as far apart as possible. Bend the right knee and stretch like a fencer, far to the right. Return to standing position and reverse. Do as many times as you like.

Inner thighs, stomach:

Lie on the floor with knees up, feet flat on the floor. Place a beach ball or basketball between your knees. Push in as hard as you can against the ball. Relax. Repeat. Relax. Repeat as many times as you like.

Stomach:

Lie on your back with feet and knees apart, feet flat on the floor and pelvis tucked forward. With elbows out, reach down and clasp the inner part of the thigh, right hand on inner part of right thigh, left hand on inner part of left thigh. Bend forward and hold the position for a count of seven. Slowly "walk" hands down to the ankles, walk them back up to the thighs, release them and raise your arms straight up as you return to the original position. Relax.

Stomach:

(This one and the next are lulus for the stomach, and may take a while to master)

Sit with back to the wall, your bottom about a hand's breadth away from it. With feet comfortably apart, point toes. Stretch legs straight out and crisscross them in scissors movement as you raise them several inches from the floor. Still crisscrossing, lower the legs to the floor. Relax. Repeat. Relax.

Same position—put your palms on the floor at your sides for support and bend your knees. Push legs up and out to make squares in the air: up, out, together, down. Relax and lower legs. Repeat. Relax. Repeat. Relax.

In the same position, with your legs apart, try to lift them. This sounds very simple, yet it's amazingly hard to do. If you can lift your legs, bring them together in front of you, then separate them, lower, and relax. If you can't raise your legs, just pull them across the floor in this exercise. It will help tone the leg and stomach muscles so that maybe next time you will get the legs up there.

A great one for the back, and for general stiffness and tension:

Clasp hands at either end of a broom or mop handle. Stand with feet apart, place the stick at the back of the neck and bend sideways from your waist. Bend over so that the stick is as nearly vertical to the floor as you can get it, then straighten, and bend the stick far to the other side. Continue going from left to right for three minutes. Now with the stick in the same position at the back of your neck, twist your torso from side to side. Continue for three more minutes.

For firming the fanny:

Stand at the kitchen counter. Bend your knees and tuck your pelvis forward. Point your right toe and push your right leg back behind you, tightening the buttocks as you push back far enough to feel the pull. Relax the buttocks as you let the leg swing back to the counter. Reverse. Do as many of these as you can, at least thirty with each leg.

For the upper arms, backs of the arms:

Hold your arms straight out in front of you, fists clenched, and make tight little crisscross motions with your fists making little over-and-under passes like drawing the letter C in the air with your knuckles; it's a bit like a cheerleader's movement, or something a semaphorist does. As you make these quick crisscross passes, lower your arms down to your waist and then up and as far over your head as you can go. Now clench your fists, palms up, and make tiny circles with your arms rigid. Keep making circles as you lower your arms to your hips, then raise them up over your head.

Reverse the direction of the circles, stretch your arms out to your sides. Relax.

These are for limberness, and good for you all over:

1. Stand with you feet apart, and your pelvis tucked forward in front of the mirror. Raise your arms, and keep the palms flat as if you were going to walk on them across the ceiling. Bend as far as you can to the left, then to the right, trying to touch your palm to the floor. (It probably won't get any closer to the floor than your knee level, but that's the direction it should be headed.) Now back up toward the ceiling and reverse.

2. Feet wide apart, knees flexed, and pelvis tucked forward, lower your knuckles to the floor. Keep your back as tabletop-flat as possible. Join your hands and swing them back and forth through your legs while you bounce your torso up and down gently following the swing.

3. Sit on the floor with your back flat against the wall. Stretch your legs out (at 10 o'clock and 2 o'clock) and bend forward to clasp your right ankle with your hands. Now bring your forehead down to touch your hands (or as far down as possible), stretch your back with a rocking motion, come back and reverse.

For the stomach, inner thigh, upper thigh and buttocks:

1. Kneel on the floor, with the pelvis slightly forward, raise your arms to shoulder level and pointing out before you, and rock back and forth slowly and as far as you can in each direction. Keep this up as long as you feel comfortable.

The "end-of-class" movement at the Lotte Berk Method classes is really fun to do:

Begin in the same starting position as for the exercise directly above, but put your hands on your hips. With the pelvis forward, describe a figure 8 with your hips, trying not to move the upper part of your body. You'll see that this is really a belly dance, done on your knees, and if you do it to music it can really get to you. Lots of people get very sexy with it. Why not? Any exercise that limbers up the lower back and the pelvic region, as this one does, *is* sexy. This also winds you down while it works all the stomach muscles and the muscles in the inner thighs.

One exercise for an all-over workout:

Make an arched bridge of your body: plant your feet and your hands wide apart and flat on the floor with your back curved upward. Now lower your head, and lead with your chin as you roll your shoulders and your body down, forward, and through your arms. Come back, with your buttocks up in the air, to resume the starting position. Repeat. Relax.

This works everything—arms, lower stomach, legs, back. It's a great reviver after a hard day.

SPECIALS FOR YOUR MAKEUP AND FRAGRANCE

• If you still haven't found just the right green fragrance for warm weather in your trips to the perfume counter, walk over to the men's department. I wear a man's cologne from time to time during the day. It's fresh and light and lemony without being too sweet. (Of course, some men's colognes now are hot and heavy.) Citrus-based scents can be very nice—all except lime. Lime fragrances, especially synthetic lime, have a tendency to irritate the skin. Just a little point to keep in mind whether you're shopping for a fragrance for you or for him.

• You can draw out a timid underlip with a paler color on the lower lip, a darker one on the upper lip. If your mouth is too pouty, go the opposite route. Your lips will look fuller if you use a richer, brighter shade in the center and go lighter in the corners. Shiny lip gloss helps the color accenting with highlights.

SPECIALS FOR YOUR SHAPE

• Try the Five-Minute Relaxer: Lie on the bed with your head hanging over the side. Arch your back and slide down over the edge of the bed until your head touches the floor. Raise your feet and brace them on the wall, about twelve inches above the bed. Now rest for five minutes in this position. It's better than a nap.

• It's time for the Seated Bikini test. Put on your bikini, sit so your profile shows in the full-length mirror. Most women on the beach tend to lie flat on their backs, or to get up to stand—quickly. It's while seated that a roll of flesh shows, a paunchy abdomen. If you don't see that in the mirror—you are in great shape. If you tend to roll over at the waist, increase the work on your middle before Memorial Day.

• Exercise before meals is relaxing. Being relaxed means you will probably eat more slowly, which in turn means eating less. The longer you linger over the meal, the better. It takes thirty minutes for blood sugar to rise sufficiently after eating for the brain to stop sending out hunger signals. If you can't get out for a quick walk or a warm-up before dinner, do have a glass of fruit juice ten minutes before dinner. It helps cut appetite in a safe, low-calorie way.

SPECIALS FOR YOUR SKIN

• Make your weekly evening for yourself (make sure that you get one every week!) a time of rest for your skin, too. First, go through your regular cleansing routine, and after rinsing, steam your face for a minute or so with a wet washcloth dipped in hot water. The ideal temperature is 93°F. (or 34°C). At that temperature the skin perspires. It throws off more carbon dioxide and absorbs almost five times as much oxygen. Just a minute of this steaming with the wet washcloth will do it. Now apply a natural pore-cleansing protein mask made from the white of an egg. Rest with your feet propped up for ten minutes, then splash off the mask with lots of cool-water rinsing. Now, give your skin a mini-vacation from everything that it usually wears. Give it an opportunity to throw off wastes overnight. Cleanse as usual in the morning and make up a fresher face. If it's to be a day indoors, you might want to continue the rest cure by moisturizing lightly but skipping all makeup. Of course, if you are going out, skin needs moisturizer for protection. Even gentle May breezes gain in velocity against naked, super-delicate skin around the eyes.

SPECIALS FOR YOUR FOOD PLANNING

• Because Vidal loves salads and vegetable dishes so much, eight years of living with him has put my ingenuity to the test in coming up with new ideas for them. Here is the latest one:

RAW VEGETABLE SALAD

½ cup sprouts (alfalfa, winter wheat, or other sprouts)
½ cup raw mushrooms, sliced
½ cup raw cauliflower buds
½ cup green beans (lightly steamed, then chilled)
1 head Boston lettuce, torn into small pieces
   Combine in the salad bowl and toss with the dressing below.

SALAD DRESSING FOR VEGETABLES

½ cup fresh lemon juice
½ teaspoon dry mustard
2 teaspoons chopped parsley
cracked pepper and sea salt or salt substitute to taste
   Mix all ingredients thoroughly.

• Marinated mushrooms are delicious, and always make me think of Vidal. Funny association? He proposed to me at an English health farm and this dish is one of the first things you eat there after a fast.

MARINATED MUSHROOMS À LA GRAYSHOTT HALL

1 pound fresh mushrooms
1 pint cold spring water
¾ cup tarragon vinegar or lemon juice
1 tablespoon polyunsaturated salad oil
1 bay leaf
pinch of thyme

Wash mushrooms. Combine water and vinegar or lemon juice in saucepan and bring to a boil. Add mushrooms and cook for 3 minutes. Remove from heat, add remaining ingredients, stir, and chill.

• Buy only what you will use within the following three days. Fresh fruits and vegetables get a bit forlorn after that, lose texture and vitamins. Onions and lemons are exceptions; lemons keep well, and lemons are juicier when the skin starts to shrivel up a little.

• Don't pay for vitamins in fresh vegetables and then peel them away. Instead, get a vegetable brush and scrub. You will save time, too, if you cook carrots washed, but not peeled, apples with the skins on. When you don't have to pare, don't.

• You cut away vitamin C when you cut up vegetables and fruits. Get the smallest sizes (cheaper!) and slice at the last minute into the largest pieces that will permit quick cooking. Here's the reason: vitamin C oxidizes and is lost when it meets air, heat, and water. Not immediately—but it doesn't take long. When fruit or leaves are cut, enzymes go to work to destroy the C. One half the C can be lost between the knife and the table.

• Keep all the vitamin A. Darker, outer leaves of salad greens usually are twenty-five times higher in A than the prettier, paler, inside leaves.

• "Which apricot? Grown where?" was Adelle Davis's skeptical response to the statement that this or that food was high in vitamins. It does help to know that vegetables are freshly picked, not trucked in from half a continent away. To insist always on local produce is too utopian in the late twentieth century—but you will save money and get fresher food if you buy local produce when you can.

SPECIALS FOR YOUR HAIR

• Want straight hair? Please don't rush into chemical straightening. It is the only salon treatment that is not guaranteed 100 percent, in even the very best salons. No matter how carefully it is done, the hair still loses resiliency and life to some degree. Your hair will look straighter if it is cut all one length. And you can dry it to look straighter. Here is the best nonchemical straightening treatment I know of: When you dry your hair, put one large foam-covered roller in the crown. Wrap all the rest of your hair around your head in one direction. Put in pins to hold it, and let it dry for thirty minutes. Take out the pins and wrap it in the other direction around your head. Pin it, and now let it dry for ten minutes. When hair is completely dry, take out the pins and brush your hair.

• From now through September, more frequent use of the Vidal Sassoon Protein Pac Treatment is desirable. Use the pac at least once a week to prevent summertime damage to hair from sun, wind, and water. Your hair will be so much more shiny and vital that you might want to make this weekly conditioning a year-round custom.

JUNE

Right now the super-exhilarating rush of warm June weather washes over you like a bracing wave.

Your program for this month will give you the glow-getting attitude to dash through summer enjoying it to the full.

This is what positive vitality is really about—the more you expend, the more you have to spend. In this form of keen excitement you spend physically without tiring because you are getting mental returns.

The only thing that can sap your energy is tedium. Avoid it.

It's a great time to attack new projects, creative pursuits that you grow with.

Going on holiday? Learn something about the history of the place you visit. Get to know the past of the area, and two weeks later you will find that not only have you enriched your enjoyment of the time you spent there but you have come home with a new mental dimension that will last far longer than your tan.

Acquire a skill. Take up knitting or macramé and make a lacy weskit in zinnia pinks or beach-pebble tints. It will be not only a pretty reminder of a string of bright blue summer days, but also a handsome asset in your fall wardrobe.

Take advantage of the long days and the warm, late twilights to get out and *do* something. Every city and town puts its best cultural foot forward in summer. Investigate the free events sponsored by your local Parks Department and museum. Use some of that positive vitality of yours to get out and support them, to enjoy them. Better yet, how about helping to organize them?

After all, isn't that what you are working for—making yourself a more beautiful person in order to be a more valuable person?

YOUR CHECKLIST AND SCHEDULE FOR JUNE

First Morning of the Month

Log your vital statistics into your diary (p. 14) *in ink.* Set your goals for the month as to loss of pounds or inches and gains in other areas, such as proficiency at yoga, say, or using the hand-held dryer. Pencil in your goals on the diary page for the last day of the month, and start the program that will help you achieve your goals.

Every Morning

Seven-Way Stretch   (p. 91)

Cup of hot water and lemon juice

Warm-up exercises   (p. 146)

Clean face and moisturize   (p. 54)

Makeup   (p. 61)

Fix hair

Vitality Drink and nutritional supplements   (p. 94)

Every Evening

Warm-up exercises to relax

Feet-up rest with pillows or on slantboard for 10 minutes

Clean face and moisturize

Bath and all-over body lotion   (p. 128)

Clean teeth before bed   (p. 259)

As Often as You Like: At Least Three Times Each Week

Exercise session of 30 minutes   (p. 242)

Yoga session of 30 minutes   (p. 96)

Shampoo and finishing rinse   (pp. 45–46)

Once Each Week
> An evening (or a day) of rest, a time for yourself
> 10-minute protective protein conditioning pac for hair
> Manicure and pedicure   (p. 201)
> Tweeze stray hairs on eyebrows   (p. 167)
> Shave legs and underarms   (p. 166)
> Facial mask   (p. 162)

Once This Month
> One night and one day of rest for the digestive system on the detoxifying Liquid Fast or the Clearing House Diet   (pp. 36–38)
>
> Haircut and any other professional hair services such as color or perm (your cutter might advise a cut more often, perhaps every three weeks. Follow his suggestion in making out your individual schedule).

VIDAL ON: MEDITATION: THE MENTAL KEY TO POSITIVE VITALITY AND REAL BEAUTY

Self-awareness is the chief tool that frees you to use all the positive vitality you have, that brings all your real inner beauty of spirit to the surface. There is one simple key to self-awareness, and it has been one of the greatest influences for good in my life. I refer to the practice of Transcendental Meditation.

Meditation is a direct route to achievement of your private goals. Not material goals, necessarily. Through meditation, you become wonderfully aware of the beauty of the physical world—but not more acquisitive. Beverly Hills has one of the highest standards of living in the world, and the people who live here have high standards of personal physical beauty. Yet these haven't always made for happiness because very often people have not achieved these goals in their own ways. Meditation will give this happiness because you assess your strengths and weaknesses, learn the way to achieve in your own way the things you want, and become almost achingly aware of the beauty of this world.

This is all lovely and highfalutin—but let me explain it on a practical level, as it applied to my life.

I grew up in the East End of London. It was more or less a ghetto area for poor Jews. At fourteen, I went to work as a shampoo boy in a salon nearby, not because it was what I wanted to do with my life (I had no plans beyond the next football game) but because my mother insisted I learn a trade.

When the Second World War ended, I was seventeen. I was a Jew who survived the war because twenty-one miles of English Channel water stood between me and the people who would have turned me into bars of soap and lampshades. Yet every Nazi had begun life as a Christian. Seemingly there were many Protestants in the world, and many Catholics, but few real Christians. I was very bitter, and very anti-Christian. Every obstacle in my way I ascribed to anti-Semitism.

An analogy today might be a poor black chap trying to make his way up, finding all sorts of obstacles before him, and becoming completely anti-white.

I was filled with hate. Hate was blocking whatever creative energy I had.

When I was twenty, I felt I had to get away from London, and from the unfulfilling work I was doing. I went to Israel and spent a year in the Palmach commando group of the Israeli Army in the Negev Desert.

Twenty is a very formative age. Along with performing much hard physical labor, I had a great deal of time to think, alone in the desert. The vast clean space of the desert reduces personal concerns to their proper perspective, even for a self-centered twenty-year-old, yet it allows you to be very much alone with yourself. I began to sort myself out.

I grew beyond anti-Christian feelings. I did not become anti-Arab, I became pro-life. I came to see how draining it is to be anti-anything; how self-defeating it is to spend time in brooding and regret.

As manual labor strengthened my body, I began to discover a sense of pride. Not false pride, but the dignity of achievement. I was not simply an object of hate, something to be despised; I was a man who was contributing something to the world, performing a valuable service during my lifetime. From my efforts something would grow that was good and would help this country as it was helping me.

I went back to London with a new dignity, that dignity necessary for all living creatures. Drained of hate, I was filled with purpose. I was, in my mother's phrase, "of this world," in the sense of being a man awake to life and all its pleasures and responsibilities.

If I was to be a hairdresser, I decided to be a damn good one. I realized at last that I was not born ordinary, that I had the juices to do it. None of us is born ordinary, we all have the juices, but we need to recognize our strengths, to channel our forces.

My life was headed up and I was working hard to keep it in that direction. At twenty-eight, I married a wonderful woman. We married, though, for all the wrong reasons and at the wrong time for either of us to grow and develop as we should. Three years later she left me.

She said that I was in love with a pair of scissors first, in love with her second. I realized for the first time that I had been devoting all my thoughts and time to my small salon rather than to my wife.

Knowing I had been at fault did not prevent me from feeling crushed. Very few people die of a broken heart, but they are miserably unhappy and dead to life for a long time. One cannot soon get over the sense of failure and the feeling of worthlessness as a human being.

My work was getting better all the time. I was beginning to have some recognition, but in my own eyes I was a total failure.

I was ready for any distraction, and one evening in 1960 some friends suggested I go with them to a shabby little hotel in London to see a guru about whom they were very enthusiastic. I was a bit skeptical but I went along.

Seated on a hard mattress in a nondescript hotel room was the Maharishi Mahesh Yogi. Much later the Beatles and Mia Farrow would discover the Maharishi, and after them a horde of cultural camp followers and much unfortunate publicity would threaten to make a joke of his name.

In those days he was an unknown man. One didn't need publicity to know that he was a great man. You hear and read of people with an aura. I felt immediately that he was surrounded by an aura and that waves of peace and power were flowing from him. I felt that he was in touch with that spirit out there that is good—call it God or whatever you choose.

He spoke to us in his soothing voice and I felt more serene than at any time since leaving the Negev Desert and the solitary thought sessions there that had done so much to melt the core of hatred which had blocked my life.

He taught me that life flows in a sure, constant stream as a river flows. So long as we move with it, the current is strong and true and supports us, giving us energy as it carries us. When we attempt to dam up the current, to block the movement and the ongoing force of life, we can only fail. The current of fresh energy becomes stagnant, and rather than being supported by life, we risk drowning.

He taught me that you cannot disallow change in yourself or in others. You cannot reach out and grab at another person to hold them to you when the current begins to carry them away from you. One or the other of you will be stifled and hurt. You must let go, and be open to the new influences, the new energies that will be positive as your life moves on; and you must be glad that you see growth and change in the person you love, you must allow that person to follow the life current.

The Maharishi taught me that good in life can come only from utilizing emotions, people, and objects for good, and at the time of your life when they are positive forces for good. Clinging to people or objects can only spoil them. Hoarding is wrong and destructive. You must keep your hands and your heart and mind open. An illustration might be a piece of fruit or a steak—it can nourish you, if you eat it when it is fresh and when you have need of nourishment. If you eat it when you have no need of food, it will make you fat; if you hoard it against the day you will be hungry, it may spoil and sicken you when you eat it. You must be open to enjoyment, to the forces for good that come into your life; then you must be willing to let them go, and to accept the new forces for good, for change.

One must not weep over failure, nor censure others for disappointing him. These good and bad experiences are all part of the stream and the flow, part of the change that is the proof you are alive.

All this can be admitted as true by the mind. But for it to help you, for it to be known emotionally, you must free your mind to concentrate on it. You must brush aside the petty outside distractions so you will be free to think about your true concern—

making the most and the best of your life. It is here that meditation comes in.

The usual prescription for a great hurt, a near-fatal blow to the psyche, is to "lose yourself" in something. Engage yourself in constant, even pointless activity, and you will "take your mind off your problems."

The answer, I realized that first evening with the Maharishi, lies in doing *exactly the opposite.* You must not lose yourself in travel, drink, drugs, sex, eating, or anything else.

You must *find* yourself.

Instead of giving yourself away when you feel worthless, you must take stock of what you really are and determine your worth.

Defeat must help you gain strength. You must learn from it to evaluate the struggle. Could you have won? Were you fighting a good fight for the right reasons, or just tilting at windmills?

Meditation will help you answer these questions for yourself, help you know yourself. Through meditation you learn to set your own pace, recognize your virtues and your mistakes.

You achieve self-awareness.

This, in so many words, is the simple and priceless value of meditation.

It saddens me that so many people have been discouraged from this way to peace and achievement because of the unfortunate publicity that has given Transcendental Meditation a crazed-hippie-dropout-mumbo-jumbo reputation.

Meditation does *not* conflict with any Western (or Eastern) religion. It is apart from organized religion, but the opening of your mind to do its given work amplifies the good of any religious beliefs you have.

Meditation does *not* have to be practiced in the lotus position in darkened, incense-filled rooms before exotic shrines and Indian symbols. The mantra is a beautiful word, a sound on which you concentrate in order to block extraneous thoughts from your mind as you reach inside yourself to tap your inner forces and get in touch with your mind while you relax. It might be an evocative word such as "sunshine" or "calm."

Meditation *does* require that you be in a comfortable position, and the lotus position is a comfortable one for some people. Sitting on a sofa, bed, or lying on a slantboard with feet elevated is comfortable, too, and might be the way you prefer to meditate.

Meditation *is* easier when your surroundings are quiet and peaceful. Everything is easier in peace and quiet. But Beverly told me of seeing a young man meditate on a New York to Los Angeles jet flight. I have been able to enter a state of meditation while walking on the street. In general, though, peace and quiet insure that you will not be distracted from your thoughts, nor have to give any attention to the world around you. A quiet church, synagogue, or mosque is a wonderful setting for meditation.

There is medical evidence of the good things that meditation does for your body as well as your mind. The Maharishi is not a simple mystic on the mountain, but an ex-physicist who knows that meditation can allow you to control your breathing so that less carbon dioxide is produced in the blood and the energy needs of the body become fewer. Research at Harvard University has shown through medical testing that blood pressure becomes lower, as does the need for oxygen. Less oxygen is dealt with, but more efficiently, so the body is working at a slower pace and getting a rest from stress.

There are many varieties of meditation, but the one I have been talking about, Transcendental Meditation, requires no props or special disciplines as some other forms of meditation do. It does not require a great deal of time, either. The Maharishi says that the greatest effects can be achieved by twenty minutes of meditation in the morning and another twenty minutes in the evening. This is the way: Get into a comfortable position in a quiet, comfortable place and begin to say "peace" or "sunshine" or "love" or whichever word you choose over and over to yourself. Let your mind go blank. Do not work at it—let yourself go. Let go and relax. In a matter of a few minutes, the world will seem to open as your forces swell to envelop you in warmth. You will feel the power rise in waves through your body to go out and to meet the forces of energy that are all around you. Things will seem clearer, and you will see them with a new eye as if your mind were above your body and the life it leads, studying them and seeing how they can be guided and directed. As these answers come, the mind can relax and plan the most direct action to settle questions and cope with problems. When the way seems clearer, life will seem better and the mind and body open to serenity and joy.

The peace of meditation is not severed abruptly when you return slowly to a state of action. The mental tranquility remains like a light, comfortable garment as you go about the chores of the day. Even the physiological resistance to stress lasts for as long as thirty minutes after a session of meditation. The psychological effects are permanent.

I cannot urge strongly enough that you devote some time to sampling the peace and strength of meditation. The relaxed time of the monthly two-day Clearing House Diet is ideal.

BEVERLY ON: TWENTY TREATS FOR YOUR SKIN— BEAUTY MENUS FROM THE BLENDER

You can whip these up in seconds using things that are right there in the refrigerator or on the kitchen shelf.

These masks, facial packs, and cleansers all work in gentle, natural ways to soothe, stimulate, relax, tone, or clear the skin. I have indicated which ones are for which problems or skin types, but you can use a tutti-frutti approach—everybody's skin is a combination of oily and dry. You might want to use a mask for oily skin on the mask of the face, which tends to be oily (nose, forehead, chin) and a mask for dry skin everywhere else.

You can take a Chinese restaurant approach, too (Two from Column A), and combine apricots from one mask with peaches from another recipe in the same skin-type category.

However you cook up your mask, apply it to clean skin and let it go to its good work for fifteen or twenty minutes while you relax. Feet up on pillows or resting on the slantboard will double the benefits of any helper you put on your skin.

Remember, skin is an all-over affair. Don't stop with nourishing just your face—spread the good work to hands, to throat and shoulders.

After twenty minutes, splash away the facial with cool or lukewarm water.

Important: Spread the facial mask everywhere *except* around your eyes. Some special suggestions for the thin-skinned eye areas are on page 165.

Five for dry skin (facial masks that are good for hands, throat, all of you):

1. Break up a large banana, toss into the blender along with half of the peel and 1 tablespoon raw honey. Blend to liquefy, pat on, let dry 20 minutes.

2. Soak 1 cup dried apricots in warm water (or use fresh ones: wash, pit, but don't peel). Toss apricots in the blender, add 1 tablespoon honey and liquefy. Pat on, let dry for 20 minutes. Rinse off with cool water.

3. Soak 1 cup dried prunes in warm water. Add fruit to 1 tablespoon sesame oil in blender. Liquefy, pat on, let dry 20 minutes.

4. Peel and pit an avocado, liquefy in the blender with 1 tablespoon raw honey. Pat on, let dry 20 minutes. Rinse off with cool water.

5. Soak 1 cup dried peaches in warm water (or use a big ripe peach, sliced, washed, and pitted and peeled) and put in blender along with 1 tablespoon dried skim milk powder and 1 tablespoon raw honey. Pat on, let dry 20 minutes, splash off with cool water.

Five for oily skin (facial masks for the face only; hands and throat are never too oily):

1. Wash and core 2 crisp apples, but do not peel. Cut into quarters and liquefy in the blender with 1 tablespoon lemon juice. Pat on, let dry for 20 minutes, splash off with cool water.

2. Wash a big, ripe tomato and liquefy the whole thing in the blender. Pat on and let dry for 20 minutes. Splash off with cool water.

3. Puree a washed, unpeeled cucumber in the blender with 1 tablespoon plain yoghurt. Pat on, let dry for 20 minutes. Rinse off with cool water.

4. Puree ½ cup ripe strawberries in the blender with 1 tablespoon lemon juice, 2 tablespoons plain yoghurt. Pat on, let dry for 20 minutes. Rinse off with cool water.

5. *The Marie Antoinette Special:*
   1 ounce cognac
   1 raw egg
   1 ounce milk

juice of 1 lemon

Blend everything together, heat slightly, then pat on the face while still barely warm. Let dry 20 minutes. Splash off with cool water. The French queen's mask still works for oily skin, even if her famous cake diet was a flop. The cognac? It dries up oils as any alcohol does, but you wouldn't expect Marie Antoinette to fool around with beer, would you?

Three nourishing masks for any skin type

1. Puree 1 ounce blanched almonds in the blender, add 1 ounce milk and 1 ounce honey, blend. Pat on, let dry 20 minutes, rinse off with tepid water.

2. Blend 2 egg yolks, 2 tablespoons honey, 3 drops almond oil. Pat on, let dry for 20 minutes, rinse off with cool water.

3. Blend 1 egg, 3 tablespoons polyunsaturated oil, 1 tablespoon apple cider vinegar. Pat on, let dry 20 minutes, splash off with tepid water. Yes, it *is* like mayonnaise. In fact, a good mayonnaise, even one from a bottle, is a nifty instant facial mask.

One clarifying facial mask good for all skins (to use occasionally. This does with gentle natural enzymes what skin-sloughing creams, peelers, and exfoliating lotions do with chemicals—it removes dead, dry skin cells on the surface to expose fresh clear skin that these hide)

Peel a ripe papaya and puree in the blender. Pat on the fruit, let dry for 20 minutes. Rinse off with cool water.

Three cleansing and blanching masks (for faded, end-of-summer tans as well as winter-drab or season-change sallow skin)

1. Add the juice of a lemon to 1 cup of buttermilk. Blend, pat on, let dry for 20 minutes. Splash off with cool water.

2. Liquefy 1 whole lemon (washed, not peeled) and ½ orange (washed, not peeled) in the blender. Add 1 cup plain yoghurt. Blend, pat on, let dry 20 minutes. Rinse off with cool water.

3. Add the juice of 3 lemons to 1 cup dry powdered skim milk. Add just enough water to make a thin paste. Spread on skin, let dry 20 minutes. Rinse with tepid water.

One cleansing mask (good as a monthly plus-and-minus treatment.

It adds proteins, subtracts blackheads and dead skin cells. Gentle enough for any skin type)

Pulverize 1 cup dry oatmeal in the blender. To this powder add 3 drops almond oil, ½ cup skim milk, 1 egg white. Blend. Pat on. Let dry 20 minutes. Splash off with cool water.

Two soothers for sore eyes (these can be piled on sterile cotton pads like open-face sandwiches, or put into wet cheesecloth, and used as compresses for eyes when the rest of the face is drinking in a treat mask)

1. Puree ½ raw, peeled potato in the blender.
2. Puree a cold, peeled cucumber in the blender. You can also use very thin slices of cucumber *au naturel* as eye compresses.

THE ONE-WEEK CUTICLE CURE

If you have been ignoring your hands, they will show it. It's easy to forget about proper nail care at this time of the year when you are doing so much with your hands and they are so exposed. Here's a quick first-aid treatment that should get them back in shape.

Every day for a week do this:

P.M. Just before bed, soak your nails in a little bowl of warm oil of almonds to which you've added two tablespoons wheat germ oil or a snipped-open vitamin E capsule. Take your hands out of the oil after ten minutes, but don't take the oil off your hands. Pat the fingertips dry, but massage oil into the nails. Massage each fingertip with the thumb from the top joint to the tip (the whole area where new nails are growing underneath). Take three calcium lactate tablets with a glass of warm milk. While this is helping you sleep like an angel, it's working like a demon on beautiful new nails (and hair, too).

A.M. Massage a little cream or oil (wheat germ oil, baby oil, or cuticle cream) into the nails. Buff your nails before you start the day. Buffing steps up the shine, speeds up the circulation for healthier nails. Whenever you think of it during the day, massage a tiny dab of cream or petroleum jelly into your nails. Drink lots of water, but touch as little water as possible. Even during your bath, avoid soaking the nails for prolonged periods. Rest your hands on the sides of the tub while you luxuriate. Work at a hobby that exercises the fingers and helps circulation and nail growth. Needlepoint, embroidery, playing the piano, and typing are great for the nails. Worried about chips? Tiny bits of masking tape on the tips will protect them.

During the day: However your eating plan shapes up, the inclusion of any of these is good news for nails: skim milk for calcium and vitamin D; raw cabbage for vitamin D; tuna, sardines, or salmon for iodine, protein, and vitamin D. Since iodine stimulates circulation (therefore, nails) and is difficult to come by except in fish and sea plants, consider adding iodine-rich kelp tablets to your diet supplements.

Wear washable cotton gloves while you work. But take them off every hour or so, and rinse your hands in cool water. Hands perspire in gloves and the acids from trapped perspiration don't do nails any good. Dry your hands, apply a bit of cream, and replace the gloves. When you wash dishes by hand, wear the cotton gloves inside your rubber gloves. Let the dishes soak first in hot water, then tackle them after the water cools down. Use handled swabbers and glass brushes to keep your gloved hands out of water as much as possible. When cooking, always rinse your hands quickly under cool running water to rinse off lemon juice and vegetable juices that pull sneak acid attacks on nails.

And use your hands, keep them in motion, for the most beautiful, graceful look while you are encouraging them to be even more beautiful. Remember, hands are very effective for flirting, but not if they're lying flat in your lap.

BEVERLY ON: REMOVING BODY HAIR

Lots of European women never bother with it, and it doesn't seem to bother European men. A number of American women refuse to shave their legs or underarms, regarding body hair as a badge of liberated womanhood. If you feel that way, don't touch the hair on your body.

I don't like body hair. My hair is dark, and that includes the hair on my forearms, so I shave legs, underarms, and forearms.

I used to have my legs waxed, but I don't think it's worth all the trouble and expense. Shaving is quick and easy. Despite what you might have heard, shaving does *not* encourage heavier regrowth.

This is the best way to shave, if you use a safety razor: Once a week, after a bath, rub lots of moisturizing lotion all over wet legs and follow with a shaving foam. Wait sixty seconds, then shave. Use long strokes rather than short ones and rinse the razor after every stroke. If the razor is clogged with foam it's harder to do a clean job. Swing your legs back into the tub and rinse thoroughly in warm, running water. Now rub more moisturizer into the skin you've shaved.

This is the best way with an electric razor: Once a week, before a bath, use lots of pre-electric shave conditioner. Use the razor all over in a sort of patting motion. Don't drag it over skin like a vacuum cleaner. After shaving, wash off all the pre-electric shave conditioner, rinse thoroughly and after your bath use moisturizer or body lotion lavishly.

That's it for legs, underarms, forearms, or bikini line.

Facial hair and hairs on your breasts are another matter. Many women tweeze out stray chin whiskers, and there are bleaches that, carefully used, can camouflage a moustache. I personally would not tweeze hair on the breasts, or any hair on a mole, and shaving the face is a touch too masculine for my taste.

If facial hair is a real problem, see if your doctor will give the green light to waxing or can recommend a good electrologist. Electrolysis is expensive, but it is the only permanent solution.

BEVERLY ON: EYEBROWS

For me, a children's toothbrush and tweezers are the only tools for eyebrow care. I don't do much with my eyebrows because luckily I am happy with the shape and the coloring of them.

If you don't like the way yours look though, there are brow beaters. To correct the shape you can try either electrolysis or tweezing.

Electrolysis is a bit expensive, and maybe a bit painful, but it is permanent. That can be good or bad. If thick eyebrows come in again, as they did in the fifties, and you have permanently delicate eyebrows, you'll have a lot of penciling to do to modernize your makeup.

Tweezing is a do-it-yourselfer, and it can be pretty painless if done properly. Here's the right way to tweeze and shape the eyebrows:

Apply lots of moisturizer over your eyebrows. Rub it in well and leave it there for ten or fifteen minutes. Get out your magnifying mirror. Brush your eyebrows up and into the arch you want. To get the best proportion for your face, there is a trick with a pencil: Hold the pencil in a straight line up from the side of the nose past the inner corner of the eye to find the inner limit. The outer limit is found by lining up the pencil from the side of the nose to the outer corner of the eye. The high point of the arch of your brow ought to be directly over the outer edge of the iris.

Now that you know where you're going, tweeze just one hair at a time, always in the direction of growth. Use your thumb to stretch the skin up on the forehead. Once you've removed the straggling hairs at the outer and inner sides of the eyebrows, start on the ones below. Never thin from above the brow line, always from below. Remove hairs row by row, working up to the thinness of brow you want. Do one brow at a time, and when both are symmetrical and perfectly shaped, saturate a cotton pad with disinfectant lotion or alcohol and wipe your brows. Be sure to clean the tweezers with alcohol before and after you use them.

If the problem isn't so much the shape as the shade of your eyebrows, you can have them dyed or bleached. This is *not* an at-home project. Only in a salon can you be sure of the results. I have a brunette friend who wound up with weird albino eyebrows because she answered the telephone while she was bleaching her eyebrows. Seconds count.

If you use an eyebrow pencil, I have two words of advice: never a dull one, and never a black one. A very sharp pencil is the only kind that can give you hair-thin feathery strokes. Even if your eyebrows are black, a charcoal gray or deep brown eyebrow pencil will give a more natural result.

I find that brushing the eyebrows up with that kid's toothbrush makes them look darker without using a pencil. Try it first before you start drawing.

One last word: so many people neglect their eyebrows. When

you shampoo your hair, wash your eyebrows, too. It's all skin and hair, isn't it?

SPECIALS FOR YOUR SKIN

• Yes, vitamins on your skin really *do* help. The skin has a remarkable ability to absorb. Putting iodine on the skin will cause traces of iodine to appear in urine within minutes. Vitamin A and vitamin E are especially good for the skin, and if your body lotion or tanning cream isn't enriched with them, why not do the job yourself? Make up only a small batch of vitamins for the skin at a time, because the vitamins oxidize quickly. You can prick a capsule of A and/or E and mix it well into the lotion or cream. Sniff the capsule before adding—vitamins don't always have the most appealing fragrances. If the vitamin smells bad, just swallow it; it will still do you good. Wheat germ oil smells wonderful, as you might expect. A fair-skinned blond friend of ours, who gets a great tan and keeps her skin beautiful, uses a mixture of wheat germ oil and avocado oil as her sun treatment.

SPECIALS FOR YOUR FOOD PLANNING

• The blender is something I can't imagine living without—especially in warm weather when the less time spent in the kitchen the better. If it's spent with the blender, it's cooler time, too. This "salad" from the blender is something our children love. They call it "The Green Glop." It comes out looking like a green gazpacho, if you'd rather think of it that way. Like gazpacho, it makes a wonderful cold first course. Add a teaspoon of curry powder when you serve it to adults.

GREEN GAZPACHO

Blend:

2 peeled tomatoes	Romaine or other lettuce
3 celery stalks	¼ cup orange juice
1 small cucumber, peeled	juice of 1 lemon, or more to taste.

Like other blender soups, you can improvise: green onions, parsley, whatever.

BLENDER PICK-ME-UP OR BEFORE DINNER COCKTAIL

Blend together a piece of fresh melon, a piece of fresh pineapple, a few strawberries, some ice cubes. A beautiful ripe pink color, and delicious. Note: the ice cubes go in last—one at a time while the motor is running.

• Zucchini is at its best this month, though available the year round. It's a great diet vegetable—only eighteen calories in a cupful.

ZUCCHINI

Get the tiniest baby zucchini. Wash but don't peel. Slice into 1-inch lengths and steam or boil quickly in a little water. The zucchini should be done, but still crisp, in 5 minutes. Just a little lemon juice does it.

• Prune Whip is a dark, smooth, delicious dessert. Very good after a light salad supper. It's easy to make if you use baby food.

PRUNE WHIP

Beat 5 egg whites till stiff. Fold into 1 cup pureed prunes with 2 table-spoons lemon juice. Chill.

• Be sure you have removed all traces of pesticides, wax and dye coatings from fruits and vegetables. Here's an easy way: Add 2 tablespoons of natural cider vinegar to a sinkful of cold water and soak the vegetables for fifteen minutes; then scrub with a vegetable brush.

• For a splendid way to begin eating for beauty and health, see The Sassoon Diet for All Seasons, p. 265.

• Salt first is not the best way to go about cooking vegetables if you want to keep nutrients in. When possible, cook first and season later.

• Health food fanatics often insist that they eat only "organic food." TV Dinners are organic food, too. "Organic" just means that the food contains carbon atoms. All food does. An *organically grown* tomato is one grown without the use of inorganic fertilizers.

• If you just plain don't like yeast, yoghurt, or liver, investigate the tablets that can be swallowed down with your vitamin supplements to give you the benefits of these great foods without the tastes.

• A pretty green-and-gold sandwich that's great for lunch boxes is this one.

AVOCADO-CARROT-WATERCRESS SANDWICH

Mash together avocado, grated carrot, and finely chopped watercress. Spread on whole wheat bread. Spinkle on a few alfalfa or bean sprouts if you like. Very tasty and it keeps well.

SPECIALS FOR YOUR SHAPE

• Exercise all you can outdoors, but *never* do any exercise you don't enjoy—it defeats the purpose. Swimming is pleasurable for almost everybody and is the finest all-around exercise, invaluable for the back. But if you don't like swimming, don't do it. Find something else that pleases you—tennis, golf, riding, bowling, roller skating, skeet shooting. It doesn't have to be a team sport or a partnership sport. If a solitary pursuit pleases you, fine. But pursue it.

• Daydream. Visualize your body in the shape you want it to be. Keep the mental picture as you go through the day,and you are already closer to your goal, because you will live in the way it takes to be the picture you have of your inner self.

• Prop up your feet at the drop of a pillow. Keeping legs up means keeping circulatory problems down.

SPECIALS FOR YOUR MAKEUP

• Get lighthearted with blusher. Flick blusher or rouge across your earlobes, your elbows, in the cleavage, your heels when you wear sandals—just a touch, well blended, makes them rosy, young, and sexy.

• Lightening your hair means lightening your eye makeup. Medium-brown mascara, instead of dark brown, looks better with pale blond coloring to me. It seems to suit that fresh, open look of blondness.

• Eye makeup can be more dramatic under glass. Practice emphasizing it so your eyes hold their own behind sunglasses or clear glasses. Frosted highlights on the eyebone, shiny highlights on the lids are two ways to bring eyes out of hiding.

• If you wear false lashes at all, wear them when you shop for glasses. It's the only way to know in advance that lashes won't brush against lenses—which they mustn't.

SPECIALS FOR YOUR HAIR

• It's debatable whether hair grows faster in the summer. I think not. The rate of growth is one-half to three-quarters of an inch per month, every month, winter or summer.

• Protecting that new growth, plus the hair already on your head, is a bit different in the warm weather months, though. Most women do a job of stripping their hair in summer that is as harsh as old-fashioned peroxide ever was: the ingredients are sun, salt water, and perspiration—all left to mix too long. It is essential that you rinse all the salt water and chlorinated water from your hair immediately you leave the ocean or the pool. Keep a conditioning pack on your hair when in the sun during the day and keep it covered with a scarf. I cannot repeat this too often.

• In summer, you should condition your hair more often, shampoo it more often, rinse in cold water to retard the return of oil to the hair and scalp.

• If hair is holding too much moisture as is often the case in humid weather and is limp, heated curlers can be a better bet now than at any other time of the year. They have a drying action that may be the solution to giving your hair a little body. But their use must not become a daily habit. Several times a week is quite enough for anybody's hair, if it is to remain healthy.

SPECIALS FOR YOUR FRAGRANCE

• Making potpourris, scented sachets, or perfume oils using the fragrant flowers in the garden is a lovely summer project. These souvenirs of your garden would make wonderful presents for friends as well as delicious treats for your own house.

ROSE SACHETS TO MAKE IN ONE DAY

Combine 1 cup of dried rosebuds, 1 cup of dried lavender, ½ cup dried thyme, and a crushed 1-inch stick of cinnamon. Pour the mixture into little cloth bags to suspend on coat hangers in your closets.

FRESH FLORAL PERFUME OIL TO MAKE IN TWO WEEKS

You will need a 1-pint glass jar with a screw-top lid, a pint of cold-pressed almond oil, a small box of sterile absorbent cotton, and petals from the most fragrant flowers you can find. Heliotrope, violets, gardenias, verbena, stock, and very fragrant roses such as 'Mirandy,' 'Talisman', or 'Tiffany' are all good choices; you can use any one alone, or any combination that appeals to you.

Proceed this way: Put a layer of cotton in the jar, saturate it with almond oil, then cover with a 1-inch layer of petals; cover with another layer of oil-saturated cotton, more petals, and so on, until the jar is tightly packed. Seal and store the jar in a warm, dark place for a week. Remove the petals at the end of the week and replace them with fresh ones; store for another week. The oil will now be redolent of flowers and can be squeezed from the cotton and funneled into tiny bottles—you now have your own tailor-made perfume. You can use it on pulse points, or add it to your bath, or even put a drop on a light bulb (before turning on the lamp) to perfume a room.

A ROSE POTPOURRI TO MAKE OVER THE REST OF THE SUMMER
(from *Potpourris and Other Fragrant Delights* by Jacqueline Heriteau)

6 cups fragrant rose petals	6 leaves dried lemon verbena
½ cup coarse salt	¼ cup dried rosemary
½ cup table salt	½ cup dried lavender
1 teaspoon ground cinnamon	2 tablespoons orrisroot powder
½ teaspoon ground cloves	1 cup dried rosebuds

Dry the rose petals to a leathery texture. Combine coarse and fine salt. In a 2-quart wide-mouthed crock, layer the petals with the salt. The petal layers should be a half-inch deep. Set away in a dry, airy place for 10 days. Stir or shake daily. When the mixture is dry, crumble it and add the remaining ingredients. Seal and cure for 6 weeks. Transfer to a decorative container and keep covered except when in use.

SUMMER

Can you feel the glow? You certainly can see it. You are in radiant shape for the open joys of summer after the clearing away of winter, the slow exchange of great new ways for tired old ones. You have done so much, come so far, and there is a whole lifetime of this delight still before you.

We are heading into the season of vacations. Even if it means a vacation for the kids, but more demands on your time, you will sail along through this summer in a way you never would have thought possible. It will take more than a heat wave to wilt the gleaming vitality you bring to your days now during the happiest season.

JULY

We hope you are taking advantage of the summer to make every evening a mini-vacation for yourself: getting in a tennis match while the light lasts; or having a late swim after work; or attending a concert in the park—acquiring new hobbies and polishing up your form with the old ones.

You haven't forgotten, we hope, to keep one night for yourself alone. You need that time to devote to the luxury of Just Stopping as much in the laze of summer as in the frenzy of winter.

Slow down, cool off, with one evening out of seven that is yours to spend in puttering, or in total bed rest.

On one of those evenings, take a good long look at you in peak form now at the year's zenith.

Study the glow of your skin, the clarity of your eyes, the shine of your hair, the suppleness of your body.

Take stock of what you've been doing for yourself lately—five laps in the pool or was it ten? A one-mile walk on the beach? Eight or nine hours' sleep?

Whatever the recipe is, remember it.

Make a mid-year's resolution to keep the pleasure and the profits of it even when you shift gears for fall. Make sure the good is on-going; it's a kind of banking and insurance that pays dividends forever.

YOUR CHECKLIST AND SCHEDULE FOR JULY

First Morning of the Month
> Log your vital statistics into your diary (p. 14) *in ink.* Set your goals for the month as to loss of pounds or inches and gains in other areas, such as proficiency at yoga, say, or using the hand-held dryer. Pencil in your goals on the diary page for the last day of the month, and start the program that will help you achieve your goals.

Every Morning
> Seven-Way Stretch   (p. 91)
> Cup of hot water and lemon juice
> Warm-up exercises   (p. 146)
> Clean face and moisturize   (p. 54)
> Makeup   (p. 61)
> Fix hair
> Vitality Drink and nutritional supplements   (p. 94)

Every Evening
> Warm-up exercises to relax
> Feet-up rest with pillows or on slantboard for 10 minutes
> Clean face and moisturize
> Bath and all-over body lotion   (p. 128)
> Clean teeth before bed   (p. 259)

As Often as You Like: At Least Three Times Each Week
> Exercise session of 30 minutes   (p. 242)
> Yoga session of 30 minutes   (p. 96)
> Shampoo and finishing rinse   (pp. 45–46)

Once Each Week
> An evening (or a day) of rest, a time for yourself
> 10-minute protective protein conditioning pac for hair
> Manicure and pedicure   (p. 201)
> Tweeze stray hairs on eyebrows   (p. 167)
> Shave legs and underarms   (p. 166)
> Facial mask   (p. 162)

Once This Month

   One night and one day of rest for the digestive system on the
      detoxifying Liquid Fast or the Clearing House Diet   (pp.
      36–38)

   Haircut and any other professional hair services such as color
      or perm (your cutter might advise a cut more often, perhaps
      every three weeks. Follow his suggestion in making out your
      individual schedule).

VIDAL ON: WIGS—WHERE AND WHEN

As I see it, there are situations in which any woman wants a wig:

   —When she wants a dramatic, short-term change of color or
style

   —When she's traveling in a difficult climate or where they
don't speak her language in the salons

   —When she's having temporary problems with hair loss or
damage (and *while* she's seeing a hairologist for treatment of these
problems. A wig can hide damage, but can't correct it)

   When you want a wig for dramatic change, the wig you choose
can be as wildly artificial as your fantasy demands. But when the
wig is supposed to look natural, it had better look good. That does
not mean it has to be an expensive custom-made human hair wig.

   I have used human hair wigs for shows, and they are something
else. But to spend ten times the price of a great-looking acrylic wig
for one made of human hair, and to go to the trouble involved in
keeping it looking right, you've got to be incredibly rich, or just
plain stupid.

   The good synthetic wigs are made to be trouble-free and they
are trouble-free. You can brush them forward or backward, restyle
them if you like, wash them at home, and they will reassume their
original shape.

   I said "good synthetic wigs," and I mean just that.

   A few years ago, everybody and his grandmother got into the
wig business. They produced badly made, badly styled wigs with
the thought, "Every woman in the world will buy four or five at
these prices, just shove them in a drawer, and buy more." A lot of
women did buy a number of cheap wigs. But they didn't keep them

in the drawer—space is too precious for that. They threw them out because most of these wigs were so unbecoming that they looked ridiculous. And they didn't keep buying.

One million wigs were dumped into Hong Kong harbor when the bottom fell out of the market. That's the rumor, anyway. Big companies lost their shirts; little ones went out of business.

I'm not happy about anybody's misfortune, but that was a red-letter day for the world's women.

The very few companies that had been making a quality product right along survived. These companies make attractive wigs that should suit your needs—If you choose wisely.

HOW TO PICK A WIG

—Turn it inside out. Look for a wide-open space base. Loose lattices of flexible ribbon guarantee that the wig will be cool and comfortable. Veto any close mesh backings: unhealthy, uncomfortable, unnecessary.

—Follow the Rule of Color: hair color must suit eye color and skin color.

—Get the total picture. A cutter wouldn't give you a haircut without having studied you as you stand and as you sit. Give yourself the same study before giving yourself a new hairstyle via the wig. Size it up in a full-length mirror.

—Come as close as possible to the style you really want. Bangs can be shortened on a wig, curls subdued, but the basic style has been baked in to stay.

—Try it on for size. First style isn't necessarily final style. But first fit is final fit. A wig won't give with wear as shoes will. It should be snug enough to stay in place through a vigorous head-shake. Do it right at the wig counter. Better to risk stares there than when your wig falls off at dinner. If it's tight enough to stay in place, but not so tight as to creep up your scalp or give you a headache, then it fits.

HOW TO WEAR A WIG

If your hair is long, section it and pin it down in wide, flat pincurls or roll it into a flat chignon. Short hair can be tucked in and under. Start at the forehead and pull the wig down on your head like a swimming cap.

HOW TO KEEP A WIG

Brush it with a good Denman-type brush to keep it clean. Wash it once a month according to the washing instructions that come with the wig. Usually it's just a swish through cool water and Woolite or wig cleaner and a cool-water rinse. Hang it up to dry. When dry, shake it to fluff it up, hit it a few licks with the brush, and it's as good as new. Don't brush when wet—you will take out the curl.

Store the wig in the original box, on a wig stand, or in a drawer (but not a jammed-full drawer). The only things that trouble a trouble-free wig are being squashed flat or being cooked on a radiator.

WHEN NOT TO WEAR A WIG

Five or six hours after putting it on. Wearing a wig for longer stretches is bad for the hair and scalp because even lightweight wigs cause heavier than normal perspiration. Take the wig off after five or six hours to give your hair the air.

BEVERLY ON: SUNBATHING

There are two attitudes on this subject around our house. Vidal likes to be as tanned as a pirate in an Errol Flynn movie; I get bored just lying there baking and would rather be doing something else than tanning, especially since so many dermatologists have warned me off the sun.

There are good things to be said for sunbathing:

1. Short sunbaths are relaxing and stimulate the circulation.

2. Acne and oily skin problems benefit from the sun's drying of excess oils.

3. Suntans are fashionable everywhere in the world, and at every season. In fact, out-of-season tans are the most fashionable.

They show you have lots of time and money to lie around resorts (or that you follow the crops as a fruit picker).

There is one bad thing to be said about sunbathing:

Exposure to sun does permanent, irreversable damage to the skin—aging, blistering, drying, blotching it, causing broken capillaries and even skin cancers.

That one little sentence should be all that's needed for anyone who cares about long-term good looks.

In the listing of assets we didn't mention the benefits of vitamin D from sunbathing for this reason: Sun stimulates the formation of ergosterol, which is carried inward and becomes vitamin D *if,* and only if, the sunbath is not followed by washing of the skin. When was the last time you had a sunbath and went to bed that night without washing? That was the last time you got your vitamin D from sunbathing. Milk, egg yolks, cod liver oil, or vitamin D in capsules will take care of your needs without demanding that you skip bathing for it.

182   *A Year of Beauty and Health*

You don't have to hide from the sun and look pasty when the world is turning golden all around you. Get enough sun to look healthy and outdoorsy, but be very respectful of sun power and take it in little sips rather than one big gulp that will make you sick.

Here are some interesting facts about exactly what the sun does, and a few ways to make it work for you rather than against you.

SUN WORKS TO TAN (OR BURN) EVEN WHEN YOU ARE IN THE SHADE OR UNDER WATER

Ultraviolet rays penetrate the swimming pool or the ocean, and they come through beach umbrellas. Moisture in the air refracts the sun; sand and water reflect it. Staying out of direct sunlight will filter the force of the sun, however. I have seen women with beautiful tans, and beautiful skins, who spent all their sun time under beach umbrellas. It takes longer to get a sunshade tan, but it's worth it.

WHAT SUNBURN IS, TECHNICALLY

Exposure to sun causes the blood vessels to dilate. Overexposure causes excessive dilation of tiny blood vessels in the dermis. Six hours later, these dilated vessels allow blood serum to enter the skin tissues and swell the dermis and skin feels taut. That is sunburn. If it is a severe sunburn, blisters will form, and the top layer of skin will peel off.

PREVENTING SUNBURN IS A QUESTION OF TIME

Still the safest way, and the quickest in the long run, is to start with five-minute sessions in the sun: one somewhere between 9 and 11 A.M., one somewhere between 3 and 6 P.M. Lengthen each session gradually until you are getting fifteen minutes in the morning, fifteen minutes in the late afternoon. Time in the sun depends on your coloring and skin type. Blondes, redheads, all those with dry, thin skin, have to ease into sunning very slowly. Brunettes and the oily-skin types can graduate quickly to fifteen-minute sessions twice a day.

SEASON AND CHRONOLOGICAL AGE AFFECT
SUN TIME, TOO

If you head down to tropic sun after having spent months in a cold climate with your body protected from any exposure, it's just plain stupid immediately to fling your bikini'd body down on a beach for an hour of sun. Before you hit the beach at home in July, you've had months of gradual exposure to a gradually strengthening sun to accustom your skin to it. A holiday is no time to experiment with shock treatments.

Cells in the body, the body's metabolic balance, the tolerance for sun, are all apt to be very different at fifteen and forty-five. Don't overdo just because "I've never had a sunburn."

YOU WON'T TAN WITHOUT B VITAMINS

The tanning pigment is called melanin. To produce it, the body requires elements from the complex of B vitamins. The more it has to work with, the better job it can do. Unless you get more B vitamins at tanning time, the body may be short of supplies for the other uses it has for B vitamins— things like insuring boundless energy, for instance. Take more B vitamins in beach weather.

B VITAMINS AND BEACHES, FINE; SUN AND SCENT,
NOT SO FINE

Fragrances all have alcohol, which is drying to sun-dried skin. Some scents contain ingredients, such as oil of bergamot, that can cause photosensitivity—not camera shyness, but blotching of the skin caused by the reaction of certain chemicals to sun. It could make you camera shy.

SKIN IS SUPERSENSITIVE IN THE SUN TO OTHER
IRRITANTS, TOO. WHEN YOU'RE THIRSTY, MAKE IT WATER

Caffeine increases sensitivity of the skin. Go easy on coffee, iced tea, cola drinks. Cool water is 100 percent thirst-quenching, with no side effects. Watch out, too, for alcoholic drinks that rob you of B vitamins needed for tanning, add pounds, and constrict blood vessels to make you feel hotter.

PREVENT SUNBURN BY PROTECTING YOUR SKIN— ALL OF IT—CONSTANTLY

Which tanning cream you use depends on your own taste. The important thing is that you use it all over, and keep reapplying it. Vidal and the children swear by Bain de Soleil in an amber-colored clear gel for quicker tanning; I prefer the creamy-white lotion kind. But we all get a heavy coat of creaming, then more after swimming, and little touch-ups now and then.

Pay special attention to thin-skinned areas. Don't forget your feet and be especially liberal with cream on the neck and throat, on the ears, the backs of the hands. Keep slathering cream on your hands every few minutes. Freckled, wrinkly hands are an awful price to pay for a suntan. Cracked, chapped lips aren't a pretty sight, either. Keep reapplying sun block, lipstick, lip pomade. (When you're buying, look for the new ones with sun screens, sun blocks built in.) You must protect your eyelids with special care. Use a sun block that you know will not irritate your eyes—read the label and ask your doctor or dermatologist. If you aren't sure, keep your eye oil and perhaps some cream eyeshadow on behind your sunglasses at the beach.

Because I burn in a second, I use sun block on the tender spots. These start with old-fashioned zinc oxide which still works even if it looks funny. Now you can get sun blocks that are invisible. Did you know that even an ultra-thin layer of foundation will act as a sun block? Not that you want to be the painted lady on the beach or the tennis court, but the foundation will protect your skin while you're out around town. Remember, with sun every minute counts, and you can get lots of sun strolling along the parking lot at the shopping mall or walking on your lunch hour.

EVEN WITH PROTECTION, THERE CAN BE SUN SIGNS OTHER THAN A TAN. THREE ARE: TINY RED SPOTS . . . TINY BROWN SPOTS . . . BIG BROWN SPOTS

Little red spots frequently show up on fair skins. These tiny burst capillaries can be removed by a dermatologist with an electric needle. The little brown ones are freckles, and these can be very becoming. Many dermatologists think they are a result of unevenly distributed pigment in the epidermis. These little color islands darken in the sun and show up as freckles. Big brown patches on the skin are another matter—have the dermatologist check them. They may indicate places where skin cancer can develop. They can be removed with an electric needle treatment or be frozen off with dry-ice treatment.

BEVERLY ON: SUNBURN REMEDIES: THREE FROM THE KITCHEN CABINET

No matter how careful you are, there is always the chance that you will get stung by sunburn.

Here are a few old-fashioned kitchen cabinet cures that have worked for me.

Cucumber compresses will relieve the swelling of sun-puffed eyes. Slice a few thin ones from a fresh cucumber and place them over your eyelids while you lie there promising yourself never to overdo again.

Salad dressing body treatment is a two-stage pain reliever. First soak a cloth in natural cider vinegar. A big silk square is great because it isn't heavy or prickly and really clings to the skin. Lay the wet cloth against your skin. Lie down and try to relax for ten or fifteen minutes. Then remove the vinegar-soaked cloth (or cloths) and very gently rub your skin with polyunsaturated salad oil (avocado oil is especially good because it has vitamins A and E, and great penetrating power). Stay oiled and vinegared for as long as you can, even though you smell like a bowl of lettuce, and have a tepid bath later. Use lots of body lotion after the bath, and air-dry your skin.

Tea facial is a de-stinger because of the tannic acid in tea. Use two tea bags to brew a really strong infusion. Toss the bags into a pan of boiling water and let it simmer for five minutes. Turn off the heat, and when the tea is cool, pat the sopping wet bags on your face. Don't rinse it off immediately, but fan yourself dry. Then rinse with cool water.

DON'T read a book, work a crossword puzzle, or do needle-point in the sun unless your sunglasses are really dark. Tinted cosmetic fun glasses will cut a little glare, but not enough to ward off damage to your eyes or all the tiny squint lines that develop around them. Get an optometrist or your eye doctor to O.K. your shades.

Don't play nature girl by drying your hair in the sun after a swim. Salt and chlorine are hair poison. Shower in fresh water after a swim, if you can. If you can't, towel-dry your hair and shower as soon as you get home from the beach.

Don't forget to count time in the water as time in the sun. Ultra-violet burning rays can come right through the water to attack.

Don't worry about getting a sunburn through the windshield. Warm, infrared rays can come through glass; ultraviolet rays can't.

Don't neglect taking vitamins when you're taking the sun. Tanning robs you of vitamin B. It works like this: to produce the tanning pigment melanin, the body needs tyrasine, an amino acid that is part of the B complex. So it takes it from your store of B's. It's up to you to replenish the stock by taking more of the B complex via food or supplements.

Don't count too heavily on the old rule of clock that says the sun is safe after three. Actually, late-afternoon sun can do a dandy job of compounding the damage done earlier in the day.

Don't let up on your burn-prevention program once you have a base coat of tan.

SUNGLASSES

Spend a day in bright sunshine without your sunglasses and you'll be blind as a bat that night. Well, half as blind, anyway.

Unprotected eyes will lose 50 percent of their night vision after a day's exposure. If you forget your sunglasses and go off for two weeks in the sun, it will take your eyes a week to recover when you come home.

Even if you don't plan to go on midnight scouting parties, your eyes have still taken a lot of punishment; and since the sun can be responsible for cataracts, it's nothing to play with.

Speaking of play, those pink or baby-blue lenses are flattering, and it's fun to see the world all rosy or delicate blue. But don't think that these lenses will do the job of sunglasses when you're driving or on the beach. The fun stops when your eyes start to sting.

Sunglasses have to be really dark. For the beach, or in any bright glare, you need glasses that filter out all but 15 to 25 percent of the light. Outdoors at home, or out driving or shopping, your lenses should allow only 30 percent of the light to reach your eyes. A good lens will block out ultraviolet rays along with the light.

Your sunglasses have to be dark, and they have to be good. Even at only seventy-nine cents, the dime-store product is a bad investment. Your eyes account for one fourth of all the energy you expend in a day. Distorted lenses (plus glare) cause that percentage to shoot way up. At the end of the day, your body will be fatigued and show it—not just in itchy, red, tired eyes, but all over.

The sunglasses to look for have ground-glass lenses. Plastic and blown-glass lenses aren't guaranteed to have bubbles, warping, irregularities or other defects, but they aren't guaranteed not to, either. Why chance it?

Check the lenses before you buy. Turn them so that an over-head light reflects on the inside, then move the glass slowly from left to right so the reflection travels across the lens. If you see any wave or wiggle, the glasses go back on the rack.

Check the frame. Plastic side pieces should be reinforced with metal for strength and to allow you to adjust them for proper fit; temples should be no more than a half-inch wide (wider ones are dangerous for driving because they block side vision); the frame and side pieces should be joined with a screw, not just a pin.

You can't check the percentage of the light that passes through the lenses if you're buying glasses in a drug or department store, but you can do this: Put the glasses on and look at yourself in a mirror. If you can see your eyes clearly, the lenses aren't dark enough, unless they are the new sun-sensitive lenses.

If you get your sunglasses at an optometrist's—and I can't

advise you too strongly to do just that—he can do all the checking work for you and leave you with the fun part: deciding on the best-looking glasses for seeing and being seen in.

SPECIALS FOR YOUR HAIR

• Naturally curly hair can become a bit uncontrollable in summer. Here is a simple trick to tame it at any time of year. While hair is wet, roll a bit of your hair around a pencil. Slip out the pencil and repeat the maneuver wherever you want to subdue curls. When the hair is dry, it will be much more manageable.

• Shampoo and condition your hair often this month. Whenever possible, use a no-rinse conditioning cream on your hair before you go out in the sun. Cover your head with a bright-colored scarf. The rest and relaxation that accompany sunbathing can be a super treatment for your hair if it is being conditioned under cover in this way.

• If you are going off on holiday, you should have a haircut before you leave. You may then wish to postpone the next haircut until you get back, or even until the first of September. If your hair will need attention while you are away, ask your cutter now if he can recommend a good salon in the town or resort you will be visiting. Don't risk your looks on the chance of finding someone good. There has been a tremendous advance in the look of hair all over America in the past five years, and there are cutters in every town now who know how to cut hair as it should be cut—to enhance beauty. But try to find out in advance just who the good cutters in another town are. You will feel more confident—and that is important.

SPECIALS FOR YOUR FOOD PLANNING

• Thirsty? This is the time for it. Thirst begins the second your body loses just 2 percent of the water that makes up about half of total body weight. Because you perspire more now, your body is constantly losing water. Once again—pure water is the best thing for you—quenches thirst 100 percent. Iced tea rates a 99+ percentage on a scale devised by Portia Morris, Ph.D., professor of food science at Michigan State University. Beer is way down the scale at 92 percent, and wine gets a 76.7. Easy does it with alcohol at any time of the year but especially on hot summer days when you want to cool off. A tall drink with vodka in it may taste cool, but it constricts the blood vessels and interferes with the body's power to release heat trapped inside. We Americans are addicted to ice cubes in our drinks—but go easy on ice if you can. Cool is more cooling than ice cold; easier on the stomach as well. Hot drinks can cool you by contrast. Hot mint tea is what the Moroccans drink to stay cool. And *that* is a hot country.

• More protein is in order. Perspiration causes a loss of nitrogen, and extra protein is needed to balance the metabolism. Cut down on carbohydrates but step up the protein with cold hard-cooked eggs, cold sliced meats and cheeses, fish.

• Our favorite high-protein, low-fuss lunch (or dinner) buffet-table special consists of one or more of the dishes that follow. Everything can be done with little or no cooking. You can set up your buffet wherever it's coolest to eat, and family or guests can pick at it whenever they like—no hassle of "Dinner is served!" It's good, too, because dieters can take only those foods that fit into their plans—low-carbohydrate, high-protein, vegetarian, whatever—without a problem; gorgers can have all they want to eat.

Make a Mediterranean salad the beautiful main attraction of such meals. In those sunny countries that are bordered by that blue sea, they know that salads are more than lettuce. They have created wonder bowls that combine proteins, minerals, vitamins, and delight with lots of variety of color and texture. Try one of these.

From France: SALADE NIÇOISE

First layer the salad bowl with some deep greenery, such as torn leaves of Boston lettuce. On it, arrange drained canned tuna, ripe black olives, strips of anchovies, quartered hard-cooked eggs, perhaps some cold, cooked green beans, capers, chopped parsley, quartered tomatoes or small cherry tomatoes sliced in halves. Toss with a vinaigrette dressing (one part lemon juice or vinegar to three parts olive oil, a pressed clove of garlic, sea salt and pepper to taste).

From Italy: INSALATA POMIDORO

On each plate, make a bed of greens such as watercress and torn Bibb lettuce or other salad greens. Lay on this a layer of thinly sliced, ripe tomato. Crush some dried basil in your palm (or use fresh if you have it) and sprinkle the tomatoes with the herb, then with some freshly cracked black pepper and sea salt or salt substitute. Cover this with another layer of tomatoes, repeat the seasoning, and top each plate with a thin slice of mozzarella cheese. Pour a dressing of lemon juice and olive oil over the salad plate and serve.

• Or you could make a Moroccan Salad by tossing fine slivers of cold roast lamb and chopped fresh mint leaves into the salad bowl; a Greek Salad with crumbled feta cheese along with black Greek olives and ripe red tomato quarters. The only limit to creating a salad is your supply of fresh, beautiful vegetables from the garden or the market and the protein supply on hand. With any of these easy-to-do platters you can set out a basket of unbuttered bread sticks, a big bowl of ripe summer fruits, and lunch or dinner is done.

• Here is a yummy low-calorie special dedicated to a friend in London, a lovely lady who happens to be a fennel freak. We all have our weaknesses, and you too may succumb to fennel, when it's done this way:

FENNEL SALAD

2 medium-size bunches of fennel
2 hard-cooked egg whites, chopped
2 tablespoons parsley, chopped
2 tablespoons polyunsaturated salad oil
4 tablespoons wine vinegar

    Chill fennel in ice water for 1 hour. Remove, dry, slice thin, and cover with the other ingredients. Toss and serve.

• This is a kiddie all-star that we like, too, for a dessert or an afternoon protein pick-me-up:

BANANA SMOOTHIE

Combine in the blender 2 cups cold skim milk, ½ cup instant nonfat powdered milk, 1½ (or 2 small) bananas, ¼ teaspoon nutmeg. Blend. Serve in tall glasses.

SPECIALS FOR YOUR SHAPE

• Use the swimming pool for exercise. The water supports your body, and even slight movements become more beneficial when performed under-

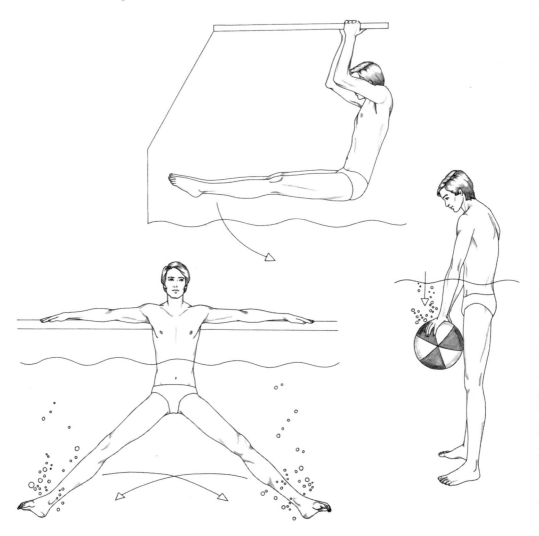

water because you have to combat the resistance of the water. Here are several suggestions for waterworks.

—Let your body go limp as you hang by your hands from the diving board. Bring your legs up to the level of your hips and keep them together as you force them down under the water to make your body a straight line. Return to the starting position. Relax. Repeat twelve times. Great for the whole body, especially legs and waistline.

—Hold a beach ball with both hands. Force it down under the water to your knees. Let it reach the surface slowly as you try to hold it down. Do this for as long as you can. Good for the arms and shoulders, it also helps the pectoral muscles, which support the breasts.

—Rest on the side of the pool, arms and shoulders holding you up, with your body in the water. Rest your back against the side of the pool and do sidewise scissors-crosses with your legs. Rest after a few of these. Keep one leg straight down, and with the other make wide circles from left to right, turning from the hips as you go. Do as many as you like. Reverse.

SPECIALS FOR YOUR MAKEUP AND FRAGRANCE

• Reserve space in the refrigerator for summer skin coolers. Keep skin freshener, eye drops, cologne, and witch hazel chilly. It makes using them four times as refreshing on hot days.

• Save perfume for time out of the sun. Sun can cause skin irritation.

• If you part your hair and tie it back loosely in summer, don't forget to use sun block on the exposed scalp of the parting. In the evening, put a little dot of rouge or blusher at the hairline and blend back toward the crown in the parting. It gives a very feminine and pretty blush.

• If you prefer not to use eye shadow in the summer, that's fine. But do give this a try: with a brush, draw a thin line of brown cake shadow just in the crease of the eyelid, and blend. Don't blend down onto the lid, just follow the crease. Do this on one eye first and note the flattering difference; then complete the job.

SPECIALS FOR YOUR SKIN AND BODY

• Stretch marks are the result of breaks in the collagen fiber below the surface of the skin. They come about through rapid weight gain or loss. Pregnancy is one, but by no means the only, time when stretch marks are made. It was during my last pregnancy, though, that I learned about a cream that can help ward them off. It's called Pre-Natol, and it restores elasticity to the skin and prevents collagen breakdown. It's a light, all-over body cream with a pleasant fragrance. You may not be expecting a baby, but if you are expecting a weight-loss, you might want to check into this cream. Try the drugstore, or ask your doctor.

AUGUST

Anticipation of a new school year gives August an edge of excitement for youngsters. How about sharing the excitement by learning something new, but with none of that old-time drudgery of study for the sake of winning grades? Now school can offer the thrill of discovery, of strengthening yourself and widening your world, with no pressure to make the honor roll or the dean's list.

Round up the adult education catalogues from your local college or the Y and see if there isn't something you would enjoy knowing more about. It might be Japanese art or jazz—something wonderfully remote from your daily concerns, such as seventeenth-century poetry, or as useful as a course in managing your money. We are busy learning something new ourselves all the time. It is a fantastic feeling to have a new body of knowledge offered you. And it means you have so much more to offer the world.

Our good friend Geoffrey Holder is a perennial source of amazement. He writes books, directs Broadway musicals, wins Tony awards, paints, dances, acts, and is a great cook! We are not the only ones to be fascinated by him. When Geoffrey and his beautiful and talented wife, Carmen de Lavallade, mention that they are having a few people in, they are beseiged by would-be guests, and no one whom they do invite ever pleads a previous engagement.

Versatility and accomplishment are magnetic. The more things you are interested in and work at, the richer your life becomes. The richer your life is, the more people flock around to be part of that life and the more in demand you are.

So many of us narrow our visions and put all our marbles in one ring. The one-dimensional life that results is unexciting to the one who lives it, and to everybody else. Dare more, learn more, and have more.

You needn't aim for the Nobel prize, but how do you know you couldn't win it unless you strike out in a broader scope? At the very least you will be a more fascinating person. And that is no mean thing to be.

YOUR CHECKLIST AND SCHEDULE FOR AUGUST

First Morning of the Month

Log your vital statistics into your diary (p. 14) *in ink.* Set your goals for the month as to loss of pounds or inches and gains in other areas, such as proficiency at yoga, say, or using the hand-held dryer. Pencil in your goals on the diary page for the last day of the month, and start the program that will help you achieve your goals.

Every Morning

Seven-Way Stretch   (p. 91)

Cup of hot water and lemon juice

Warm-up exercises   (p. 146)

Clean face and moisturize   (p. 54)

Makeup   (p. 61)

Fix hair

Vitality Drink and nutritional supplements   (p. 94)

Every Evening

Warm-up exercises to relax

Feet-up rest with pillows or on slantboard for 10 minutes

Clean face and moisturize

Bath and all-over body lotion   (p. 128)

Clean teeth before bed   (p. 259)

As Often as You Like: At Least Three Times Each Week
 Exercise session of 30 minutes   (p. 242)
 Yoga session of 30 minutes   (p. 96)
 Shampoo and finishing rinse   (pp. 45–46)
Once Each Week
 An evening (or a day) of rest, a time for yourself
 10-minute protective protein conditioning pac for hair
 Manicure and pedicure   (p. 201)
 Tweeze stray hairs on eyebrows   (p. 167)
 Shave legs and underarms   (p. 166)
 Facial mask   (p. 162)
Once This Month
 One night and one day of rest for the digestive system on the detoxifying Liquid Fast or the Clearing House Diet   (pp. 36–38)
 Haircut and any other professional hair services such as color or perm (your cutter might advise a cut more often, perhaps every three weeks. Follow his suggestion in making out your individual schedule).

VIDAL ON: WHAT NOT TO LOOK FOR IN THE FASHION MAGAZINES

Any time now, the fat, glossy fall numbers of the magazines will be on the stands. This is a good moment to talk about what you should expect from them, and from yourself.

You know they will contain sumptuous presentations of smashing models wearing super new clothes, furs, and jewels, extraordinary hair styles and makeup.

Page after page of women who look the way you should. Right? Wrong.

The models in the magazines don't even look the way *they* should look—or do look—away from work.

For they are hard at work, projecting for you a kind of heightened reality, or a fantasy, if you will, in which the real-life element: say, a dress of 100 percent rayon—is given an otherworldly glamour. The simple dress would look fine, perhaps, if you tried it on. But it won't have much appeal in cold, hard print unless something is done with the photography to enhance it.

That's where the talented fashion editors, beauty editors, photographers, and models come in. Adding real emerald clips, a sable jacket, a dramatic setting, and an attitudinizing star to wear it gives the dumb little dress distinction by association and makes it seem very desirable.

Fine. And fair. You can read the caption and see that it is really only rayon. But you don't read what happens off camera to make an attractive girl (with good bones, but far from perfect hair and features) become a confident, glamorous woman in the photo. The sad thing is that many women have their own hang-ups reinforced as they think, *She* has a perfect nose . . . beautiful skin . . . great hair; if I only had that . . .

"She" doesn't. One of the most beautiful models in the world now, Lauren Hutton, calls her nose "a banana" and wouldn't think of straightening it, any more than she would have dental surgery to correct a wide gap between her two front teeth. Because she is confident about the things that make her beauty unique, she projects her good features and her so-called flaws in the unself-conscious way without which there is no real beauty. But she makes her living in a world where the plastic beauty standards count. We all are involved to some degree in the world of artificial standards of what is, and is not, beautiful. We cannot escape it. So Lauren Hutton has learned to use makeup with great skill to make the shape of her face symmetrical for the camera. She has a small plastic filler, made by an orthodontist, to slip over the space in her teeth when photo sessions demand it.

Like every person whom we see as beautiful, Lauren has taken herself in hand and judged by her own standards which things about her looks and her life are good and beautiful, which things are correctable faults, and which things are essential parts of her and go along with her other characteristics to make her individual. Once any human being has set about the correction of those things that need correction, and made the most of the others, then they can forget about an "image" and begin creating a personal style.

This personal style is not arrived at overnight. It takes years of interest and involvement in the world. It takes years of getting to feel at home in your skin. When your mind and your skin truly fit, you will never again make a real mistake in your looks or the way you project yourself. You have a style of your own—you leave a sharp-focus memory image with people. And they will remember and notice those things about you that you wish them to see.

Quick. What does Mrs. Jacqueline Kennedy Onassis look like? Describe her looks.

I am willing to bet that you left her legs out of the description. This powerfully beautiful woman has a great sense of style, her own personal style. She has tremendous grace of movement, a dazzling smile, great healthy hair, a fascinating voice, beautiful eyes, a lithe, lean figure. Unobtrusively, automatically, she can distract attention away from a less attractive feature to more attractive ones. That is personal style—not all of it, but an important element.

Neither she nor any of the great beauties of this or past ages arrived at this self-awareness overnight. Look some time at a photo of Mrs. Onassis taken when she was the wife of the junior Senator from Massachusetts. She was a bit plumper, a bit fussier, with the hair, which is now a great, free mane, curled tightly about her face, making that wonderful head seem a trifle out of proportion with her shoulders. It took time, and a certain amount of genius, to set off the bone structure of her face with a full, loose flow of shining hair.

Not until after her thirtieth birthday was she to come into her own. Now, past her fortieth, Jacqueline Onassis is one of the sexiest, most beautiful women in the world.

The fashion model, on the other hand, is usually "over the hill" at thirty, for a very good reason: she has become too much her own woman. Her style and her beauty are too definite, too personal. Stylists and photographers want a pretty blank on which they can superimpose many looks, many styles, many women. A successful model is a chameleon, changing roles at the click of a shutter. "Is that the same girl?" is a question that means money in the bank to a model. If she can look like ten different women for ten different jobs, the public will not tire of her face, and she will not be restricted to any one small area of modeling.

It's not completely true for the big stars, like Lauren Hutton or Margaux Hemingway, but most models have to play the role of the pretty girl whom nobody remembers. Think what that can do to the ego.

There is also a physically damaging side to modeling. Having her hair yanked, pulled, set, dried, reset, and overdried so it can look different for each dress or job of the day is a beauty killer the model must endure. Not only must she submit to having her hair damaged, but she cannot even wear it in the way that would be most flattering to her individual bone structure or to its texture and growth pattern.

The fashion model must have an unfashionable cut and stick with it if she wishes to make money. If that sounds mad, let me explain. At a time when short hair is the new fashion, the model must have bouncy, shoulder-length hair. When the newest look is long hair, the model must have hers at shoulder length. The magazines and the advertisers fear that an advanced style (that is to say one not worn by the overwhelming majority of the women in the country) will alienate some proportion of the people who see the ad. The model who wears her hair in a fashionable way will lose work because she looks "far out," or "too high-fashion." So by cutting her hair, she cuts her income.

Still, it can be a financially profitable career, and the model learns through exposure to develop the sense of style we are talking about. By the time she has developed this sense, and has achieved real beauty and real style, she is usually far away from the camera, busy pursuing a life that is personally rewarding.

If thirty is the age when real style and beauty begin, the true shine comes at forty. Lady Hamilton and the Empress Josephine hit their stride after forty, and Sarah Bernhardt didn't hit the top until her fifties. The light of beauty needn't go out: the famous French courtesan, Ninon de l'Enclos, was taking new young lovers at eighty-five!

To me the real spellbinder is a woman of that uncertain age that is called "a certain age" who cares for her body, her skin, and her hair, and who cares visibly about the people and the world around her. She is filled with enthusiasms and is always in demand.

One of the most sought-after guests at parties given by the young movers and shakers in New York is Mrs. T. Reed Vreeland, although she has grandchildren who are young adults. One reason that people are drawn to Diana Vreeland is her dynamite and red pepper enthusiasm for life, for the new in every field of creativity. It makes her irresistable, and I would wish her youthful glow for us all.

BEVERLY ON: TIME ON YOUR HANDS (AND FEET)

Beauty care consumes the most precious thing we have—time. I've discovered it's not how much you spend, but how. Some drawn-out beauty routines are just time-wasters; some time-savers are beauty-killers.

Never try to beat the clock with your hands. A really good manicure takes an hour or so every two weeks, but it's a good investment. And time spent on keeping your feet in good condition is crucial to feeling good.

In New York, I used to spend fifteen dollars a week on a professional manicure. Now I do my nails myself with the manicurist's blessing.

The pros want you to be self-sufficient so that you don't become an enemy if you break a nail just before a big evening and can't be fitted into the day's appointments at the salon. So they are happy to have you carry on their good work for yourself, and save the visits for occasional treats to yourself.

We can all stand to save a little money these days, so here's how to give yourself the fifteen-dollar manicure at home.

First, set out the things you will need. Have:

A bowl filled with warm, soapy water. I add a little scented bath oil or oil of almonds to the water because it's good for the skin and the cuticles, as well as giving a nice fragrance.

Emery boards. If you have a steel file, use it for digging around in your house plants to aerate the soil, but not for your nails. Steel is just too tough, and leaves rough, ragged tips. Use the fine side of an emery board to file your nails.

Orange stick with the tip wrapped in sterile cotton, or Q-Tips

Sterile absorbent cotton in balls

Nail buffer

Polish remover—the best you can get. Some of the newest contain more ingredients that are gentle to nails, fewer that are harmful.

Nail brush

White towel. Why white? because it looks professional, and because every nail-polish color sings out against white.

Cuticle cream or petroleum jelly. Cuticle creams may or may not be more beneficial than plain petroleum jelly, but why not have the pleasure of a cream that can be a pretty pink, with the scent of ripe apricots?

Nail polish

Polish sealer

Clear base coat polish

Nail Menders Glue

Facial tissue

THE MANICURE

—Lay everything you need out on the towel.

—File your nails first, while they are dry and protected by the old polish. This helps keep ragged edges at a minimum. Hold the finer side of the emery board at a 45-degree angle to the nail. File toward the center, and in one direction only. Sawing back and forth leads to rough nail edges. Don't file into the corners, your nails will split and break easily if you do. I don't believe in filing the nails into squares or other exaggerated shapes. The object is graceful fingertips, and an oval is still best.

—Remove every trace of old polish now. Soak a cotton ball in polish remover and press it down firmly on the nail. Give the remover a second to work, then slide the pad off the nail, slipping the old polish off along with it. If there is still a bit of lacquer left on the nail, do a second press-and-slip with the remover. The idea is to get it off—all off. Remover, too. Acetone, which is a natural substance and a great polish remover, does have a way of lingering in the corners of the nails. In time, acetone does battle with the nails. So wipe off every trace of remover you can see, then wash off the polish remover you can't see. Use a soft nail brush and warm, soapy water. Rinse in cool water and dry.

—Massage the nails with cuticle cream or petroleum jelly. Rub it into the sides of the nails, then soak for a few minutes in warm, soapy water.

—Gently push back the cuticles with the Q-Tip or cotton-wrapped orange stick. When I say gently, I really mean it. Poking at the cuticle leads to hard, noticeable cuticles that can split into hang-nails, and even invite infection at the nail base. If you have one of those cuticle-clipping gadgets, by the way, use it to snip loose threads off your clothes, or invent some other use for it, but get it out of your manicure kit. If you ever have a torn cuticle, cut off only the loose flap of skin, never into the cuticle itself, which guards against infection to the nail bed. If you take care of the cuticle with creams you never will have a torn cuticle.

—If you have a minor split, or a cracked nail, now is the time to repair it, and here's the method: Tear off a tiny shred of facial tissue the size of the disaster area. Lay it on the towel, and saturate with Nail Menders Glue. Plop it over the break in the nail and, using the thumbnail of your other hand, press the tissue down. Slide it toward the center of your nail and flatten it over the split; see that there are no air bubbles or loose fiber. When the glue dries (about five minutes), apply a clear base coat, and go on to paint your nails as usual. For a real break, twist off a tiny bit of cotton wool and proceed as you would with the tissue, but use the emery board to even out the surface of the nail after the glue-and-cotton-wool patch is dry.

—Apply a very thin coat of clear base.

—Now apply a thin first coat of color. Don't stop at the tip of the nail, but pull the brush over and paint the backs of the nails. It somehow looks less startling and more natural. It also helps protect the tips. Try it and you'll see. Five minutes later, apply another coat of color and give it five minutes to dry.

—Now a top coat of clear sealer. I promise you will never again have a coat of chipped polish on your nails if you apply another top coat and coat of sealer every other night. At the end of two weeks, it all comes off and you start at Go.

THE PEDICURE

The only equipment you need that is different for foot care is a bigger basin to soak your feet in—and you might want to use a toenail clipper. It's nice to have a big bottle of body lotion, or spray cologne and dusting powder handy.

—Soak your feet in warm soapy water for ten minutes. Wriggle your toes around and really relax; or do this foot-strengthening and relaxing exercise: Stretch out your feet. Heels resting on the bottom of the basin, roll the toes up and back toward the body, then curl them down toward the ball of the foot. Without lifting heels, or moving feet, pull as if to draw them up toward your body. Then, dry your feet.

—Rub moisturizer or body lotion into the feet and rub the heels and sides with pumice stone to remove dry, dead skin. *Never* use a razor to pare off calloused, horny patches.

—File or clip toenails straight across rather than in an oval shape.

—Rub cuticle cream into the toenails, and use a Q-Tip or cotton-wrapped orange stick to gently push the cuticle back.

—Slather lots of body lotion on them, and, before you move, pull on little white socks or slippers. Otherwise, you have fuzzy feet from walking across the carpet.

—In the morning, give your feet some more moisturizer, a dusting of powder, and a spray of cologne. Walk out light-footed and light-headed.

SPECIALS FOR YOUR SHAPE

• The average American gains one pound per year every year after the twenty-fifth birthday. Why should you be average? But be realistic. Your ideal weight, physically and psychologically, is the one at which you feel well. Lose pounds until you reach it. Below it, though, you will be irritable and easily tired and you will look tired and drawn. When that happens, gain weight! Get to your ideal, and work to maintain it. It can be done. Vidal doesn't weigh one ounce more now than he did at twenty—which was twenty-seven years ago.

• Get plenty of rest whether you are trying to lose, gain, or maintain. Calorie-burning goes on, by the way, even while you sleep. The body burns ½ calorie per pound of body weight per hour in sleep.

• Relax tensions, slim thighs, and work all the muscles of the body by skipping rope. It's better with your shoes off for fullest benefits. Even when not skipping, walk barefoot whenever you can to strengthen feet and relax them.

• Make love. It's the best exercise for the middle back, among other benefits.

SPECIALS FOR YOUR FOOD PLANNING

• Fresh summer vegetables are plentiful and good buys. Good for the colon and cholesterol level, too. Plant fiber, or "roughage," moves through the small and lower intestines taking bile and cholesterol with it, preventing the body from reabsorbing the potentially dangerous wastes.

• Carrots are made better sources of vitamin A by cooking. Most other vegetables and fruits are delicious raw. Before you cook it, taste it. Will it really be better in taste and texture after it's cooked? If not . . .

• Make salads. A pretty one that's green and white and tan is this:

Dice a celery stalk, an unpeeled green apple, an avocado. Tear some watercress into small pieces and add along with ¼ cup chopped cashews, almonds, or walnuts. Toss with vinaigrette dressing and sprinkle with wheat germ.

• If you have fresh mint handy, chop up a few leaves and add them to a cucumber salad.

• You already know that yoghurt is a wonder food. But did you know that it probably reduces cholesterol? Jane E. Brody wrote, in *The New York Times*, of a study indicating that eating yoghurt may discourage the body from producing cholesterol of its own (it does, you know) and thus help lower the cholesterol level in the blood. Here's a yoghurt salad dressing:

1 egg yolk (hard-cooked, mashed)
1 egg yolk (raw)
1 teaspoon dry mustard
2 cups yoghurt
2 teaspoons lemon juice
pinch of salt substitute

SPECIALS FOR YOUR SKIN AND BODY

• "Cold sore" is a misnomer. Miserable as cold weather and head colds are, they are not responsible for this particular plague. Strong sunlight is an aggravating factor, along with tension and fatigue. Protect your lips this month with sun block cream on lips. There are clear, amber creams that look like lip gloss. Lipstick with sun blocks is around, too—check it out.

• The heat wave hasn't broken, but you're about to? Resist the impulse to drown in a cold shower. The cooling effect of a lukewarm or tepid bath lasts. It dilates blood vessels all over so the body can release trapped heat. Soak for half an hour if you can. Walk slowly into the bedroom while you're still wet. Lie down and spray yourself all over with cologne. Think cool thoughts while you air-dry. Use lots of dusting powder later.

• Mosquitoes are a good argument for preserving a tranquil disposition. They are far more interested in highly emotional types. They also seem drawn to people who consume a good deal of sugar. Honestly.

• If you suffer, even mildly, from hay fever, it's a good idea to stay away from chlorinated pools, alcohol, and chocolate. All have ingredients that sensitize your system.

SPECIALS FOR YOUR MAKEUP AND FRAGRANCE

• Pack eyedrops in your beach bag and use them. Wind and sun irritate the eyes, and perspiration and sun lotions are killers!

• Step up the manicure and pedicure schedule. Building sand castles tears down nails. Keep cuticle cream handy, and use it.

• Get a golden glow on in the evening. Even the best tan can look drab at night. Use the lightest suggestion of gold gleamer on your shoulders, your collarbone, along the nape of the neck.

• Gather rosebuds. Summer flowers dried in the sun can go into big bowls of potpourri for the house for a really beautiful fragrance this fall. You'll find a potpourri recipe on page 173.

SPECIALS FOR YOUR HAIR

• Make the appointment for your September haircut well in advance. Salons are incredibly busy after Labor Day, and so are you. If you put it off, your cutter might not be free at the time that suits you.

• So that no heavy repair work for hair is needed in the fall, keep up the conditioning regime this month.

• Flat beer makes an excellent setting lotion. The reason for using it flat is that once it's flat the chemicals in it will have dissipated. Put it into a mist-spray bottle and spray lightly on damp hair. The smell of the beer will leave but the body will stay.

• Just a reminder about using conditioners—the dry ends of hair need conditioning, not the scalp.

• Shampoo as often as you like through the hot weather, when oil glands (and you) are most active. Among other things, giving yourself a shampoo is a marvelous way of relaxing tension. But always remember the ABCs of a good shampoo. And never omit the finishing rinse, or conditioner.

SEPTEMBER

Like so many other things that will make your life smoother this year, the habit of making lists is probably getting to be second nature for you now.

So as summer ends and the first bright days of fall arrive it's a good idea to review where you've been, where you're going, and do a little mental reorganizing.

Kids start a new school year with a fresh stock of sharp new pencils, fat blocks of pristine paper, and new-smelling satchels. There is a wonderful, anticipatory sort of aroma to a stationer's store at back-to-school time.

Why don't you spark up your attitude toward list-making this month with a pile of memo pads? Little canary-yellow pads and new parrot-green felt-tip pens, or pink paper and scarlet ink, might free your thoughts and inspire you to write love notes to your mate as well as shopping lists.

Why don't you take a few minutes to cover a big bulletin board in sky-blue felt and post it in the kitchen or wherever your lists will be up-front evidence of what you have planned, not untidy scraps at the bottom of your bag or a desk drawer?

Why don't you, while you're thinking of it, list in *one* place and in the diary that's always with you the telephone numbers of everyone who is apt to be important on the spur of the moment—the florist when you have to order at the last minute, the taxi company when your car breaks down, the parents of your children's friends when you're going to be late picking them up? Why not let your fingers do the walking when you have to rush? The numbers of the dealer and the service company of all the appliances you own (along with appliance model and serial numbers) go on the emergency list, too. Especially if you work. You can always call from the office, but you can't go back home to check the model number of an out-of-whack dishwasher and what the warranty date is.

YOUR CHECKLIST AND SCHEDULE FOR SEPTEMBER

First Morning of the Month
> Log your vital statistics into your diary (p. 14) *in ink.* Set your goals for the month as to loss of pounds or inches and gains in other areas, such as proficiency at yoga, say, or using the hand-held dryer. Pencil in your goals on the diary page for the last day of the month, and start the program that will help you achieve your goals.

Every Morning
> Seven-Way Stretch   (p. 91)
> Cup of hot water and lemon juice
> Warm-up exercises   (p. 146)
> Clean face and moisturize   (p. 54)
> Makeup   (p. 61)
> Fix hair
> Vitality Drink and nutritional supplements   (p. 94)

Every Evening
> Warm-up exercises to relax
> Feet-up rest with pillows or on slantboard for 10 minutes
> Clean face and moisturize
> Bath and all-over body lotion   (p. 128)
> Clean teeth before bed   (p. 259)

As Often as You Like: At Least Three Times Each Week
  Exercise session of 30 minutes   (p. 242)
  Yoga session of 30 minutes   (p. 96)
  Shampoo and finishing rinse   (pp. 45–46)
Once Each Week
  An evening (or a day) of rest, a time for yourself
  10-minute protective protein conditioning pac for hair
  Manicure and pedicure   (p. 201)
  Tweeze stray hairs on eyebrows   (p. 167)
  Shave legs and underarms   (p. 166)
  Facial mask   (p. 162)
Once This Month
  One night and one day of rest for the digestive system on the
    detoxifying Liquid Fast or the Clearing House Diet   (pp.
    36–38)
  Haircut and any other professional hair services such as color
    or perm (your cutter might advise a cut more often, perhaps
    every three weeks. Follow his suggestion in making out your
    individual schedule).

VIDAL ON: CHOOSING A CUTTER/STYLIST

Devote as much thought to this as you would to selecting a doctor.
Your cutter will be a doctor for your morale.

Do a little groundwork and research. Look at people at parties,
on the street, in the supermarket. When you see someone who has
a super cut, don't be shy about asking who does it. Everyone loves
the combination of a compliment plus the chance to be helpful
without going to any bother.

If the same name comes up two or three times, you've probably
found your cutter. Don't commit yourself to a cut then and there.

Go to the salon. Ask to watch the work, and if schedules permit, to meet the cutter. No good stylist minds having an audience—
a real pro is always happy to have his work seen—and getting to
know new clients gives the cutter more time to study them, so better
haircuts result. If you feel foolish going in alone, go along on a
friend's appointment.

Either way, you will feel more at ease with the cutter when you go back for a cut. That's important because, believe me, you will be in the cutter's hands when you sit in that chair. Your cutter needs a chance to see how you stand, how you walk, how you hold your head. Only then can the two of you work together on a haircut that will show you both at your very best.

A show-and-tell session is important, too. When you go for the first cut, tell your cutter the important things:

How much time can you spend on your hair every day?

Are you good at drying, setting, styling your hair?

Are you happy with the basic look of your hair, or do you hate your curls or your straight hair?

What do you like least about your looks? Most?

Do you share your life with someone who is adamant about seeing you with long hair or short? Or with someone who will be happy with your looks if you are happy?

If you see a photo in a magazine or newspaper of a haircut you really like, take it along; it is difficult for most people to describe a haircut. But don't expect your cutter to give you an exact duplicate of the photo. If your bone structure, hair texture, and skull were exactly the same as the other person's, you could get a carbon copy and it would be boring, as carbons are. But you are not the same. Remember that you are unique. No one in the world can look exactly like you, and your cut will be yours alone.

VIDAL ON: ELEVEN THINGS YOU SHOULD KNOW ABOUT HAIRCUTS

1. A good cut has a lifespan of four to six weeks. If you want your hair to look first-rate always, then always have a monthly cut.

2. Hair must be cut long, not just hang long. Even if you want to grow your hair very long, you must have ¼ inch nipped off the ends every month. It is the only way to eliminate the wear and tear of the past thirty days. As hair grows at the rate of ½ to ¾ of an inch per month it sounds a maddeningly slow route to long hair. But it is the only route if you want shining, swinging long hair.

3. Hair can be any length at any age. Long has no more to do with teenage than short has to do with maturity. Bone structure,

not age, determines cut and style throughout life. What should change is the degree of softness and movement to the style. When a woman is older she will find that a softer edge, a less severe geometry, waves or curls will be more becoming.

4. Never let a stylist interfere with the natural hairline on the neck.

5. Never *ever* let a stylist use a razor on your hair. The hair that needs thinning is rare. But even in those cases where hair is so extremely thick that it requires thinning, the cutter should use scissors. A pruning motion with the scissors can thin out just the hairs he would like to remove. The first time I saw this done was by Raymond in London. In general, my philosophy is that hair should be as thick at the ends as at the roots.

6. Beware the stylist who wants to "effolate" you. Such razoring and chopping the hair can be done by a clever stylist to look fine as you get up from the chair, but wait a few days and the effect will be diabolical. It is the worst thing a hairdresser can do to your hair.

7. Hair should always be cut wet. The cut should be checked while still wet. Then the hair should be dried, and checked again when dry.

8. Cutting your own hair is a dangerous hobby. It looks easy enough to cut a simple, chunky bob, but it can take a haircutting student up to three years of study to get it right. Complicated sectioning at the back of the head is needed to get that marvelous look of hair that is one length all over. Simplicity is always the most demanding thing. I can see why a woman who is far from a good salon or incredibly pressed for time might want to trim her own hair. No real harm will be done by nipping off a quarter inch from the ends of hair that was well cut to begin with. But please don't try to give yourself a complete new cut. It can take months for your mistake to grow out.

9. Don't be discouraged if the cutter cannot give you what you want on the first visit. I have often told a client to go home and let the hair grow for six weeks. Say you want a short, chunky bob. We can shorten the back and trim the sides so that you are on the way to the cut you want, but very often the hair is too thin at the sides to do a chunky bob right off. We will suggest treatments and a diet that will encourage hair growth; then later you can have the cut you want.

10. All hair should be blunt cut. If a stylist comes at you with thinning shears to thin the hair, run a mile. If he picks hair up and back-combs it, then "effolates" off what's left in his hands, run two miles.

11. Sculpting a head of hair with scissors is an art form, is drama, is the inexpensive version of cosmetic surgery. The pair of scissors is basically an extension of the expert's hand. Long, short, or mid-length, all good hair work depends upon a first-class cut. And should you have a perm or color afterward, these will look their best only if the cutting has been of the highest quality.

VIDAL ON: SOME QUESTIONS ON HAIR CUTTING

Q. What if the cutter insists on a style I can't wear?

A. No good cutter will. You have to be guided by his expertise to create a cut that will be sexy and easy for you to manage, one that will suit your hair and your bone structure. But perhaps you know it won't suit your life style. It's up to you to be honest with the cutter about the life you lead, what you are willing to do for your hair and what you want it to do for you. This information will help the cutter to make a decision about what is really the best cut for you.

Q. What if I don't like the cut?

A. Say so then and there. Chances are it can be styled differently. But don't go into a panic. There is a psychological timing for a cut—when you feel the need of a change—and there is also a physical period of adjustment. Give your eyes a chance to adjust to the new look, the new shape.

Q. What if I cannot get adjusted to the new shape?

A. Even a top cutter cannot satisfy 100 percent of the people. We do please a very high percentage, but since we are innovators, once in a great while we do come a cropper with a cut. On the very rare occasions when that happens, the client is our guest and is invited to come back to allow us to correct the mistake.

VIDAL ON: TOP TALENTS FOR YOUR HAIR: A FEW OF THE GREAT CREATORS

I think that you couldn't do better than to come into a Vidal Sassoon salon for your haircut. But, as Sly Stone sings, "Different strokes for different folks." There is a chance that you might be happier with a frills-and-pastels approach rather than our simpler one. With our methods we have been enormously successful in suiting the individual needs of many thousands of men and women, but no truly innovative cutter or stylist can please everyone. There are other first-rate approaches to creating with hair, and that is at it should be. Great as the architect Mies van der Rohe was, this would be a poorer place if he had designed all the world's buildings. We would never have seen the work of Breuer, Le Corbusier, Saarinen or Frank Lloyd Wright.

Here are just a few of the top talents who are making enormous contributions to our craft, but with approaches and statements very different from mine:

In New York, there are salons like Cinandre, Kenneth, and Monsieur Marc, as well as our own offshoots like Charles Booth at La Coupe, David Daines and Ian Harrington at Davian, and the best creative cutter of them all, Roger Thompson. In London, Leonard and Michael John are two of the top hair designers in the world. In Paris, Alexandre and Carita do some extraordinary work; Jean-Louis David and Maniatis are names to remember. In Los Angeles, Gene Shacove, with his great natural talent, became the father of Californian hairdressing. Carrie White proves (as the Carita sisters in Paris do) that women make super hair stylists.

New talents and new approaches are constantly being developed within our own organization. The greatest charge I get is in going around to our schools and salons to see this happening. Without being pretentious I can honestly say that many of the world's great cutters studied with us and many of them are still with us. Although I cannot mention them all I must single out Christopher Brooker. Our Artistic Director, he has been with us for fifteen years. During that time he has constantly produced line after line. He has developed a keen feeling for what is *now* and has consistently proved his point with artistic flair. His unerring sense of style puts him in the forefront of the world's hairdressers.

Many of our top talents make up my international show team. They work with or without me, giving demonstrations of our methods and techniques around the world to audiences of professional hairdressers. At a recent show in Tokyo, there were 2,500 professional hairdressers on hand to see and to learn, in Paris, 3,000, and, at a two-day show at the Royal Albert Hall in London, 5,000.

Whether on the show team or in the salons, these new lights have an opportunity with us to grow and develop on their own, to travel and to learn. Their creative juices ensure that our profession will be an exciting one in the future as it is now, and it is exhilarating to think that really super creative talent is always developing in Rio and in Topeka; that the next great look can come from a young whiz out of Chicago as easily as from New York, London, or Paris.

Years of study, discipline, and training are required, but there is enormous scope in what we do. I consider it a craft, an exciting adventure, and no mean art form.

Whether you have your cut at a Vidal Sassoon salon or elsewhere, I hope that you view the cutter's work with some of my sense of enthusiasm.

SPECIALS FOR YOUR HAIR

• If your hair is very damaged after a summer in the sun, a tiny bit of no-rinse conditioning cream can be put on the very ends of the hair. Not a heavy slathering, but a slight film on dry, split ends will help prevent more damage until you get to the cutter.

• Perhaps you want a new look for fall. Even if not, the haircut is especially important this month to get rid of summer punishment to even carefully cared-for hair.

• A salon treatment for your hair to condition it, along with a relaxing and stimulating massage for neck and scalp, is a marvelous idea and a super treat for yourself. If you can swing it, do. If you can't take the time, then pay close attention to conditioning at home. Make the protein pac conditioning a weekly ritual along with your finishing rinse at every shampooing.

• Color probably needs freshening this month. Make the appointment with your colorist now. If your hair is very drab and you can't get to the salon at this time, you may want to use a shampoo-in color rinse—but take extra care if your hair is dry or damaged. Better to nourish the hair this month, in that case, and save coloring for next.

SPECIALS FOR YOUR SKIN AND BODY

• Speed off the dead skin that can make a lingering suntan look muddy. Scrub with the loofah sponge in your bath. A clarifying bath with the juice of three lemons per warm tub will help to encourage that flaky, last-rose-of-summer look to go away.

• There never was a better time for a real production number of a manicure and pedicure (see page 201) to repair summer damage. Pay extra attention (using skin-sloughing lotion or pumice) to the toughened skin that summer has produced on heels and sides of feet. Always gentle your pumice stone with a cushion of soap smeared across it before use. Knees and elbows can stand a bit of extra-gentle pumice polishing, too.

• If your face seems a little yellowish with a fading tan, try one of the mauve color-correcting moisturizers. Now is also a good time for a thorough facial cleansing. Go through your regular cleansing procedure, then, before moisturizing, apply a facial mask made of buttermilk and yoghurt in equal parts. Pat the thick paste all over face (except around eyes), throat, shoulders, and hands. Let it dry while you relax with your feet up. When the mask dries, rinse it off with lots of cool water.

SPECIALS FOR YOUR FOOD PLANNING

• Lunch boxes guarantee that your children at school (or you at the office) will get food that fits into the body-improving plan you follow at home. Small cellophane packs of toasted soy nuts, Tiger's Milk bars, carob-covered raisins, fresh fruit go into them. A sandwich made with whole-grain bread and fresh peanut butter (not the hydrogenated kind, but fresh from the health food store or your blender) provides complete protein and can be made the night before with no loss of flavor, texture, or nutrition. You can make it even better and better tasting with a sprinkling of Bac • O bits or chopped dried apricots. Hot tomato juice with brewer's yeast, cold skimmed milk, hot or iced herb tea with honey and lemon could go in a thermos.

• Mae West says ginger is the secret of long-lasting sexual powers. Who's going to argue with Mae West on that score? She grates it into tea. A fruit salad can always stand a pinch of ginger.

• Brighten the flavor of cauliflower buds when you serve them steamed by tossing some caraway seed into the water.

• Don't wait until Thanksgiving to serve Turkey (remember the 20 Best Protein/Calories Buying chart on p. 135). It's available all year. Cold sliced turkey along with celery sticks stuffed with cottage cheese make one of our favorite light dinners.

• Eggs will stay fresher if you store them in the carton in the refrigerator. Large end is the Up end. Cook them at the lowest heat to keep the protein and all the other nutritive values intact. They taste better, too.

• Summer fruits and vegetables tend to be better buys now than earlier in the summer. Buy a little more than you think you need. They are beautiful decoration for the house in baskets and bowls.

SPECIALS FOR YOUR MAKEUP AND FRAGRANCE

• First two weeks this month are for shopping and experimenting. Buy new makeup for fall in warmer tones. If you are keeping up a tan, then get into bronzy shades. I tend to be too pink, so I stick with ivory and beige coloring. If you have the opposite problem and look a bit sallow, get into the pink, but not spicy, tones. Second two weeks are for presenting a new fall face.

• Mascara is back in your life. Always make sure eyelashes are bone dry when you apply it. Use dark brown or dark gray for the prettiest, softest effect. Black is too hard.

• Retire the pale pink highlighter eye shadow and switch to pearly grays and shell beiges. Never ever use white to highlight; it's too harsh.

• Your lips have got to be there. Timid mouths are bad news any time, especially in fall. Get a ripe, fruity red lipstick. Stay away from color with a blue cast for fall. Give your lips a soothing coat of lip gloss before you put on the color if they are chapped by summer weather.

• Experiment with scent. Start warming up to the heavier, more mysterious ones. Rich, fruity fragrances are great in fall. Start with the cologne, move up to the perfume as evenings get longer and cooler.

September 217

SPECIALS FOR YOUR SHAPE

• We all tend to get careless about now with our exercise program. New duties—school, job, shopping for clothes—tend to replace tennis, swimming, and the other exercise that put us into such great summer shape. Get out and walk whenever you can: when you take escalators, don't stand there—walk; get off the bus, or park your car, a few blocks before your destination and walk the rest of the way—briskly. Get out the skipping rope and jump up your circulation. Book yourself into the gym now for a specified number of visits on a regular basis, and stick to the schedule. If you can exercise out-of-doors, do. Textbooks and needlepoint, too, take well to the fresh air, and so do you.

• Suntans tend to make you look slimmer. But when the tan goes, you might want to drop one or two pounds.

• If you're back at your desk, hard at work, make it easy on your back. Always sit with one foot in front of the other slightly elevated if possible. This defeats backache and tension. Raise your arms over your head from time to time and stretch them up above your head, then out to the sides, and relax. You'll nip neck and shoulder tension in the bud.

AUTUMN

This is the rich, rewarding season of holidays and parties, of cooler days and long, promising evenings, the fruitful season, and the annual time of gathering in. It is an appropriate time to look back over the really marvelous achievements you have made during the year that is drawing to a close.

If this is the first season in your personal year of beauty and health, it will be a full and exciting one. You will tap hidden stores of energy for a glowing, expansive attitude that will enable you to enjoy this time of closeness and sharing as you never have before.

The changes in the way you look, think, and feel will continue in an upward spiral as you continue your pattern of balancing discipline with pleasure, climbing with growth.

OCTOBER

Seasonally, this is the month for reaping, for harvest moons and everything that goes with gathering in the rewards of a long season of development.

As this book is a sort of record of ongoing development for you, and a recap of some of the ways we ourselves have found useful in our development, it seems a good time to speak of the results—of what was expected, and what has been achieved.

As you go through this year together with us, you will become a far more beautiful person spiritually and physically.

There is always the possibility, however, that you expect even more—more of yourself, more from yourself. That is healthy, and we are with you. Never ever sell yourself short, or be satisfied with less than the best you can be. We are not.

We are almost paranoid about standards. Mediocrity frightens us. And we will go to great lengths in order to better ourselves. We hope that you feel the same way. As a matter of fact, we are sure you do—else you never would have stuck with us this far.

What we hope you are not doing is to set unrealistic and false goals for yourself. To explain:

Each of us is born with a certain kind of body, a physical frame that is, practically speaking, inalterable.

These frame types have been very broadly classified in terms of "morphs." There are ectomorphs—long-boned, narrow, tall, and rather frailly angular; endomorphs—voluptuously curved, all soft rounds and rather short; mesomorphs—the outdoorsy figures in the middle, broad-shouldered and a little muscular. Bones are bigger than those of the ectomorphs; the mesomorph is not quite so plump as the endomorph, and is flatter of body.

No one is 100 percent pure ectomorph, endomorph, or mesomorph. But we all have more characteristics of one than of the others. The bones are there, the frame is there, and the endomorph will not change her body into an ectomorph's with all the diet and exercise in the world.

She will make her unique frame as supple, as beautiful as any body in the world—but it will be her own. It will be beautiful in a unique way. It is that individual beauty you are working for, not some phantom image pieced together from what you have found attractive in others.

By the same token, trying to look seventeen all one's life is foolish. And it is as futile as wishing away bone structure.

We would wager that right now you look far younger than many of your contemporaries.

Because you are spending time in caring for your mind and your body, you are involved in development, not in deterioration. Development is the real and central ingredient of "youthfulness."

The best example we know of continuing development is Cary Grant, whom we admire enormously. Well into his sixties, he walks about on the balls of his feet like a youngster.

I [Vidal] remember working with him in Washington on a Fabergé promotion. His transatlantic flight had been delayed, so he had been on the plane for almost twelve hours; he barely had time for a quick shower between landing and going out on the job of being charming to several hundred strangers and making friends for Fabergé.

We went up to his suite, and I waited while he had a quick shower, singing loudly to himself, and then he was out, all raring to go.

I have never seen such a pro in action; and peak physical performance is very much a state of mind. Cary Grant knows that he has

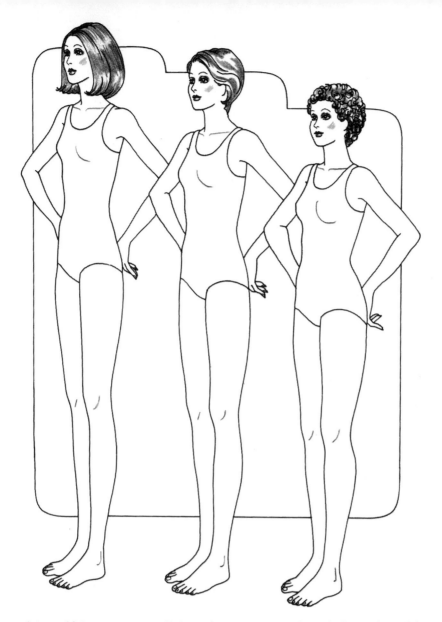

put himself into top condition, has organized and disciplined his life so that he functions at peak efficiency when peak efficiency is demanded of him.

He has prepared his mind to function as if in neutral during times of unavoidable tedium (as on a delayed flight, when becoming agitated would only tire him to no avail) so that he has stores of energy to function at top speed when he wants or needs to.

He knows the value of pacing himself, and he knows the value of taking a course of action when you can effect a desirable change by acting; he knows when to relax and remain tranquil in the face of the inevitable.

This mental assessment is necessary in every step of life if our lives are to be rewarding and not filled with regrets and frustrations.

As an example of something in my life that took a good deal of thinking about, and my eventual resolve to undertake a change that has effected my life for the better, I [Vidal] would like to tell you later on about my plastic surgery. Perhaps it will help you organize your thinking about a mental stumbling block of your own.

YOUR CHECKLIST AND SCHEDULE FOR OCTOBER

First Morning of the Month
> Log your vital statistics into your diary (p. 14) *in ink.* Set your goals for the month as to loss of pounds or inches and gains in other areas, such as proficiency at yoga, say, or using the hand-held dryer. Pencil in your goals on the diary page for the last day of the month, and start the program that will help you achieve your goals.

Every Morning
> Seven-Way Stretch   (p. 91)
> Cup of hot water and lemon juice
> Warm-up exercises   (p. 146)
> Clean face and moisturize   (p. 54)
> Makeup   (p. 61)
> Fix hair
> Vitality Drink and nutritional supplements   (p. 94)

Every Evening
> Warm-up exercises to relax
> Feet-up rest with pillows or on slantboard for 10 minutes
> Clean face and moisturize
> Bath and all-over body lotion   (p. 128)
> Clean teeth before bed   (p. 259)

As Often as You Like: At Least Three Times Each Week
> Exercise session of 30 minutes   (p. 242)
> Yoga session of 30 minutes   (p. 96)
> Shampoo and finishing rinse   (pp. 45–46)

Once Each Week
- An evening (or a day) of rest, a time for yourself
- 10-minute protective protein conditioning pac for hair
- Manicure and pedicure   (p. 201)
- Tweeze stray hairs on eyebrows   (p. 167)
- Shave legs and underarms   (p. 166)
- Facial mask   (p. 162)

Once This Month
- One night and one day of rest for the digestive system on either the detoxifying Liquid Fast or the Clearing House Diet (pp. 36–38)
- Haircut and any other professional hair services such as color or perm (your cutter might advise a cut more often, perhaps every three weeks. Follow this suggestion in making out your individual schedule).

MAKING THE WHOLE THING WORK

Because time and temper are short just before the holidays, and so much effort and conditioning have gone into persuading us that this is the time for love and peace, this is the championship season for fights and misunderstandings between husbands and wives.

All the recipes and formulas for making your life rich and beautiful mean very little when a fight (or the prospect of one) with your mate makes you feel miserable.

Sharing your life with someone you love has got to be the most rewarding, and difficult, way of living it. It poses a million questions and problems that only the two of you can work out together.

We cannot give you any foolproof formula for dealing with the body blows that every marriage suffers. But we can pass along some of the positive decisions for making the partnership work that we have arrived at through our own ups and downs in the course of our marriage that, usually, has been unusually happy.

—First rule is to get it out in the open. If you don't like the way he forgets to replace the cap on the toothpaste tube or anything else on up the scale, say so. And say it now. Don't dwell on it for days, practicing the devastatingly clever line you will use and how you will deliver it. Just get it off your chest.

—Take your annoyances to the one who annoys you. This is a second part of the first rule. A sympathetic friend or relative is *not* the ideal listener. Conversations with a friend that begin "Well, Marge, he did it again . . ." can end your marriage. And if not, they are embarrassing for you and for Marge once the storm has blown over.

—When you think that yours is the divorce case Louis Nizer has been waiting for, and that you have been singled out for suffering, don't talk but listen. Go to a gathering of members of your own sex—a women-only lunch, for example—and you will hear lots and lots of talk. Much of it will have to do with the problems other people have with their partners. Listen well and you will probably discover that your problems are far from unique. In fact, they may pale by comparison.

—Follow up on the comparison-listening session by trying to find some one of your friends, married or single, whose life seems ideal—someone with whom you would trade places in every respect. Chances are you won't find this paragon. Then you should consider what goes into making your own life so right for you, and pinpointing the false notes in it. Then you can get busy correcting them and the marriage. If you do come up with another couple who are leading an ideal life, who have what you think is an ideal marriage, then pay the closest attention to how they operate. Your research may turn up the fact that part of the success lies in their attention to details or problems that you neglect or do not work on.

—Often the marriage gets a new lease on life if you begin thinking of yourself as a person, not just as half a couple. I [Beverly] went through a little identity crisis of my own a while back there. When we moved to Los Angeles, I was back in my home town. Before we were married, I had known that I was Beverly Adams, and I was an actress with a career in the making. Now I was Mrs. Vidal Sassoon and I wasn't quite sure just what that meant. To talk about "finding yourself" always sounds pretentious; but I know that it has helped my own happiness and sense of value to do a few things on television and to act again, as well as to have my life with Vidal and the children. I'm not out to become Liv Ullman, but it is wonderful to do something of your own that you enjoy and that enlarges your life. And it doesn't have to be a great big thing. Nobody said you have to win the Nobel Prize. But you can go out of the house and have a job that puts you in contact with people, gives you a sense of accomplishment, and something more to talk to your husband about than what happened when the washer broke. You don't even have to go out. Best-selling novels have been written at the kitchen table, and there are lots of women whose lives and bank accounts are fuller because they let some of the creativity that goes into homemaking spill over into creating for profit, working at home to produce cakes, ceramics, or something else that they can offer to the world.

VIDAL ON: PLASTIC SURGERY: HOW AND WHY I DECIDED ON IT FOR MYSELF

We must stress the importance of taking oneself in hand—the importance of deciding for oneself where positive action should be taken and where to draw the line in going along with the plastic standards of what is and is not beautiful. Knowing, accepting, and liking yourself means not wasting precious time in wishing for longer legs or blue eyes.

That would seem to rule out plastic surgery, wouldn't it?

I think not. Not if you consider it carefully. And, believe me, I considered it very carefully before my own operation. Let me tell you the story.

Four years ago, when I was forty-three, I decided the time had come to do something about the very pronounced bags under my eyes. They were a hereditary trait, and had always been there. When I was twenty-two and looked younger than my years, the bags were of no great concern. In my forties, to wake up to see those puffy eyes in the mirror was not a morale booster.

It could not be particularly appealing to Bev, either. I thought to myself, One morning she's going to wake up and say, "Christ, hasn't he changed. Isn't he old!"

My immediate throught was that my concern indicated a love affair with myself—that the necessary bit of vanity we all have had grown in me like mushrooms after rain. I did a lot of very serious thinking about it.

I came to the realization that once I had chosen my clothes, showered, shaved, combed my hair, and dressed, I didn't look at myself in a mirror for the rest of the day.

So it couldn't be self-love. But self-esteem is something else. And it's a healthy thing.

Whenever I had encountered an obstacle to my self-esteem at any point in my life, I had assessed the possibility of removing or correcting it. I had tried and done every possible form of therapy to become the person I knew I could be—exercise and proper nutrition, meditation and as much reading in philosophy and literature as I could find time for, even voice lessons to correct the questionable handicap of a Cockney accent. I had worked to earn my own self-esteem.

I was damned if something as easily correctable as this was going to handicap me.

I considered the effect it would have on my family. Not to make them love me more. That is not something that surgery can do. One is loved or not. A scalpel will not change it. But I did want to look as young as I felt with my young family.

On the advice of a friend who is also a brilliant medical man, I made an appointment with a plastic surgeon.

In a lengthy interview he probed my reasons for wishing surgery. When at last he was satisfied, a time was arranged for me to be in his office on Central Park South in New York.

The operation was done then and there. Removing the heavy bags under my eyes took just two hours. I was given a local anesthetic, but was not put to sleep. This work is done taking into account the shape of one's eyes, the way one uses them, so the patient must be awake and busy doing eye exercises, looking left, right, up, down, forward. I could watch the doctor's hands as he worked. Beautiful hands, incredibly sensitive, with a deft touch. Knowing how difficult it is to perfect even a minor art, such as the cutting of hair, I was astounded by the marvel of this man who can carve in skin and flesh and bone.

My eyes were bandaged after the operation and Beverly led me to the Essex House Hotel next door. I was to rest there for the next twenty-four hours. Like any operation, this one is a shock to the nervous system, so complete rest is vital.

Bandages were removed the next day, and I wore dark glasses to rest the eyes until the stitches were removed two days later.

I was given special creams to hasten healing and minimize scarring. It was imperative that I stay out of the sun for two months since scar tissue darkens in the sun at a more rapid rate than the rest of the body.

Two months later, it was as if nothing had ever happened. But this operation had given me five years and banished the "yech" feeling I had when I looked in the mirror.

Plastic surgery, or cosmetic surgery, did not change my life style, my habits, my friends. It did not do any of this for me, nor has it done this for any of the many people Beverly and I know who have had surgery.

To expect this kind of miracle cure is asking too much of plastic surgery. You are the only one who can effect these changes in your life. The surgeon can merely remove certain physical impediments to the fullest expression of your pride in yourself and joy in life.

How fantastic it is that today surgeons are able to rebuild the body. I was privileged to observe (with the patient's permission) while a brilliant surgeon in Los Angeles, Dr. Steven Zax, performed an operation to enlarge a woman's breasts.

The operation is an augmentation mammoplasty and is done with a self-contained implant, a silicone gel that is inside a sterile container. This eliminates the danger of the silicone's shifting once inside the body.

Seeing this operation gave me a better understanding and a completely new insight into plastic surgery. I see now that it is a marriage, as Dr. Zax says, of technical adroitness, esthetics, and psychology.

Today with the right surgeon (but only with the right surgeon) this way of aligning physical form with mental attitude can no longer be classified as merely an expensive way of satisfying a whim. It is a real and invaluable tool which can be employed in realizing one's own greatest potential. It is, in short, another way to arrive at the ideal of positive vitality.

If you are considering plastic surgery in any form, or have even toyed with the idea, I cannot urge you too strongly to get hold of *Psycho-Cybernetics,* the book by Dr. Maxwell Maltz. You can find it in the library, or in a paperback bookstore. It is a real mind-shaker that may revise your thinking in many areas.

After reading the book, do some more thinking. Discuss the

idea frankly with your friends and your family. Then make your decision.

Once you are realistic about what plastic surgery can do, it can do great things. I know.

FACIAL EXERCISES

Often, cosmetic surgery might have been unnecessary had the patient practiced wiggling his ears. Facial exercises look ridiculous, but they are simple to do and are very effective in preventing the droop and sag that are the inevitable end result of keeping a stiff upper lip. If you will spend a few seconds a day stretching that stiff upper lip in funny-looking ways, you will be repaid by a younger look years longer. But exercise in private or you will be rewarded with some very curious looks as well; watchers tend to think you've gone mad as you wiggle your ears, cross your eyes, and wag your jaw.

Here are four exercises to try:

1. *Eyes shut* (to prevent baggy lids): Close your eyes and squeeze them tightly shut, now even tighter; now slowly release the squeeze and lift your eyebrows. Stretch the lids upward as far as you can without opening your eyes. Slowly lower your eyebrows. Relax and repeat five times.

2. *Toothless smile* (for lines from nose to mouth): Press lips together and turn corners of your mouth up in a smile as you slowly open your mouth. Keep teeth covered by lips. Smile, with corners turning up, until you feel the tension, then slowly bring your mouth into an O shape. Relax. Repeat.

3. *Forehead smoother* (to get rid of lines): Lie with head hanging over the edge of the bed, raise eyebrows as high as you can, relax them. Repeat twenty times.

4. *Jawline shaper* (to get rid of jowls): Clench back teeth then release and drop your jaw. Slowly bring jaw up again and bite down hard on the back molars. Repeat ten times.

GIVING YOUR MOISTURIZER A
HELPING HAND

Fuel bills aren't the only thing you save when you turn down the thermostat. Cooler is better as far as your skin is concerned, too. You will feel more comfortable at lower temperatures if the level of humidity is a bit higher.

Hot air indoors in winter is usually dry as a bone. Interior decorators often suggest a humidifier to keep antique furniture in good condition. The odds are pretty good that if the furniture needs humidity, so does your skin, so you will avoid looking like a not-so-rare antique.

The smallest and simplest electric humidifiers cost only a few dollars, but shop for a good model. As with any equipment you buy, it's better to save for it and wait for quality. A really cheap article is hardly a bargain if it breaks down quickly.

Even without a humidifier, there are a number of ways to get more moisture into the air. The simplest don't cost a dime.

If you have radiators, you can soak a terry cloth bath towel in cold water and drape it over the radiator. Not so pretty, but effective. If you have forced-air heating, put lots of plants in your life. Keep them well watered and mist-spray them daily. The humid atmosphere that's congenial to plants will be kind to your skin. In fact, the famous dermatologist Dr. Norman Orentreich likes to compare the skin to a delicate plant, since both need air and moisture to thrive. A cheerful note at this time of year would be forcing some spring bulbs set in a wide low bowl filled with pebbles and water. Another trick is to set a shallow pan of water in an inconspicuous place where it won't be upset, and then get double benefits by adding a few drops of your perfumed bath oil to the water. Don't add bath oil or any kind of perfume to the humidifier, though. Even a drop can gum up the delicate works.

YOUR CLOSET THIS FALL

This is not so much about the new additions to your wardrobe, as it is about the place you store them, and how you organize it. Closets shouldn't be disorganized any more than you should be—but they have a way of getting out of hand in a hurry.

Before you put any new addition away, why not spend some time (perhaps on your weekly evening for yourself) on shaping up your storage. It can be a very easy means to a feeling of super-efficiency.

Be ruthless in taking out every single thing you haven't worn in a year. If you didn't like it this summer, you won't grow to love it by the next. Perhaps someone else will. Call the charity thrift shop to take it all away.

Hang the things you do love on the proper kinds of hangers, and cover them in plastic zipper bags. Bags give an extra-tidy look to the closet as well as protecting clothes. Do not hang your sweaters, knit dresses, or knit trousers. They tend to "grow" with suspension. Instead, fold them and store on shelves or in drawers.

Shoes, with trees in them, should be kept in boxes. If you have see-through plastic boxes, fine. If not, mark the outside of the box with colored magic markers so you will know at a glance what shoe is inside what box.

Accessories such as scarves, belts, and necklaces can easily fall into tangled heaps, but that can easily be prevented with the kind of metal tie racks that the dime store sells. Hanging accessories saves hunting and digging.

A final thought on the organized closet: Never put anything into the closet that needs repair. The broken zipper won't be mended or remembered, and will come as a shocking surprise the next time you are dressing in a hurry.

Splurging on something pretty for the closet—padded hangers or scented flannel drawer liners—is an inducement to maintaining apple-pie order at all times.

CIGARETTES

We know. You have already heard all the good reasons for not smoking. We thought we had too. But in the course of working on this book and reading books and articles on nutrition and health we came across a few new shockers; and the daily newspapers have a fair share of chillers as well. Some of the good arguments against smoking we have come across are these:

A child's chance of getting pneumonia or bronchitis in the first year of life nearly doubles if both parents smoke. Even if only one parent smokes, the child's chance of disease is 50 percent greater than for a child of nonsmoking parents. (From *The Lancet,* the British medical journal)

Smoking as long as six hours before flying can seriously impair a pilot's eyesight, manual dexterity, reflexes, and the ability to estimate time intervals. Carbon monoxide from inhaling cigarette smoke goes into the blood and destroys oxygen in the red blood cells. For a one-pack-a-day smoker, the reduction of oxygen supplied to the heart and brain may be as much as 15 percent. It takes four to six hours to expel the carbon monoxide from the body, or overnight for heavy smokers. (From a report in the *Los Angeles Times* on a study by Dr. I. Herbert Scheinberg)

Dangerous blood clotting can lead to sudden death from arterial thrombosis. Dr. Peter Levine's study at Tufts-New England Medical Center showed that only five minutes after smoking a cigarette, volunteers all showed an accelerated activity of platelets, the blood compoments that stick together to aid the clotting process. (From *Circulation,* a journal of the American Heart Association)

Women who smoke heavily run the risk of bone disease that can weaken bones and even cause the collapse of the spinal column. Smoking increases acidity in the bone tissue. That probably allows the structural minerals in the bones to drain away. Dr. Harry W. Daniell, of California, cites as evidence of the mineral loss the greatly increased calcium level in the blood after volunteers had smoked three cigarettes. He also found that menopause occurs several years earlier among smokers, suggesting that smoking affects sex hormones. (From *Vogue*)

Pregnant women who smoke are more likely to experience miscarriage, still birth, the death of the newborn child, and to have babies that weigh less at birth. (From *The New York Times*)

Because women get more Pap tests now, and smoke more cigarettes now, lung cancer has replaced uterine cancer as the third leading cause of cancer death in American women. (From the *New York Daily News*)

One cigarette destroys 25 milligrams of vitamin C.

Cigarettes destroy lecithin in the bloodstream. You need lecithin to break down fats and keep them from being deposited on the walls of the arteries as cholesterol. (From *Prevention* magazine)

You already know about the larger horrors of smoking, but don't forget the relatively minor ones—stained, smelly hair and hands, discolored teeth, poor complexion, and premature wrinkles—none of which seem minor when they turn out to be your personal problems.

VIDAL ON: SMOKING AND SEX

We have already discussed the absolutely terrible effects of smoking on the skin, lungs, blood, hair, and nails. These apply to both men and women.

I would like to add a small, totally male chauvinist note here, though: Smoking is anti-sex. To kiss a beautiful woman, even if she is wearing the most feminine of scents and has the softest skin and moistest lips, is—if she smokes—like kissing a little old man. I associate smoker's breath with whiskery old codgers and with my army buddies—neither group do I kiss. The smoking woman may have come a long way, baby, but it's down the wrong street.

Because Beverly hates the smell of onions I got her to stop smoking during the day. I kept an onion with me, and whenever she started to smoke a cigarette, I took a big bite of raw onion. She now smokes occasionally in the evening, but she always uses mouthwash before we kiss goodnight.

SPECIALS FOR YOUR MAKEUP AND FRAGRANCE

• Are you wearing a heavier moisturizer now for the coming winter? Do!

• More time under artificial light means retiring any lipstick with a bluish or brown cast. These can make you look like Dracula's daughter under fluorescent lights.

• If you use face powder, try substituting baby powder. It has a youthful sheen and transparency.

• Foundation should be paler unless you have a winter suntan. I use the palest shade of ivory from now until spring comes along. The top makeup professional Pablo Manzoni says that trying foundation on the back of your hand is all wrong. The skin tones of your face and the back of your hand are different. Try it on the place you'll use it.

SPECIALS FOR YOUR SHAPE

• Keep moving. A brisk twenty-minute walk burns off 50 calories. Stair climbing is even better—10 calories a minute!

• Consider that if the average mind were allowed to deteriorate in the same fashion as the average body, most of the populace would be blithering idiots.

• Keep an eagle eye on snacks during cooler weather. One extra daily cookie at 25 calories will put 2½ pounds of fat on you if you keep it up for a year.

SPECIALS FOR YOUR FOOD PLANNING

• Chicken is something we enjoy often. One recipe we love is:

VINEYARD CHICKEN

1 roasting chicken
lemon juice
1 tsp. paprika
salt substitute
fresh green seedless grapes
    Rub chicken with seasonings. Stuff with grapes and bake at 300°F. for

20 minutes per pound, about an hour and 20 minutes for the usual 4-pound roasting chicken.

• Hot soups sound good again, and chicken is a natural for them.

CHICKEN BROTH

3- or 4-pound hen
celery, stalks and leaves
onion, peeled but whole
carrots, washed, unpeeled
bay leaf, parsley

Put chicken in the pot, add water to cover, and simmer, covered, with the vegetables and seasoning for about two hours. Remove the vegetables and the chicken from the pot. Put the vegetables into the blender to puree. Remove meat from the bones of the chicken. Cut the chicken into small pieces and return to the soup along with the pureed vegetables. Heat together and serve.

• Baby eggplants are beautiful things, no longer than your hand, and are delicious scrubbed, cut up unpeeled, and quickly stir-fried in a little poly-unsaturated vegetable oil or margarine.

SPECIALS FOR YOUR HEALTH

• Keep your feet in shape for the heavier shoes and boots that are on the agenda. Pumice lightly every day, massage feet with body lotion after the bath, push cuticle back gently, and keep feet dry by using powder after the massage. Switch shoes often, and give them 48 hours (with shoe trees in place) between wearings. It's a great idea to switch frequently from lower to higher heels. High heels should have a thicker platform sole for best support. To wear around the house, you might try a pair of the new "earth shoe" designs that have low heels and built-up arches and toes. The idea is to simulate the natural position of bare feet walking on soft earth or sand. When you shop for shoes, late afternoon is the golden moment. Your feet are larger then than they are in the morning, and you will get the best fit. Pantyhose or socks have to fit properly, too, for happy feet. A half-inch longer than the big toe is ideal.

• It's a good month to have your eyes checked by an opthalmologist. Sooner is better when it comes to the well-being of your eyes. Glaucoma can get started on its evil work when you are only thirty years old.

• With your glowing health, you aren't a likely subject for sniffles at the season's change, but remember that colds are bad for ears, too. When you blow your nose, it's one nostril at a time to prevent ear damage.

SPECIALS FOR YOUR HAIR

• If you like the extra shine and body your hair has because of your weekly use of the Vidal Sassoon Protein Pac Treatment, then keep it up through the steam-heat season. Otherwise, the extra conditioning you have been giving your hair over the summer can be relaxed a bit now, and you may use the conditioner every other week. But do not omit the Vidal Sassoon Finishing Rinse after each shampoo.

• Gray hair? Please don't feel that you must color it. I think that gray hair in beautiful condition has tremendous elegance. Many women rush into color at the first few gray hairs. If you do color, don't get rid of all the gray. My personal preference is to see a bit of gray with color. Our colorists use blends of tints on gray hair that tone the gray, and allow it to be seen against a varied tonality that will highlight it and give the hair a lively, becoming quality that merely "covering gray" could never have. The effect is quite smashing. Many of the women who accuse their gray hair of aging them are pointing in the wrong direction. Any woman (or man) who allows the body to deteriorate slowly, who becomes fat and lazy, can dye hair. They then become puffy blondes or brunettes, with middle-age spread, and look no younger despite the color of their hair. Diet, exercise, and mental attitude are the keys to a youthful appearance at any age.

NOVEMBER

The countdown to Christmas and New Year's Eve is on. Even noise takes on a different, holiday character for the next sixty days. Ideally, there should be the silvery sounds of carols and little bells and children's laughter, buzzing anticipatory sounds of parental conferences and hidden crackling noises of presents being wrapped. Ringing doorbells and car horns signal people paying calls, going to parties, speeding along on errands that have to do with pleasure-giving.

That ideal is real if—and only if—you are in mental trim for the rushing and racing of the year-end Olympics.

One key is the preservation of a sense of the ridiculous. It can save your temper in frustrating situations—jammed stores, traffic jams, and long lines at the supermarket. Vidal always likes to imagine how the Marx Brothers or Jacques Tati would behave in the same deadly fix he finds himself in. Another of Vidal's secret fantasies, when on an elevator with that terrible Muzak playing, is to imagine bowing to a stranger standing next to him; next thing, they are dancing to the music until the elevator stops, then bowing, they get off the elevator without saying a word. That kind of mental foolishness can really reduce the pressure.

Pull out every trick in your bag that can help you relax in a hurry. Yawn widely to relieve tension while you're driving . . . yoga breathing whenever and wherever the adrenalin starts to pump . . . unobtrusive stretching and relaxing exercises at your desk . . . five-minute relaxers whenever there is a break in the schedule . . . quickie muscle-toners in the kitchen. . . . We have two new 30-minute relaxers and rechargers for you to do when you get home from a strenuous day, and some "invisible" exercises to do in your seat at the children's Christmas pageant or anywhere you're apt to develop a bit of squirming impatience.

YOUR CHECKLIST AND SCHEDULE FOR NOVEMBER

First Morning of the Month
> Log your vital statistics into your diary (p. 14) *in ink.* Set your goals for the month as to loss of pounds or inches and gains in other areas, such as proficiency at yoga, say, or using the hand-held dryer. Pencil in your goals on the diary page for the last day of the month, and start the program that will help you achieve your goals.

Every Morning
> Seven-Way Stretch   (p. 91)
> Cup of hot water and lemon juice
> Warm-up exercises   (p. 146)
> Clean face and moisturize   (p. 54)
> Makeup   (p. 61)
> Fix hair
> Vitality Drink and nutritional supplements   (p. 94)

Every Evening
> Warm-up exercises to relax
> Feet-up rest with pillows or on slantboard for 10 minutes
> Clean face and moisturize
> Bath and all-over body lotion   (p. 128)
> Clean teeth before bed   (p. 259)

As Often as You Like: At Least Three Times Each Week
> Exercise session of 30 minutes   (p. 242)
> Yoga session of 30 minutes   (p. 96)

Shampoo and finishing rinse   (pp. 45–46)
Once Each Week
An evening (or a day) of rest, a time for yourself
10-minute protective protein conditioning pac for hair
Manicure and pedicure   (p. 201)
Tweeze stray hairs on eyebrows   (p. 167)
Shave legs and underarms   (p. 166)
Facial mask   (p. 162)
Once This Month
One night and one day of rest for the digestive system on
either the detoxifying Liquid Fast or the Clearing House Diet
(pp. 36–38)
Haircut and any other professional hair services such as color
or perm (your cutter might advise a cut more often, perhaps
every three weeks. Follow his suggestion in making out your
individual schedule).

ALCOHOL

The advice you probably expect to find in a book on health and
beauty is "Never touch a drop of alcohol." It is very good advice,
and you will be both richer and healthier if you never patronize a
wine merchant.

But, since we both enjoy a bit of wine on occasion, it would not
be very honest of us to pretend otherwise and to advocate abstinence for you.

We like to splurge occasionally on a bottle of Dom Perignon. It
is superb, but fiendishly expensive, so we don't drink it in great
quantity. It's so good that, rather than following it with the letdown
of another wine with dinner we often have a glass of fresh fruit
juice instead.

We always serve wine with dinner when we have guests, because it is festive, and wine stimulates a party mood as well as the
digestion. It needn't be an expensive wine. Wine snobbery is just
one more form of fanaticism and stress that your life will be richer
without.

Another form of fanaticism, at least for us, is that idea that no dinner is complete without wine. Why? Reserve the wine for a party, or for a meal that it will complement. With other meals, fruit juice, milk, tea, or water might be more suitable, more thirst-quenching, and healthier. You should never, in any case, swallow food with great floods of liquid to "wash it down." If you chew properly, the food doesn't need washing down.

Wine can be used in cooking whenever you like. The heat causes all the alcohol and 85 percent of the calories in a dry table wine to evaporate.

In the world of alcohol, wine is not the major thief of your looks and your health. Distilled liquor is. Since this habit-forming and lethal drug is so widely advertised and so available, we think you should know what you are dealing with when you drink it.

Liquor is labeled according to "proof." Proof is the percentage of pure alcohol, doubled. Thus, 86 proof Scotch is 43 percent pure alcohol, and 100 proof liquor is 50 percent pure alcohol. Wines are labeled with the percentage of alcohol. Wines are not usually more than 12 percent alcohol by volume. This means they are 24 proof. The lower proof will prove better for you. Beer is the alcoholic drink lowest in alcohol. By law, it must contain more than 1/2 of 1 percent alcohol by volume, and most domestic beers are about 4.5 percent alcohol, or about 9 proof.

You should know, too, about the calories and the carbohydrates and nutrition values (or lack of them) in the liquor you drink. Various "drinking diets" have made it common knowledge that there are no carbohydrates in gin, Scotch, vodka, etcetera; no minerals, vitamins, or any other valuable nutrients either. But lots of calories. Dry table wines do have carbohydrates, traces of minerals, and calories. Beer is higher in carbohydrates than either liquor or wine, but *lower* in calories ounce for ounce, and contains more nutrients than wine.

Here is the calorie breakdown for one jigger, (1½ ounces) of alcoholic beverages.

> 86-proof liquor—105 calories
> dry table wine—37 calories
> domestic lager beer—19 calories

The counts are rounded off, and some wines may be a few calories higher or lower. Bourbon whiskey will be higher in calories than vodka; some beers are lower in calories than others. Also, nobody ever drinks just a jigger of beer. Still, it is a much maligned drink as a source of calories. It's the carbohydrates that get you in beer: 53 grams of carbohydrate, but only 150 calories in a 12-ounce can.

When figuring out the calories in a drink, alcohol is only part of the story, unless you drink in Western movie style: a straight shot of old red-eye. Tonic water or ginger ale add lots of calories to the glass. One Tom Collins can represent a hefty 210 calories, but it has none of the energy builders your body needs along with the calorie rations for the day.

That sort of drink depletes the body's store of B vitamins, hinders the metabolism of other nutrients, and adds extra work for the liver.

Let's look at the visible effects of alcohol on the work of the body, and the measurable internal effects.

When you drink, liquor goes into the alimentary canal, then into the bloodstream to raise the alcohol level in the blood. The body needs time to metabolize the alcohol so as to keep the level in the blood from rising. For most people, one ounce of whiskey or four ounces of wine can be metabolized in an hour without raising the level.

Two moderate drinks in an hour raise the level to 0.5 percent. You can see the effect: slightly carefree, a bit more effusive.

Beyond that point, it's all downhill. Clumsiness at .10 percent; crying jags or other emotional outbursts at .20 percent; stupor at .30 percent; possible death at .50 percent.

It's difficult to imagine anyone going through more than twenty ounces of whiskey in an hour; but the cumulative effects of liquor on the liver can spell death as surely as polishing off a fifth in one sitting.

OUR FOOLPROOF THIRTY-MINUTE RECHARGERS

If any season of the year has a corner on pressure, this one does. Between Thanksgiving and New Year's Eve, there seems to be a constant demand that you function round the clock, and grace under pressure is tested severely.

What you need is a personal private trick to recharge your store of energy and enthusiasm—fast. We each have our own, and it really works in that half-hour between the day's rounds and the evening's.

BEVERLY: I take fifteen minutes to get the old feet off the ground. Lie down on a slantboard, or with pillows propping up your feet and legs. Concentrate on tension sliding away from your feet, your legs, your back, your hips (it's the mental relaxer of the first yoga pose I told you about, the savasana, p. 100). Then a nice, warm bath with oil in it and the bathroom door *shut*, so the children can't come in for a question-and-answer session. That takes care of ten minutes. Then I'm up, I brush my hair, and on with the smile and I'm off. . . .

VIDAL: I take twenty minutes to relax, lying on the bed with my feet braced high on the wall, my head and shoulders hanging over the side of the bed. If you're really fagged out, it's a marvelous reviver. Then, if you can do a yoga headstand or shoulder stand, do it. Two minutes will give you a great surge of energy, and you will think clearly.

Do these while you are sitting down. Total time for tension and relaxation of muscles is nine seconds for each one. Total visible movement is zero. Only your muscles know for sure.

1. Tighten buttocks. Count to 3. Relax for a count of 6.
2. Tighten only the left buttock. Count to 3. Relax for a count of 6.
3. Tighten only the right buttock. Count to 3. Relax for a count of 6.
4. Tighten the stomach. Count to 3. Relax for a count of 6.
5. Press hands into your thighs. Count to 3. Relax for a count of 6.
6. Hands on thighs, pull up, but without raising hands. Count to 3. Relax for a count of 6.
7. Press feet hard into the floor. Count to 3. Relax for a count of 6.

One of our best, prettiest, and busiest friends is Shirley Lord. She always has the fresh, cool bloom of an English rose and never loses her wonderful sense of enthusiasm and fun. We first knew Shirley in London where she was a top newspaper editor. She then came to America to be Beauty Editor at *Harper's Bazaar* and, later, Beauty and Health Editor at *Vogue*. Shirley is now a corporate executive of Helena Rubenstein and in private life Mrs. David Anderson. She has a nonstop day and evening schedule and, as every busy woman has, a trick for keeping looks and energy at peak:

"At the end of a hectic day my impulse is to simply collapse in a heap while David gets me a vodka-and-tonic. But if I did, I would fall asleep, so instead I exercise. Exercise then is a bit like going to church—you really don't want to do it, but afterwards you feel marvelous. I'm a bath person and in the morning I have a tub, but after a long day I get under the shower and do five minutes of stretching exercises. Then I shampoo my hair, giving my scalp a good massage. After the shower I take a few minutes to elevate my feet on a pile of cushions with a witch-hazel mask on my eyes. The combination of exercise and rest is unbeatable."

BEVERLY ON: DRESSING TO MAKE THE MOST (OR THE LEAST) OF YOUR BODY TYPE

There isn't a single figure "problem" that cannot be minimized by the proper choice of what you wear. Because I want to look a little taller than I am, I almost always aim for a fluid look of one color (or tones of one color) from neckline to toe. I like to wear dark pants, navy blue for instance, with a navy top and perhaps a blue-and-white scarf. I might wear a black turtleneck and black boots with a black jumper for a total one-color look. If on the other hand, you are too tall for your taste, distract the eye from your long line with lots of separates, lots of colors and lots of textures.

Here are some thoughts on clothes camouflage for specific problems:

For a large fanny: Avoid jeans or any other pants with pockets and detailing on the back. Wear pants with straight legs that hit the waist. Wear pants that are long enough (almost every woman seems to wear them too short) to lap over the shoe for the longer line you need. Wear a shoe or boot with a higher heel. Wear narrow belts and avoid belts that contrast with clothes.

For a big bosom: Nothing too clinging; a dress with a gathered yoke is a good idea, as are looser fits in general.

For big hips: Blouson tops are terrific; so are overblouses and other things without definite waistlines—wider sleeves will balance the proportion. A low neckline is good and so are earrings, scarves, and necklaces that call attention up and away from the problem area. Bracelets aren't such a hot idea because they do the opposite.

For big shoulders and heavy arms: The dolman sleeve and the raglan sleeve were made for you. A lower armhole is always a good idea—a sleeveless dress or tank top never is, Yes to hats; no to shoulder bags.

SPECIALS FOR YOUR HAIR

• Leaves fall in an annual cycle, and there is a natural cyclical pattern of normal hair loss on the human head, too. The greatest amount of hair loss occurs in November; the least amount in May. A single hair grows on your head for a little less than three years. Then it rests. After about three months of rest, it falls out and a new hair grows in its place in the same hair follicle, and the cycle begins again. This is the end of that resting period for old hair, so you can expect heavier accumulations than usual in your brush and comb. Up to one hundred hairs a day may fall out in the normal course of things, but healthy new hairs are growing as you read this. If you suspect that your hair loss is greater than normal, count the hairs that come out in your comb. If the total is higher than one hundred, take measures. See the hairologist at a good salon for treatments. Avoid any chemicals that might further damage hair. That includes the chemicals in perms or coloring agents. Do not use rollers in your hair. If you pull your hair back into a chignon or a ponytail, change the style. Protect your hair from temperature extremes and any other punishment.

SPECIALS FOR YOUR SKIN AND BODY

• Ancient Roman beauty trick for dry-skin time (which this month is): Every other bath, massage with body lotion *before* getting into a warm tub. No soap in the water, but one pint of fresh milk or one cup of instant powdered nonfat dry milk crystals and three drops of almond oil. Soak for ten minutes, then get busy with loofah and bath brushes to polish off every cell of dead, dry skin. Rinse quickly in tepid water. Pat yourself dry and rub in more body lotion, with extra dollops on hands and feet. Your skin will be whistle-clean but oil-rich.

• In cold weather, the principle of wearing layers is one that works for skin as well as clothing. Three thin layers are much better insurance than one shoulder-hunching heavy one when it comes to sweaters and coats. Layer your makeup, too: A thin slick of lip gloss, then color, then a shiny topcoat of gloss; a creamy film of moisturizer on your eyes, then shadows and highlights using creamy formulations.

• Apple season, and great for your teeth (crunching on raw apples is cleansing as well as pleasurable).

• If your cheeks look rose red on long country hikes, that's not so good—especially if the red is surrounded by snow white. It can be an early warning signal of frostbite. Protect with moisturizer, wool mufflers to there, and even a wool ski mask if you go for very long walks in snow country.

• If you don't have one already, or haven't been using it lately, get out your bath thermometer. Tepid is 85 to 90 degrees; warm is 90 to 100 degrees; trouble for skin is anything above that.

SPECIALS FOR YOUR MAKEUP AND FRAGRANCE

• Your jawline can look more clear-cut than ever with this trick for evening: Lift your head and draw a light curve of blusher just under the jawbone from ear to ear. Blend well, up and inward toward the chin.

• To accentuate the cheekbones for evening makeup, use a liquid foundation, a shade lighter than usual, applying it in little taps on the tops of cheekbones into the corners of the nose. Blend.

• Help false lashes and real ones look uniformly natural by brushing both with a little mascara after you apply the supplementary ones.

SPECIALS FOR YOUR SHAPE

• Get your leg and ankle muscles in shape now for skiing, ice skating. Here is one ankle strengthener/slimmer: Hold feet above the floor while seated on a chair. Angle heels down and make arcs from left to right with the feet (as if they were windshield wipers). Do 10 arcs. Rest.

• Shape up your thighs: Sit on the floor with hands flat on the floor behind you, left knee bent. Straighten and raise the right leg off the floor. Bend the right knee and slip the leg under the left knee. Don't touch the floor. Straighten the right leg, then return to the original position. Relax and reverse.

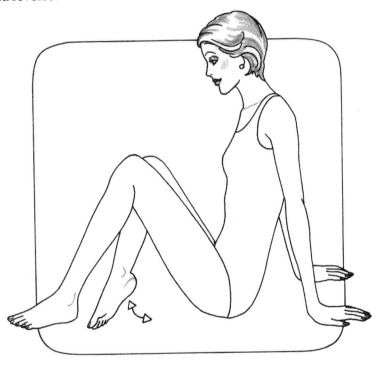

SPECIALS FOR YOUR FOOD PLANNING

• This is the start of party time on a nonstop basis. Here are two appetizers that don't wreak havoc with your shape plans and are delicious additions to the carrot and celery stick and raw cauliflower trays, and the bowls of toasted soy nuts.

BEEF TARTARE BALLS

1 pound ground lean beef
1 raw egg yolk
1 teaspoon lemon juice
½ teaspoon white pepper
chopped parsley
   Mix first 4 ingredients, make into little balls, roll in parsley.

STUFFED RAW MUSHROOMS

Wash mushrooms, remove stems. Boil stems quickly in a little water. When tender, chop stems. Whip a cup of cottage cheese with a tablespoon of skim milk. Mix chopped stems and chopped chives into cheese mixture and use it to stuff raw mushroom caps. Chill.

• Warm milk drinks are soothing in cold weather; for extra protein and richness, you can add a tablespoon of skim milk powder to skim milk. For flavor and nutrition, blackstrap molasses or honey or carob powder is great. Instant malted milk powder is high in carbohydrates, but encourages sleep. When you heat milk, *always* cover the pan tightly and use the lowest heat. Protein will separate and form a skin or stick to the pan otherwise. The riboflavin in milk is destroyed by lots of light. So keep heating slow and dark to keep milk full of B vitamins and protein.

DECEMBER

Jingling sleigh bells are festive accompaniment to this holiday month. Jangling nerves are not. Happy holidays for you and for those you love depend on your being relaxed. To derive fullest enjoyment of this big holiday month, start today to plot out your time. Pacing and timing now will pay off in a full store of energy and beauty when the big day arrives.

Make a list of top priorities and schedule everything now. Call today to slate your haircut, perm, or coloring for a day not later than two weeks before the holiday. Book time well in advance, too, for any other professional visits (one to the dentist's office for a cleaning, perhaps). Pre-holiday parties and preparations go more smoothly if you are not worried about the state of your health, and appointments are almost impossible to get in the last minutes before a holiday.

Demands on your time will be heavy, and all the bustle and excitement is a big part of the fun. But a happy holiday will depend on a good balance. Balance busy times of sharing with quiet restful times for yourself. Set aside one evening each week for attention to your manicure, a conditioning treatment for your hair, a thorough cleaning and nourishing for your skin, a good night's sleep. Try to fit a few five-minute sessions of stretching, toning, and relaxing exercises into your daily schedule. This time for yourself is vital in making the holidays happy for those who share them with you; if you are exhausted, no one benefits.

When planning holiday food treats don't neglect sound nutrition. As you are going like mad all day, you should be especially zealous about having a high-energy Vitality Drink to start the day. Be smart about holiday party foods, too. In the Food Specials for November you will find two appealing and healthy suggestions; Stuffed Raw Mushrooms on page 248 are another pretty-to-look-at, easy-to-fix, delicious-and-good-for-you addition to parties. Complicated candies and cakes are often associated with holidays. They are also associated with spreading waistlines and tooth decay. Save time and your family's health: Instead of making sugary confections, put out big bowls of nuts and raisins, huge baskets of shiny red apples and tangerines. Popcorn is a marvelous "nibble." There are just fifty calories in a cupful of plain popcorn. If you like it buttery, use margarine or polyunsaturated corn oil.

Just a little rethinking and preplanning will make this holiday season in your year of beauty and health the happiest and best ever.

YOUR CHECKLIST AND SCHEDULE FOR DECEMBER

First Morning of the Month

Log your vital statistics into your diary (p. 14) *in ink.* Set your goals for the month as to loss of pounds or inches and gains in other areas, such as proficiency at yoga, say, or using the hand-held dryer. Pencil in your goals on the diary page for the last day of the month, and start the program that will help you achieve your goals.

Every Morning

Seven-Way Stretch   (p. 91)
Cup of hot water and lemon juice
Warm-up exercises   (p. 146)
Clean face and moisturize   (p. 54)
Makeup   (p. 61)

Fix hair
Vitality Drink and nutritional supplements   (p. 94)
Every Evening
Warm-up exercises to relax
Feet-up rest with pillows or on slantboard for 10 minutes
Clean face and moisturize
Bath and all-over body lotion   (p. 128)
Clean teeth before bed   (p. 259)
As Often as You Like: At Least Three Times Each Week
Exercise session of 30 minutes   (p. 242)
Yoga session of 30 minutes   (p. 96)
Shampoo and finishing rinse   (pp. 45–46)
Once Each Week
An evening (or a day) of rest, a time for yourself
10-minute protective protein conditioning pac for hair
Manicure and pedicure   (p. 201)
Tweeze stray hairs on eyebrows   (p. 167)
Shave legs and underarms   (p. 166)
Facial mask   (p. 162)
Once This Month
One night and one day of rest for the digestive system on
either the detoxifying Liquid Fast or the Clearing House Diet
(pp. 36–38)
Haircut and any other professional hair services such as color
or perm (your cutter might advise a cut more often, perhaps
every three weeks. Follow his suggestion in making out your
individual schedule).

BEVERLY ON: SCENT—IT'S THE LITTLE TOPPER

All that exercise, the right food, perfect posture and makeup are really aimed at one thing—making you feel better about yourself so you will be more attractive to men, and to people in general.

One of the best, most pleasurable little toppers for your self-image is putting on a really great perfume that you love.

One of my favorites is Bal à Versailles. It's wildly expensive and makes me feel mysterious and beautiful. Maybe that's because it was given to me by an early boyfriend when I was eighteen.

But I don't wear it all the time; I wouldn't do that with any perfume. I think it's exciting to change your scent. It's like the rest of your life: Why do the same thing every day?

I know some women who wear the same perfume forever, and never ever change. After a while, everything they touch carries a little of that perfume—it's in their clothes, their houses, even in their cars. The scent becomes like the theme song in a movie, and you can never smell that scent without thinking, "God, that reminds me of Mary."

That's fine, provided you feel the same way *all* the time.

But I don't. I like to switch my scent around, depending on my mood, the time of the day, the season of the year.

There's another argument for switching, too. Did you know that your nose becomes deadened to a scent when you wear it all the time? It's nice that other people can still smell it; but if you can't, where's the fun?

I like tiny little sample bottles, enough for one evening or so, of perfumes that I'm still experimenting with, just to try them out. I buy a little larger bottle of something that's a favorite, but I never buy a big bottle of anything. Once you open it, you'd better use it. A great big bottle saved for special occasions is a great big bottle lost—perfume just evaporates and turns if you don't use it.

It lasts longer, of course, if you keep it out of the sunlight and heat, which speed up evaporation. It lasts a *lot* longer if you keep it out of the reach of the kids. Those are the only two rules about perfume you have to worry about. From there on, it's just fun.

I classify perfumes as mysterious—like Bal à Versailles, Cabochard; romantic, like Carnet de Bal; and the open-air, fresh country-girl ones like Charlie or Calandre.

The open-air perfumes are the ones to use in cologne, because they're the very fresh, youthful daytime scents that you splash on. You might find that your favorites in this category are labeled "For Men." Go ahead and buy them. One of my treasures is a light man's cologne which I can really pour on; I feel fresh and know that I smell good, but not as though I bathed in perfume. I don't feel masculine, either. There are lots of men's colognes that are perfect light colognes for women. I'm told that Greta Garbo never wears anything but Monsieur de Givenchy, and I wouldn't call her exactly male.

Even in the winter, I don't like too heavy an oil scent—musk or patchouli, for instance. If you do like perfume oils, though, be careful with them—oils tend to rub off on clothes rather easily, and they really linger. Be sure you like the scent. If you have very dry or very acid skin, you might want to look into oils.

They contain no alcohol at all. So, no irritation from alcohol on dry skin, and some people say they find that perfume doesn't go through funny changes on very acid skin when it's in a perfume-oil form. Try it with the bath oil of one of your favorite scents.

Speaking of bath oil, it's part of a whole shelf-ful of scents that you may enjoy. You can bathe in scented water and dust yourself with scented talc, then put on perfume to match for a total immersion in one perfume.

But please skip the perfumed soap. It smells wonderful, but it doesn't last. Sure, it smells great, but it will have a longer life if you tuck it into your dresser drawers. It smells luxurious while you're washing with it—but don't you plan to rinse the soap off your skin? Won't the perfume be rinsed away too? Get luxury into your bath with milk, almond oil or bath oils, foaming gels or bubbles—and get your perfume from dusting powder or straight from the bottle.

Use the bottle stopper instead of your finger if you want to keep your perfume pure—they say. I personally don't think it makes much difference, but that's the official line. What matters more is where you put your perfume.

I use a little perfume in a circle from the top of the cheekbone (you can feel the pulse beat there), over the ear to the ear lobes, at the wrists and elbows, behind the knee, at the ankles, between the breasts and under them. Put perfume any place that will tend to perspire. Eventually your body will bring out the scent. But avoid your neck. For some reason, perfume can irritate sensitive skin there.

Take along a little atomizer in your purse so you can top off the topper whenever you feel the need of a lift. One note of caution: Take off your jewelry before you spray. You can ruin jewelry if you get perfume or cologne on it. Perfume and pearls are natural enemies. That goes for the real thing as well as for the stuff that looks like it.

The last word on perfume is price. If you're lucky enough to receive your favorites as gifts—great. If not, go ahead and get them yourself, and look at it this way: Amortizing the cost over a month or so, your perfume costs less than cigarettes or a cocktail at dinner, and you look, feel, and certainly smell much better for spending the money on perfume instead.

WATER: WHAT'LL IT BE, HARD OR SOFT?

You heard a lot about hard water, but do you really know what it means? Hardness refers to the presence of calcium and magnesium in water and is often measured in grains of these minerals per gallon.

0 to 1 grain per gallon is soft water.

1 to 3 grains per gallon is moderately hard water.

3 to 7 grains per gallon is hard water.

7 grains and up per gallon is very hard water.

Only about one-quarter of the country has water that is soft or only moderately hard. The soft-water belt is primarily along the East Coast, but New England is largely a hard-water area. Hardness is one of those things that varies from town to town.

Some cities treat water to soften it. Others treat soft water to harden it because the acidic state of soft water is more corrosive to pipes. Corrosion of old lead pipes (these are still in use in Boston) can allow lead to leach into water. Newer piping systems can leach such dangerous substances as asbestos and cadmium into the water supply if corrosion occurs.

Soft water makes the removal of soap and bacteria easier when you wash. But for drinking, studies suggest that the calcium and magnesium in hard water help prevent heart disease and high blood pressure as well as reducing the body's absorption of lead.

You should get the softest water you can for washing, and get your supply of calcium and magnesium from food and food supplements.

THE PUREST WATER—THE BEST?

The purest water you can come by is triple-distilled water. Fine for steam irons, it isn't particularly palatable. Those minerals put the sparkling taste in water.

You do want clean water, though. It's harder and harder to get. Studies last year by the U.S. Environmental Protection Agency revealed that the stuff that comes from the tap can have all sorts of noxious additives. Because of the things we do to the environment, we mess up the water supply, too. Pesticides and herbicides and nitrate fertilizers seep into the ground and then into the underground water supplies. Inorganic chemicals—arsenic, cadmium, mercury—as well as organic ones—carbon tetrachloride, chloroform—become water-borne threats.

Our own answer to purified water is a tap in the kitchen that has activated charcoal filtration built into it. It works only for the cold-water tap, but that's the only one you should use for drinking and cooking water, anyway. Hot water is more corrosive to pipes, and you know what that means. Always let the water run for a minute to flush out the pipes, and then bring cold water to a boil for cooking. Never save time by using hot water from the tap—it's no saving. If you don't have a filter, boiling water before using it drives off the chlorine taste and makes water purer, more palatable. Let it boil for a good five or ten minutes.

ON TAP OR BOTTLED?

If the local water simply tastes bad, buy bottled water. The concern about drinking water has really boosted the sales of bottled water all over the country. The good taste of bottled waters keeps most people coming back for more. We still lag behind the French in consumption of bottled water. Their average is thirty-three liters a year, but then, the French believe that the right bottled mineral water can cure everything from a tried liver to a flagging sex drive. The water for weight loss is Evian. Those taking the Evian cure drink two glasses before getting out of bed, two glasses at noon, two glasses before dinner, and one glass before going to bed. Two glasses of *any* water right before a meal will reduce your capacity for food, so you are bound to lose weight.

Bottled waters can range in price from next to nothing all the way to special-occasion luxury. On the next page is a chart of some of the waters that you will find around the country; check out the domestics and sample the imports. Connoisseurship in water is even more subtle and sophisticated an art than in wine. Cheaper and better for you, too.

We have put the ones we like best at the top of the list in each category. Part of the fun is learning the ones *you* like best so you can disagree. We have limited comments to little historical footnotes. What we classify as "bland" or "blah," might be exactly what you love. Vichy Celestins, for example, is a world-wide best-seller that we really dislike. The price guide is based on New York and Los Angeles prices as we write. Prices may come down and pigs may fly, but who can say when? Also, we've worked out a system of pricing by the quart. Some waters come in 18-ounce bottles, others by half-gallons. We've evened it all out. * means up to 25 cents a quart; ** means up to 50 cents a quart; *** means up to 90 cents a quart.

Still Waters	Availability	Cost	Comments
Domestic			
Mountain Valley	National	**	This is the one DeSoto found the Indians drinking for their aches when he came to Hot Springs, Arkansas, in 1541.
Sparkletts	Far West	*	
Poland Natural Spring	East Coast	***	
Hinckley & Schmitt Natural Spring	Midwest	**	
Deer Park Mountain Spring	East	*	
Great Bear Natural Spring	Northeast	*	
Blue Rock Mountain Spring	Northeast	*	
Imported			
Evian	National	***	From springs at Evian-les-Bains in the French Alps, it is the best-selling bottled water anywhere.

Still Waters	Availability	Cost	Comments
Fiuggi	National	***	Michelangelo said it cured his kidney stones; the Borgias didn't report on the effects, but they drank it. It comes from central Italy.
Contrexeville	National	***	From the Faucille Mountain in France, it's loaded with calcium, lithium, and magnesium.

Sparkling Waters (Because the sparkle isn't pumped in, but comes naturally, it lasts and lasts)

	Availability	Cost	Comments
Domestic			
Saratoga Vichy	National	**	
Imported			
Perrier	National	***	400 million of the green Perrier bottles are filled each year at the source near Marseilles; that means that more than Frenchmen can't be wrong about Perrier. It's a great mixer all over the world and fine all by itself.
San Pellegrino	National	***	
Apollonaris	National	***	
Vichy Celestins	National	***	

BEVERLY ON: VOICES

I have known some of the most fantastic women—chic, well groomed, everything about them perfect—to open their mouths and blow the whole thing. Not by what they said, but how they said it.

A loud, screechy voice, or a very high-pitched one, especially with nasal sounds, is just awful. So many people don't seem to be aware of their own unappealing voices and accents.

I don't think people should work for perfect diction—that can sound phony; but I am all in favor of your working with your voice, on your own with a inexpensive tape cassette machine or even with a voice teacher.

A fantastic teacher here in Los Angeles helped me to get over a really terrible way of speaking. When I made my first screen test, I was given a scene from *Born Yesterday* to do. I did the Judy Holliday part, Billie Dawn, a screechy-voiced dumb blonde. Everybody liked the test, but they didn't know that that was my real voice. With Judy Holliday it was an act. Not for me. Then I did *The Ozzie and Harriet Show* on TV, and it was all right to say "Hi Mom, hi Pop" way up there in my nose. At last, though, I had to do something about the way I sounded, and I studied with a lady who had been the voice coach at M-G-M for years. She worked and worked and worked with me.

She made me so self-conscious that I was afraid to use the telephone, especially to call her. I would rehearse my speech while I was dialing. But I know that it was worth the effort.

Do get a tape machine, and keep it with you. Talk into it and sing to it while you're alone in the house, or take it with you in the car and talk away on the highway. As you play back the cassettes, you will have some very unpleasant surprises, but after a while you will begin to hear the improvement. Keep at it.

Even without a tape cassette, you can help your voice by reading aloud, especially poetry. The rhythm will creep into your reading and help correct the monotone that afflicts so much speech. Give it lots of expression, ham it up, and some of the rise and fall of inflection will spill over into more normal everyday speech.

Keep practicing your yoga breathing. Do the exercises that relax tension in the neck, yawn often to relax the vocal cords. All of these are important to a good voice, because beautiful sounds don't come out of a tense, pinched throat or a lazy diaphragm.

As you go along, you will find that you are speaking up, too. There are few things worse than people who shout, but the whisperers can be pretty tiring, too. Those breathy, little-girl voices never win women friends, and eventually they bore men who can't hear what it is you're saying.

Your voice makes a big difference in the way people feel about you—whether they see you as dumb or bright, sexy or not, efficient or sloppy—and children react immediately to the tone of your voice, even more than to what you say. Make sure it's a good reaction.

TEETH

There is a very amusing mystery movie on the Late Show circuit called *And Then There Were None*. The same title fits another not-so-amusing mystery: Why are twenty million people in the United States completely toothless when tooth decay is responsible for only 2 percent of the loss of teeth?

The villain of the piece is periodontal disease (which used to be called pyorrhea) and of the 90 million adults who do still have all or most of their teeth after the age of thirty, three out of four have some periodontal disease. For one out of every four, it is advanced.

Part of the horror of periodontal disease is that it doesn't hurt a bit. So you aren't even aware of it. To deal with it, you have to recognize it. The first stage is known as gingivitis, and red, inflamed gums are the least serious sign. Red gums or swollen gums or bleeding indicate increasing severity. You should know that there is no such thing as "normal" bleeding of the gums. A pink toothbrush means that your gums are ulcerous—and that is serious. Soft, puffy, ulcerous gums are draining infection into the system as surely as a festering wound would do. The mildest side effects are low-grade fevers and listlessness, but heart ailments can result as well.

Periodontitis begins where the gum tissue meets the tooth. The healthy gum tissue has tiny salivary glands that function to flush the tooth surfaces with saliva, keeping them washed. If the diet includes lots of fresh, raw vegetables and other roughage, the glands work as they were meant to. But the average diet—high in soft, sticky, sugary foods—literally gums up the works. Here's how: Sticky food and refined white flour and refined white sugar combine with the bacteria in saliva to form a film known as bacterial plaque. Minerals in the saliva cause the plaque film to harden and adhere to the surface of the tooth. Plaque builds up, as do stalactites of limestone in caves, to produce a hard crusting over the enamel surface of the tooth. Inside this crust, called tartar or calculus, the bacteria in plaque ferment food particles to form an acid that goes to work dissolving the calcium of the tooth. All these waste products irritate the gum tissue. The body attempts to fight back by dilating the blood vessels in the gum tissue, and sending up white blood cells. The gums swell when this happens. As more plaque forms at the tooth and gum, the body starts removing the top of the bony socket that holds the tooth in place. This is to provide more room for more white blood cells. By this time, the protective gum tissue recedes further down the root of the tooth. Pus pockets form in the areas where bone was lost. From there on, it's just a matter of time until the tooth is lost.

If you prefer happy endings, there is an alternative. Once each day, by using the right combination of brush, string, and stick, you remove the day's accumulation of plaque before it can solidify. This is done in less than ten minutes before bedtime, and you keep your teeth for life.

We are great believers in prevention—proper diet and exercise so that you never have an overweight problem to deal with; a balanced supply of vitamins and minerals so that you will never have to deal with diseases that attack the body that suffers from vitamin deficiencies. Not all branches of the medical profession are attuned to the idea of preventive medicine, but the American Dental Association certainly is. The best time to do something about saving your health by saving your teeth and gums is right this minute, before you think they are in jeopardy.

If you have been hiding a dimmed smile off in a cave somewhere, come up for re-education now before plaque destroys your teeth. One of the first things you'll learn (if you haven't seen your dentist in a while) is that everything you learned at mother's knee about oral hygiene was wrong.

Your dentist will remove all the plaque from your teeth and then instruct you in the best way for you to remove the plaque every day.

Dr. Ron Odrich, a brilliant periodontist in New York, undertook our re-education. That he is a good friend as well as a medical man made the learning process more enjoyable. This is the new way to brush as he taught it to us:

Use a very soft toothbrush with rounded nylon bristles. The old up-and-down brushing is now recognized as ineffective in removal of plaque. The brush should be held at a 45° angle to the tooth, aiming into gum line and moved in tiny, gentle back-and-forth strokes on the surfaces of the teeth. For getting at the inside of the front teeth, the brush is placed vertically and pushed gently up and down to the gum line. Even more important than brushing is the correct use of unwaxed dental floss, which can remove more than 75 percent of the plaque. An eighteen inch length of floss is wrapped around the middle finger of each hand, leaving a taut four inches of floss that is employed in a gentle sawing motion between the gum and the neck of each tooth. This takes care of most of the plaque between the teeth. For the surface of the tooth, floss is curved around each tooth and scraped up and down several times.

For the space between the gum and the tooth, a round toothpick is used. The wooden tip of the toothpick polishes the tooth's surface down where it meets the gum and in the space between the tooth and the gum, known to the dentist as the "sulcus."

After this sulcular brushing with a toothpick comes the brushing with a toothbrush. This can be an extra-soft standard toothbrush, multi-tufted with rounded nylon bristles, or an electric toothbrush such as the Broxodent by Squibb. Five minutes of brushing in the manner prescribed; then all the bacteria dislodged by the floss, the toothpick, and the brush are flushed away with the Water Pik. The last step is massage or stimulation of the gum tissue using a Lactona Stimulator with a little flexible rubber tip. Five rotations of the Stimulator at the gum line, outside pointing in and then inside pointing out.

The total plaque removal is done before bed. In the morning you use only the toothbrush. Some dentists feel that with proper methods of plaque removal, toothpaste is superfluous. Both toothpaste makes a big difference in the clean taste and feeling of the mouth, so we use it. Do, however, use the toothpaste your dentist recommends. The abrasiveness of dentifrices varies widely, and so do individual needs. Beware the toothpaste that is too abrasive for your teeth.

When even the choice of toothpaste is best left to your dentist, doesn't it make sense to make an appointment as soon as possible so you can start doing the things that are sure to be good for your teeth rather than just guessing at a program of good care?

If money is holding you back, see if you can't manage a bank loan for dentistry, or a system of prorated payments with the dentist. Spread out payments for the life of your teeth if you must, but guarantee a long life for them. Another tooth- and money-saving thought is to check the dental clinics found in most university medical schools. The cost of superior dental care tends to be very low in these clinics.

The cost of any dental care is low if you think of the inestimable benefits it pays in terms of overall health and lifelong good looks.

SPECIALS FOR YOUR MAKEUP AND FRAGRANCE

• You need a little extra color for evening makeup. Makeup artist Way Bandy gives this tip: Circle the outer edges of the face very lightly with blusher and blend with feathery strokes. It focuses attention on your eyes and mouth.

• Just a thought for skiiers and vacationers in the sun:—You've been out of the sun for a long time. Take it slower than ever. Did you know that an ultra-thin layer of foundation will block sun? In a deeper tone than the pale winter one you use at home, it will help you adapt to suntan climate quickly and safely.

• If you've been hoarding perfume, stop. It will just evaporate on your dressing table. On you, it makes the holidays more festive. Besides, replacements may be on the way, and unless they know what you wear because you're wearing it now, how will they know what you want?

SPECIALS FOR YOUR SKIN AND BODY

• Your skin renews itself every three weeks. New cells work their way up from the subcutaneous layer to the epidermis, or top layer of the skin. When the old, dead cells are sloughed off, the new skin is exposed. Paying close attention to your diet and skin care on the first of the month will mean you start reaping benefits by the first of next month. A great way to start a new year!

SPECIALS FOR YOUR SHAPE

• When you sit on the edge of the chair, with the back bones of the pelvis carrying your weight you not only strengthen the back but help prevent thigh and buttock spread.

• Crossed legs and varicose veins are natural allies. Crossing legs at the knee cuts circulation in the legs.

• A thought we like is this one from Dr. Grant Gwinup's book, *Energetics:*

262   *A Year of Beauty and Health*

"We are a people at a state of rest unparalleled in nature, and obesity is part of the price we pay."

SPECIALS FOR YOUR HAIR

• The smoke-filled atmosphere you have to cope with at many holiday parties means more frequent shampooing. If your hair is very dark, very curly, or chemically colored, it tends to be more porous and thus to absorb odors of cigarette smoke and other pollutants more easily.

• Be on the alert for tension through this extra-busy month. Prop your feet up or do a yoga head- or shoulder-stand whenever you have the time. Massage your neck and scalp at every opportunity. Stimulating the flow of fresh blood to the scalp is vital to the health and beauty of your hair.

• Your next haircut will probably be due at the beginning of a new year. We hope this one has been a wonderful year for you. All the good, healthy hair care habits you began are now second nature, part of your lifelong routine. But there is nothing routine about the really fantastic quality of your hair. Keep it as beautiful as it is today.

Once again—many very Happy New Years.

SPECIALS FOR YOUR FOOD PLANNING

• Cook with wine. It adds wonderful flavor to foods—*and* a dry table wine loses 85 percent of its calories, all of its alcohol, when it is used in cooking. Since a five-ounce glass of dry wine has about 125 calories in the bottle, in the finished dish it will add only about 11 calories, but considerable festive taste.

• Vidal is really the one to speak about wine and festivity and food this month:

"We are all tempted into feasting, even into gluttony on occasion. On a holiday, especially when you are a guest in someone's home, I think it rude to insist that this or that is not on your diet. When your hostess has put a great deal of time and love into preparing the meal, you should eat as much of the wonderful things presented as you like. Enjoy it, and enter into the spirit of the company and the time. Tomorrow will be the day for eating lightly, or for fasting. Life must be a balance. There is a time of feasting, and a time for fasting. So long as you do more fasting than feasting, you will live a beautiful life. That beautiful life will be mirrored in everything to make you the beautiful person that the world sees."

THE SASSOON DIET
FOR ALL SEASONS

It's happened to almost all of us. Everything seems fine. Then one day you can't get into your clothes; the mirror and the scales have turned against you. You've lost the battle with calories. It's easy to do because the enemy is silent, invisible, and omnipresent. You don't even know there's a war on until you wear the badge of defeat around your hips. Cheer up. You've lost a battle, but you can win the war. The trick is to know your enemy. Calories alone are powerless: you can eat tons of food and not gain an ounce if you work like a longshoreman—or you can live on next to nothing and gain weight if you spend all your time just lying around. But you must understand your caloric intake, and then plan to use all the calories you get if you are to avoid storing them away as fat.

Counting calories has always seemed to us a boring way of approaching the enjoyable subject of food, but it is essential to understanding the subject. The only nice thing about calorie counting is that, like learning to ride a bicycle, you need go through it only once; it's something you never really forget.

First, let's clear up the question of what calories are, then move on to ways of handling them. Next, we've plotted a diet built around approximately 1200 calories a day.

CALORIES

—Are simply units of measure. One calorie is the amount of energy necessary to raise the temperature of one gram of water by 1° Centigrade. This heat is of course invisible; but three drops of honey conceal one calorie, and so does half an asparagus tip. As a rule, there are four calories per gram in proteins and carbohydrates, nine calories per gram in fats. The challenge (and it can almost be fun) is to get the most food, in the best balance, for the lowest cost in calories. But you need more than a calorie counter. It is imperative that you balance meals by consuming some fats, some carbohydrates, some proteins, some natural sugars. Otherwise, the low-calorie diet means low-grade energy, and a low beauty quotient for skin, eyes, hair, all of you. We'll talk more about the proper balance later; for now, let's concentrate on how many calories you need and then decide on where to find (and how to lose) them.

—Must be supplied to the body in a fairly exact number to meet the body's needs for energy and rebuilding of cells. To find out your individual requirement, here's the formula: Jot down your perfect weight (a realistic one for your frame, the weight at which you know you feel and look best). Now multiply that number by 15 if you are between ages thirty-five and fifty-five. If you are between eighteen and thirty-five years old, add 200 to the figure arrived at. If you are between fifty-five and seventy-five, subtract 300. That is the number of calories needed to maintain your perfect weight.

Example: Perfect weight = 125 pounds

$$\frac{\times 15}{1875} \text{ calories (ages 35–55)}$$

1875 cal + 200 = 2075 calories (ages 18–35)
1875 cal − 300 = 1575 calories (ages 55–75)

O.K. That's the maintenance figure for your ideal weight. Now do the same arithmetic trick with your actual current weight. Let's say you are currently ten pounds over the line at 135. Multiplying by 15 again, the figure is 2025; which means you are currently getting a daily oversupply of 150 calories for the ideal body inside. Giving the body fewer calories, at least 150 fewer each day, is part of the answer.

Only part of the answer because each pound of fat you carry represents a previous oversupply of 3500 calories. So in addition to cutting down on the now and future intake, you have to reduce the calorie stockpile. Whenever you overeat, the body stores away the excess for future needs. Now you have to get to work to force the body into surrendering that hoarded energy. The way to do that is to get to work.

Calories are burned constantly. Even while you sleep, your body is using calories. But it burns them fast or slow, depending upon needs. Sleep demands an output of only about a half calorie per minute. Sitting up in bed raises the calorie burning to 1.3 per minute. But if you get up and go for a walk, you burn 5.2 calories per minute. Twenty-five minutes of running, or forty-five minutes of swimming would wipe out 500 calories. Actually, you needn't carve out a big chunk of time from your day to seriously undercut the hoard of calories. Just put a little more body English on everything you do. (See the list of quickie exercises to do during housework or at your desk on page 143.) And you burn the same number of calories by walking five miles at a clip or by walking five miles in the course of a day. For some people, lots of light exercise is the better way, because the appetite is not stimulated. We ourselves don't come back from a workout at the gym feeling ravenously hungry, but many people do. And burning off all those calories is pointless if you are going to indulge in an eating binge after exercise. If that's your story, then get more frequent short sessions of exercise instead of one marathon stint.

We think that any diet can be made a pleasanter experience if you consider it as an enjoyable new way of thinking about food, a long-delayed new program of doing good things for your body after a long period of insulting it. Because you have led yourself astray for such a long time, though, the body is apt to rebel against the new, stricter discipline. That's why we urge you to begin your new food life with thirty-six hours of the Liquid Fast or the Clearing House Diet on pp. 36–38. There are three reasons for this:

1. Willpower is greatest at the start of a diet, so you will be better prepared then for a period of almost complete abstinence.

2. The body is accustomed to receiving food in great quantities now. After a thirty-six hour "cooling off" period, it will be more amenable to accepting smaller portions.

3. The Liquid Fast or the Clearing House Diet will give almost

immediate visible benefits in terms of weight loss (loss of water retention, too), and so will strengthen your resolve for the days and weeks to come when loss of poundage is not always so constant.

But, you must *not* continue the Clearing House Diet for longer than thirty-six hours. After that, your body must have a daily allowance of no fewer than 1200 calories. That is the minimum for safe, healthy weight reduction. Some doctors believe that 1400 calories is even better for some dieters. While we are on the subject, we strongly urge that you see your doctor before beginning this or any other diet plan. The diet we outline is perfectly safe and well balanced. But you may have special problems that neither we nor you are aware of. If there is some history of diabetes in your family, a diet that includes lots of fruits could trigger a problem for you. There are other problems and individual reasons for seeing a nutritionally aware M.D. before changing your eating patterns. It could be that he will advise an even more stringent diet than this. What we have outlined is our own maintenance diet. Given our bodies, activities, and preferences, this diet keeps us in peak condition. For your body and life, it can be a weight-loss diet. You can add to the portions to make it a maintenance or even weight-gaining diet, if that's your aim.

OUR DIET FOR ALL SEASONS–A ONE-WEEK SAMPLE

Asterisk * indicates that recipe appears in the book.

MONDAY

	Calories
Breakfast:	
1 cup hot water and lemon juice	0
1 glass Vitality Drink *	230
1 slice whole wheat toast	55
tea, coffee, Sanka or herb tea	0
Mid-morning:	
1 glass V-8 juice or other vegetable juice with 1 tablespoon food yeast stirred in	100
Lunch:	
Salade Niçoise *	325
1 slice whole wheat toast	55
tea, coffee, Sanka, or herb tea	0
Mid-afternoon:	
½ glass Banana Smoothie *	118
Dinner:	
Spinach Salad *	200
6 ounces Grilled Fish *	150
Marinated Cucumbers *	12
½ cup Lemon Freeze *	12
coffee, tea, Sanka, or herb tea	0
Bedtime:	
½ cup of yoghurt, or a small apple	75
TOTAL:	1332

TUESDAY

Breakfast:

1 cup hot water and lemon juice	0
1 glass Vitality Drink *	230
1 slice whole wheat toast	55
coffee, Sanka, tea, or herb tea	0

Mid-morning:

1 glass grapefruit juice with 1 tablespoon food yeast	100

Lunch:

Greek Salad *	218
1 slice whole wheat toast	55
coffee, Sanka, tea, or herb tea	0

Mid-afternoon:

1 glass Blender Pick-Me-Up Drink *	95

Dinner:

2 stalks raw celery stuffed with 4 ounces uncreamed cottage cheese	117
4 ounces cold roast turkey	304
1 cup Icy Green Gazpacho *	32

Bedtime:

½ cup yoghurt, or medium pear	75
TOTAL:	1281

WEDNESDAY

Breakfast:

1 cup hot water and lemon juice	0
1 glass Vitality Drink *	230
1 slice whole wheat toast	55
coffee, tea, Sanka, or herb tea	0

Mid-morning:

½ cup yoghurt with 1 teaspoon honey	100

Lunch:
 Smooth and Crunchy Lunch Sandwich *   375
 coffee, tea, Sanka, or herb tea

Mid-afternoon:
 Hot Vegetable Broth * with 1 teaspoon food yeast 40

Dinner:
 Cold Consommé   75
 1 small Cornish Game Hen *   250
 green salad   25
 Steamed Green Beans *   25
 Cinnamon Grapefruit *   70
 coffee, tea, Sanka, or herb tea   0

Bedtime:
 ½ cup yoghurt, or hot skim milk with
  1 teaspoon honey, or a medium peach   75
          TOTAL: 1320

THURSDAY

Breakfast:
 1 cup hot water and lemon juice   0
 1 glass Vitality Drink *   230
 1 slice whole wheat toast   55
 coffee, tea, Sanka, or herb tea   0

Mid-morning:
 1 glass tomato juice with 1 tablespoon food
  yeast stirred in   100

Lunch:
 Mushroom, Raw Spinach and Hard-Cooked
  Egg Salad *   220
 1 slice whole wheat toast   55
 coffee, tea, Sanka, or herb tea   0

Mid-afternoon:
 ½ cup yoghurt with 1 teaspoon honey and
  wheat germ   140

Dinner:

1 cup vegetable bouillon	25
tomato salad	35
Asparagus Vinaigrette	175
Baked Salmon *	204
Golden Fruit Sherbet Cup *	48
coffee, tea, Sanka, or herb tea	0

Bedtime:

½ cup yoghurt or skim milk with honey	100
TOTAL:	1387

FRIDAY

Breakfast:

1 cup hot water and lemon juice	0
1 glass Vitality Drink *	230
1 slice whole wheat toast	55
coffee, tea, Sanka, or herbal tea	0

Mid-morning:

1 glass vegetable juice with 1 tablespoon food yeast	100

Lunch:

Insalata Pomidoro *	190
1 slice whole wheat toast	55
coffee, tea, Sanka, or herbal tea	0

Mid-afternoon:

½ glass Banana Smoothie protein drink *	118

Dinner:

Crabmeat and Lettuce Salad Vinaigrette	100
Vineyard Chicken *	250
Steamed Asparagus with lemon juice (or Steamed Zucchini with lemon juice)	25
fresh fruit compote	80

Bedtime:

1 small apple	80
TOTAL:	1283

SATURDAY

Breakfast:
1 cup hot water and lemon juice	0
1 glass Vitality Drink *	230
1 slice whole wheat toast	55
coffee, tea, Sanka, or herbal tea	0

Mid-morning:
1 glass grapefruit juice with 1 tablespoon food yeast	100

Lunch:
Brunch Salad *	400
coffee, tea, Sanka, or herb tea	0

Mid-afternoon:
½ cup yoghurt or skim milk	75

Dinner:
1 Artichoke Vinaigrette	75
Broiled Lamb Chop with Basil and Lemon *	250
½ cup Steamed Zucchini *	18
½ cup Carrots Braised in Water and Soy Sauce *	25
½ cup strawberries with orange juice	25
coffee, tea, Sanka, or herbal tea	0

Bedtime:
½ cup yoghurt	80
TOTAL:	1233

SUNDAY

Breakfast:
1 cup hot water and lemon juice	0
1 glass Vitality Drink *	230
1 slice whole wheat toast	55
coffee, tea, Sanka, or herbal tea	0

Mid-morning:
1 large orange	75

The Sassoon Diet for All Seasons   273

Lunch:

Moroccan Salad with Cold Lamb and Raw Vegetables *	225
1 slice whole wheat toast	55
coffee, tea, Sanka, or herbal tea	0

Mid-afternoon:

½ cup yoghurt with honey	100

Dinner:

1 cup Clam Chowder	100
6 ounces Sautéed Calves' Liver	160
½ cup Broccoli with Lemon Juice	50
1 Grilled Tomato with Basil	25
½ cup Prune Whip *	125

Bedtime:

½ cup skim milk	75
TOTAL:	1275

and in between . . .

The only workable diets are the realistic ones. If you are an inveterate between-meals eater it is best to face the fact. Breaking your snacking habit at the same time as trying to lose weight is just too much to ask of yourself. Instead, eat whenever you like; but . . . keep within your calorie limit and switch from high-calorie snacks to tasty lightweights. Below are 25 suggestions at 100 calories or less.

SNACK	CALORIES
Apple (*1 average-size raw*)	80
Apricots (*3 average-size fresh*)	55
Banana (*1 average-size*)	85
Brazil Nuts (*4 or 5*)	100
Camembert cheese (*1 ounce*)	85
Carrot (*1 raw*)	25
Cashew Nuts (*7*)	75
Caviar (*1 ounce pressed*)	90
Cherries (*1 cup fresh*)	80
Cinnamon Wafers (*4 wafers*)	80
Figs (*3 small fresh*)	90

Grapes (*1 cup Thompson seedless*)	95
Hazelnuts (*10*)	100
Honeydew Melon (*¼ melon*)	65
Nectarine (*1 average-size*)	30
Orange (*1 average-size navel*)	60
Oatmeal Cookie (*1 average-size cookie*)	60
Peach (*1 average-size*)	35
Popcorn (*1 cup, plain*)	54
Pretzel Sticks (*15 small*)	60
Provolone Cheese (*1 ounce*)	95
Raisins (*1 ounce*)	60
Swiss Cheese (*1 ounce*)	95
Tangerine (*1 average-size*)	40
Wheat Thins Crackers (*10*)	100

GENERAL INDEX

[*Index of Recipes and Menus follows.*]

Exercise (*cont.*)
   dancing as, 72; tennis as, 110, 138, 171;
   for thighs, 146–47, 247; timing and, 144;
   "togetherness" in, 144; walking as, 218,
   235; warming up for, 146; in winter, 40;
   for women, 145–50; yawning as, 111
Eye(s): care of, in winter, 40; checkup, importance of, 236; color, and choosing wig,
   180; makeup for, 64–66, 171; protection
   for, in summer, 187–89; soothers for,
   165; and vitamin A, 84
Eyebrow(s): cleaning, 137, 168–69; coloring,
   168; pencil, use of, 168; shaping, 167–68
Eyedrops, for eye protection in summer, 206
Eyelashes: curling, 111; false, 66–67, 172
Eyelids: exercise, 230; sun and, 185
Eye shadow. *See* Makeup

Face: exercises for, 230; makeup for, testing,
   235
Facials, 162. *See also* Skin
Fall: hair coloring for, 78; makeup for, 217;
   perfume for, 217
Fanny: exercises for, 146–47, 148; large,
   244
Farrow, Mia, 158
Fashion: magazines, and sense of heightened
   reality, 197; model, as beauty "image,"
   198–99; model, style problems of, 198–99
Fasting, thirty-six-hour, 34, 35, 36–37, 132
Fatigue: as source of "cold sores," 206; and
   vitamin C, 86
Fats: functions of, 127; hydrogenated vs.
   animal, 127; as storer of vitamin A, 84;
   and vitamins B₆ and D, 85. *See also* Oils
February: beauty plan for, 42–70; checklist
   and schedule for, 43–45; food-planning
   specials for, 68–69; specials for hair in,
   70–71; specials for makeup and fragrance
   in, 69; specials for skin and body in, 70
Feet: care of, 203–204, 236; elevated, and
   circulation, 90–91, 171; exercise for, 33,
   205; and shopping for shoes, 236
Female hormones, and vitamin E, 82
Fencing, as exercise, 72, 138
Fields, W. C., 131
Figure problems, camouflaging, 244
Fish, value of, as food, 120
Five-Minute Relaxer, 150
Floor mop, 17
Flynn, Errol, 181
Folacin, 85–86; and vitamin B₁₂, 85
Food(s): needs, individual, 119; and Nutri-
   tion Board (National Research Council),
   119; organic, definition of, 170; as relax-
   ant, 129; to get rid of, 38–39; healthful

cooking of, 39; as sources of vitamins
   and minerals, 80, 83–84; supplements, in
   tablet form, 170–71. *See also* Diet
Forearms, removing hair on, 166–67
Forehead, exercises for, 31, 230
Foundation. *See* Makeup
Fragrance(s), 41, 217; duration of, 69; how
   and when to buy, 136; men's, for women,
   150, 252; and sunbathing, 184; switching,
   importance of, 252. *See also* Perfume
Freckles, 186
Friction, 132
Frostbite, protection against, 246
Fructose, natural, 21
Fruit(s), 217; fresh, storing, 152; juices, nat-
   ural, 39; removing pesticides from, 170;
   and vitamin loss in peeling, 152

Gable, Clark, 142
Garbo, Greta, 252
Ginger, and sexual powers, 217
Gingivitis, 259
Glasses: and false eyelashes, 172; and hair-
   styles, 39–40
Glaucoma, 236
Gloves, cotton, for care of hands, 166
Glucose, 21
Goals, for health and beauty, 12, 15; un-
   realistic, setting, 221–24
Golden Door, The, 138
Golf, as exercise, 110, 171
Grant, Cary, as example of continuing de-
   velopment, 222–24
Grayshott Hall, 34, 35
Green peppers, as source of vitamin C, 85
Growth, and iron, 89
Gwinup, Dr. Grant, 263
Gymnastics, value of, 144

Haig, Kenneth, 34
Hair: and biotin, 86; brush, how to clean,
   48; brushes, 18; caring for, in summer,
   172, 187, 189; conditioning, 207; damaged,
   110, 215; dryers, types of, 18–19, 39, 49–
   53; facial, methods of removing, 167; falling, normal vs. abnormal, 245; fine, man-
   agement of, 40; frizziness, avoiding, 53;
   gray, 77, 237; line, natural, 212; methods
   of drying, 49–53; naturally curly, 189;
   pins and clips, 19; rollers, 19; rollers,
   heated, 19, 39, 172; salon treatment for,
   215; setting lotion, proper, 138; and
   smoking, 263; spray, how to use, 60–61;
   static electricity in, 39; straightening, 153;
   style, and age, 211–12; style, choosing,

280   *A Year of Beauty and Health*

Salad-dressing treatment for sunburn, 186
Salmon: iodine in, 166; protein in, 166; vitamin D in, 85, 166
Salon treatment for hair, 215
Salt: cooking without, 170; iodized, 88; sea, 21, 130; sea, and iodine, 88; substitute, 21
Sardines, as source of iodine, 166
Sasangasana (rabbit pose), 108
Sassoon, Beverly: 34, 161, 228, 234; on baths with extra benefits, 128; on blender skin treatments, 162–65; on care of hands and feet, 201–204; on clothes in winter, 95; on dressing for your body type, 244; on energy recharging, 243; on exercise for women, 145–50; on eyebrows, 167–69; on favorite dishes, 120–27; on makeup, 29, 61–68, 96; on marriage, 226–27; on removing body hair, 166; on scent, 250–54; on sleep, 89–90; on sunbathing, 181–86; on sunburn remedies, 186–87; on Vitality Drinks, 94–95; on voices, 257–58; on water, 131; on yoga, 96–109
Sassoon, Vidal; 151, 152, 181, 185, 205, 222, 226, 238; on choosing hair cutter/stylist, 210–11; on Clearing House Diet, 37–38; on energy recharging, 243; on English Health Farm program, 34–36; Finishing Rinse, 48; on food and festivity, 263–64; on haircuts, 211–13; on hair spray, 60–61; life history, 157–58; on plastic surgery, 224, 227–30; Protein Pac Treatment, 153; Shampoo, 47; show team of, 214–15; on sleep, 89–91; and Terry Robinson's exercise program, 142; on therapeutic touching (massage), 132–33; on top hairdressers, 214–15; on transcendental meditation, 156–62; and vitamins, 79; on what not to look for in fashion magazines, 197–200; on wigs, 179–81
Sassoon Diet for All Seasons, 170, 265–74
Scalp: baldness, 110; massage, 71; massager, 19; poor circulation, 110; in summer, 193; and traction alopecia, 71
Scheinberg, Dr. I. Herbert, 233
Schmidt, Dr. Alexander, 85
Sea salt. See Salt
Seated Bikini Test, 150
Seeds, as source of lecithin, 87
Self: -awareness and trancendental meditation, 156, 160; -control, and yoga, 97; feeling about, and beauty, 13–14
Savasana (dead man pose), 99, 243
September: beauty plan for, 208–18; checklist and schedule for, 209–10; food-planning specials for, 216–17; specials for hair

in, 215–16; specials for makeup and perfume in, 217; specials for shape in, 218; specials for skin and body in, 216
Seven Standing Sins, 15, 30–32
Seven-Way Stretch, 40, 91–93, 145, 146
Sex: hormones, and smoking, 233; and smoking, 234
Sexual development, zinc and, 89
Sexual performance, and vitamin E, 85
Sexual powers, and ginger, 217
Shacove, Gene, 214
Shampoo: ABC's of, 45–46; benefit of, in summer, 207; tips on, 46–49; use of conditioner after, 48; Vidal Sassoon, 47
Shaving, for body hair, 166–67
Shellfish, cholesterol and, 121
Shoes, shopping for, 236
Shoulders: big, 245; exercises, 31–32, 193
Shower, cold, 206
Skeet shooting, as exercise, 171
Skiing: care of skin for, 41; as exercise, 110
Skin: "acid mantle" on, 137; aids to, 70; allergic, care of, 56–57; basic care for, 53–59; and biotin, 86; blender treatments for, 162–64; cancer, 182; cleansing masks for, 164–65; color, and choosing wig, 180; combination (dry and oily), 55–56; damage to, by sunbathing, 182; dead, removing, 216; drinking water and, 131; dry, 53, 54, 130, 163, 245; facials for, 163, 164, 216; and fats, 127; freshener, 54, 55; and hormone creams, 59; and humectants, 58; "hypo-allergenic" products for, 56–57; moisturizers for, 57; irritation, and perfume, 193; Marie Antoinette Special for, 164; and minerals, 88, 89; need for moisture by, 59, 231; older, and moisturizers, 59–60; oily, 53, 55, 59; protecting, while sunbathing, 185, 206, 262; protecting, in winter, 40, 41, 245–46, 262; renewal of, 262; sallow, hints for, 111; sensitive, care of, 56–57; spots on, from sunbathing, 186; stretch marks on, treatment for, 137, 193–94; types of, 53; types, and sunburn, 183; "vacation" for, 151; and vitamins, 84, 169; washing, 137
Slantboard, 70
Sleep: afternoon naps, 89; aids to, 89–91; calorie-burning during, 205, 267; individual need for, 89; and sleeping pills, 89–90
Sleeping pills, 89–90
Smith, Alexis, 97
Smoking: as anti-sex, 234; and calcium, 88; dangers of, 233–34; and vitamin C, 86
Snacks, 235; healthful, 39, 216
Soap, perfumed, 253

INDEX OF RECIPES AND MENUS